BUILDING BETTER UNIVERSITIES

Building Better Universities provides a wide-ranging summary and critical review of the increasing number of groundbreaking initiatives undertaken by universities and colleges around the world. It suggests that we have reached a key moment for the higher education sector in which the services, location, scale, ownership, and distinctiveness of education are being altered dramatically, whether universities and colleges want it or not. These shifts are affecting traditional assumptions about both the future 'shape' of higher education institutions, and the roles of—and relationships between—learners, teachers, researchers, managers, businesses, communities, and other stakeholders.

Building Better Universities aims to bridge the gap between educational ideas about what the university is, or should be 'for,' and its day-to-day practices and organization. It roams across strategic, operational, and institutional issues; space planning and building design; and technological change, to bring together issues that are often dealt with separately. By analyzing the many challenges faced by higher education in the contemporary period and exploring the various ways universities and colleges are responding, this powerful book aims to support a step-change in debates over the future of higher education and to enable senior managers and faculty to develop more strategic and creative ways of enabling effective twenty-first-century learning in their own institutions.

Jos Boys is currently an academic developer at the University of New South Wales, Sydney. She trained originally in architecture, followed by many years' experience teaching design and contextual studies in a variety of higher educational institutions at different levels. She has also worked as an educational technologist and academic developer, developing ways to enhance learning through both technology-rich and pedagogically sound resources and delivery. She has been a consultant for the UK Joint Information Systems Committee and has written several books on higher education, including *Towards Creative Learning Spaces: Re-Thinking the Architecture of Post-Compulsory Education* (2010) and, with Peter Ford, *The e-Revolution and Post-Compulsory Education: Using Business Models to Deliver Quality Education* (2007).

BUILDING BETTER UNIVERSITIES

Strategies, Spaces, Technologies

Jos Boys

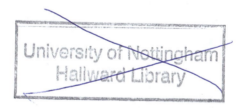
 Routledge
Taylor & Francis Group

NEW YORK AND LONDON

First published 2015
by Routledge
711 Third Avenue, New York, NY 10017

and by Routledge
2 Park Square, Milton Park, Abingdon, Oxon OX14 4RN

Routledge is an imprint of the Taylor & Francis Group, an informa business

Library of Congress Cataloging-in-Publication Data
Boys, Jos.
   Building better universities: strategies, spaces, technologies / Jos Boys.
      pages cm
   Includes bibliographical references and index.
   1. Education, Higher—Aims and objectives.   2. Education, Higher—Effect of technological innovations on.   3. Educational change.   I. Title.
   LB2322.2.B72 2014
   378.01—dc23
   2014017954   *10 0732491*

ISBN: 978-0-415-85931-8 (hbk)
ISBN: 978-0-415-85932-5 (pbk)
ISBN: 978-0-203-79888-1 (ebk)

Typeset in Caslon Pro
by Apex CoVantage, LLC

MIX
Paper from
responsible sources
FSC   FSC® C013056
www.fsc.org

Printed and bound in Great Britain by
TJ International Ltd, Padstow, Cornwall

Contents

List of Figures

List of Textboxes

INTRODUCTION

THE SHIFTING BOUNDARIES OF HIGHER EDUCATION

[T]here are few more idiosyncratic conglomerates than the modern university . . .
—*Kevin Carey (2011)*

In the current period—as universities and colleges face many challenges—
there is a considerable amount of research and criticism analyzing the impacts
of factors such as marketization, internationalization, new technologies and
neo-liberal approaches on higher education. These are generally perceived
as either negative or positive effects, depending on whether authors place
greater emphasis on opportunities for economic innovation or on how education should be valued in society. We now have many publications suggesting
that, on one hand—for supporters—universities are becoming more innovative (Christensen and Eyring 2011; Barber et al. 2012), entrepreneurial (Clark
2004; Shattock, 2003), corporate (Meister 1998; Prince and Beaver 2001), and
central to the "creative economy" (Araya and Peter 2010; Florida 2012). On
the other hand—for critics—the contemporary university is in ruins (Readings 1997), in dissent (Rolfe 2013), in turmoil (Knight 2008), corporate
(Donoghue 2008; Cote and Allahar 2007, 2011) has become a form of academic capitalism (Slaughter and Leslie 1997; Slaughter and Rhoades 2009);
or is reaching its 'end times' (Brennan and Shah 2011).

Many of these concerns about the challenges higher education faces are not
new. When we reviewed the state of UK universities and colleges in a previous

publication (Boys and Ford 2008), authors such as Ernst et al. (1994) and Dolence and Norris (1995) were already suggesting that institutions needed to better understand the depth of shifts occurring in higher education, and to make strategic rather than defensive and piecemeal changes to their educational models and systems (Table 0.1). In that book, *The e-Revolution and Post-Compulsory Education*, we also argued that public universities and colleges

Imperative: increase administrative productivity	
Adhocratic	**Planning centric**
Cut expenses across the board	■ Develop a vision ■ Identify academic priorities ■ Rethink mission/markets ■ Nurture internal growth sectors
Cut administration deeper	■ Redefine administration ■ Eliminate unnecessary work ■ Dismantle unproductive policy ■ Reengineer processes ■ Leverage the IT infrastructure ■ Attack paperwork
Tighten procedures and seek scale through centralisation	■ Empower employees ■ Leverage the private market ■ Embed procedural controls in IT infrastructure

Imperative: enhance controls and reporting	
Old strategies	**Emergent strategies**
■ Introduce new rules ■ Introduce new forms ■ Acquire additional signatures ■ Centralise approval authority	■ Specify desired outcomes ■ Negotiate acceptable risk ■ Embed controls in IT ■ Measure and elevate continually

Imperative: adopt a consumer orientation	
Old strategies	**Emergent strategies**
■ Do things right ■ Assure compliance ■ Foster specialisation ■ Manage by exception ■ Safeguard institutional data	■ Do the right things, right ■ Become a problem solver ■ Empower generalists ■ Create centres of competency ■ Promote access to information

Imperative: facilitate organisational change	
Old strategies	**Emergent strategies**
■ Add vertical layers ■ Enhance vertical communications ■ Create functional 'stovepipes' ■ Use the chain of command	■ Create a network of networks ■ Reduce information float ■ Promote cross-functional integration ■ Use the network

Table 0.1 New business imperatives for higher education
Source: Ernst et al. (1994); reprinted from Boys and Ford (2008: 5).

tended to be risk adverse and were only making small-scale and additive changes to their structures and services. International campuses were being developed through opportunistic connections, rather than as part of a critical overview. New technologies and spaces were often being generated at the level of small-scale prototypes and pilots that ceased when funding ran out or when a particular educational enthusiast left. Most crucially, universities and colleges were *reacting* to changes, rather than *proactively* leading in national and international learning and teaching debates or locating themselves strategically and explicitly within a global and increasingly hybrid higher educational sector.

This book aims to show that this situation is moving on in some important ways. Whilst the larger context—particularly in the English-speaking countries across the globe—remains that of financial constraints, policy changes, risk aversion and short-termism, many more universities and colleges are acting to improve their educational services through strategic, organizational, technological, curricular, and physical changes. They are doing this for a whole variety of reasons: because of their educational beliefs, to educate students more appropriately for an increasingly complex and hybrid world, to offer distinctiveness in an increasingly competitive global market, and to operate more effectively and efficiently. This has been aided by more explicit—and public—arguments about what education is for, the sharp realities of competition from for-profit education providers, increasing opportunities for new kinds of partnering both within and beyond the higher education sector, a developing maturity (and ubiquity) of information and communication technologies, and the emergence of learning spaces as an academic discipline in its own right, aiming for rigor in integrating issues of learning and the space in which it takes place. In addition, the global financial crisis of the first years of the twenty-first century has intensified the pressures on higher education in many countries to do more with less—whether because of austerity measures cutting back on public spending, or through demands for immediate growth in student numbers where expanding education is part of attempts to 'kick-start' struggling economies or to produce step-change in growing ones.

We are therefore reaching a key moment for the higher education sector. There are now an increasing number of powerful and robust initiatives aimed at building better universities and colleges by rethinking educational strategies, spaces, and technologies. This is not just about an abstract question (what universities are 'for') or the content of 'mission statements,' but about how various, often contested, ideas of the university are being translated and implemented through their everyday practices. It is about the actual, changing patterns of 'unbundling' and 'rebundling' of different aspects of learning, teaching, and critical enquiry currently taking place. By bringing together examples under a number of key emerging themes, *Building Better Universities* aims to support and focus debates over the future of higher education institutions (HEIs) and to inform senior management and faculty decision making as they critically consider effective and creative ways for providing higher education, appropriate to the twenty-first century, in their own universities and colleges. In bringing themes and examples together across educational strategies, spaces and technologies, I also aim to bridge across areas that are often dealt with separately to provide a critical overview of the very many initiatives that are happening in higher education today.

Crucially, however, the examples outlined here are *not* offered merely as expressions of good practice, to simply be adapted by others. Rather, they allow us to critically investigate, and ask questions of, how some universities and colleges are attempting new or adapted forms in the current period. A central argument will be that now is a crucial time for universities and colleges to go 'back to basics' by engaging with, and debating, the key characteristics of higher education in the twenty-first century. We need to move beyond merely following current fads and trends, by asking what kinds of education we should be offering, and what alternative kinds of relationships we should be making between learning, teaching, research, enterprise, and communities; and among learners, scholars, citizens, and employers. And we need to ask how such educational services can be offered both effectively and equitably.

A Critical Background

This book does start from the belief that many existing universities and colleges are no longer fit for purpose. Whether in the public or private sector, higher education in the English-speaking world has a variable and uneven record in enabling high levels of student retention and achievement, in providing value for money, in maintaining standards and resisting grade inflation, and in increasing equality of access. This is in a context where universities are faced with many external demands and considerable constantly shifting political and economic changes. This means that the location, scale, ownership, services, and distinctiveness of higher education are being altered dramatically, whether universities and colleges want it or not, as existing boundaries shift and slide.

However, in *Building Better Universities* I aim to show how these challenges and difficulties are most often argued over (and distorted through) two dominant tropes in educational and political debate: first, the perceived opposition between public/nonprofit and private/for-profit educational providers and second, a series of ubiquitous concepts such as 'knowledge economy,' 'globalization,' and 'ranking' that have come to the fore in recent years. The former is affecting how debate about what universities are for is framed, and the latter is producing many 'bandwagon' effects, as universities appear to unthinkingly merely follow current trends. Here, the aim is both to expose the unfortunate results that such simplistic oppositions and clichéd expressions produce and to consider just what kinds of criteria we need to more clearly understand how to build better universities and colleges. I suggest that the underlying issue for contemporary higher education is what Siemens (2013a) calls the complexification of education, that is, the dilemmas, tensions, and even contradictions that are arising for HEIs (particularly in the English-speaking world) as they struggle to fulfill an ever increasing and shifting number of interconnected and hybrid roles. Many universities and colleges now teach many more students on fewer resources than they used to. At the same time many are required to produce much more research, which can be both quantified and applied to the real world. They are expected to innovate, particularly in support of business research and development. They collaborate with other institutions and add global networks and campuses to their portfolios. They may have to show explicitly how they are improving employability, research-informed teaching, and their impact on economies and societies. In the UK at least, the emphasis on research and enterprise performance is leaving many academics having to fit education—students' learning—into the interstices of what they do. In this context in *Building Better Universities* I focus on learning and teaching rather than, for example, higher education governance, management practices, or technological infrastructures. But this is also a contemporary focus on learning and teaching – recognizing that these days it is necessarily integrated with other roles, such as research, and business and civic engagement, and that these can all benefit and support learning, rather than simply compete for resources with it.

Beyond the Rhetoric?

How, then, should universities and colleges develop in the future? How do we frame students in this changing world? Are they consumers, clients, or members of a community; creative producers; citizen-scholars; or something else? Are teachers still lecturers or are they facilitators, coaches, mentors, or curators? How do learning, teaching, and critical enquiry relate? What is or should be the role of scholarly activity in society? How will the growth in for-profit universities and increasing international competition affect existing public-oriented provision in the US, the UK, Europe, Australia, and elsewhere? What are the impacts of new kinds of collaboration and competition between and across different educational providers and among these providers, businesses, and the wider community? And what are the effects of new information and communication technologies, both in offering new templates for learning within the university and in developing new types of learning 'places' connected to, or outside of, it?

Starting from these kinds of questions is a way to more critically challenge the limitations of existing dominant discourses and to creatively rethink educational models and future initiatives. To do this properly, I suggest that HEIs need to do three things: first, interrogate their own internal dynamics and assumptions; second, engage critically and creatively with external

pressures; and, third, develop ongoing educational research and relevant analytical data that can properly inform strategic decision making. I next briefly
look at these points in turn.

Like all organizations, contemporary universities and colleges are the result
of a historical, additive accumulation of functions, roles, and cultures into particular shapes and not others that can become both obvious and normal and are
hard to challenge and change. Higher education's history of academic autonomy, for example, needs unraveling in terms of what is merely embedded—and
stagnating—tradition and practice, and what remains important and essential
to knowledge production and reproduction (Boys and Ford 2008). Similarly,
the common structures of higher education need critical reviewing. Why, for
example, do so many universities still tend to feel obliged to offer a wide range
of subjects, organized by levels over a number of years and assessed by credit
hours? How does higher education deal with the competing pressures for
increasing subject expertise and reputation on the one hand and the need for
more cross-disciplinary hybridity on the other? How do they revisit the tendency to proliferate departments and subdivisions? As Capaldi (2009) notes,

> Customarily, universities organize their academic operations into depart-
> ments constructed around disciplines, whose standards and boundaries
> the departments patrol. In response to the growth of knowledge and the
> proliferation of disciplines as the sum total of knowledge has increased,
> the number of academic departments has risen dramatically since they
> were first introduced in the United States. Columbia University had 42
> departments at the beginning of the 20th century and started the 21st
> century with more than 85, for instance, with traditional departments
> such as history and literature dividing into ones focused on specific areas:
> Asian Studies, African Studies, and so on.

At the same time, this growth and these complications are being expanded
in another direction, through new business—research—learning projects and
other forms of collaboration, both globally and locally. Universities and colleges need to ask themselves about whether they are 'over-stretching' their
capabilities because of unthought-through assumptions about higher education being a kind of 'all-purpose' institution that can and should just go on
adding new activities.

This brings me to my second point, which is the extent to which contemporary universities and colleges find themselves continually 'reacting to'
externally imposed trends and pressures. As already suggested, this is both
about the considerable impact on higher education of governmental policy
and its regulatory frameworks, and about the willingness to rely on simplistic

shorthand—'the knowledge economy,' 'the entrepreneurial university,' 'the new managerialism,' 'excellence'—and the whole supporting paraphernalia of league tables and mission statements as a means of both framing and competing in the higher education sector. So, for example, as Rolfe writes (following Reading 1997), the concept of excellence—ubiquitous in the UK education system—is "in itself an empty signifier bereft of any ideological intent, a unit of measurement rather than something to be measured" (2013: 9). Anything can be excellent (education, vegetables, a book) and excellence can be measured in numerous ways, which are not inherent to the concept itself. It therefore needs to be given content—which can either be a quality or a quantity. Rolfe argues that excellence in many UK universities has come to be predominantly defined in terms of a quantity—position in a national league table, number of first-class degrees, external research income—rather than any specific qualities embodied by higher education:

> The aspiration towards excellence, seen in the mission statements of so many universities, can only be demonstrated through a crude quantification of targets that is the very antithesis of the quality to which those universities previously aspired.
>
> (Rolfe 2013: 9)

This 'empty' concept of excellence is, in turn, linked to hierarchical 'labeling' systems for higher education, through various ranking systems:

> As Calhoun has written, this results in the equation of 'excellence' with being 'better' than somebody or something else (Calhoun 2006). Indeed, for higher education to play its role in the legitimation of social inequalities effectively, it is clearly necessary to at least 'pretend' that some universities are 'better' than others, and that they are better at 'everything'. Thus, their students are to be socially advantaged for the rest of their lives, not because of their advantaged backgrounds and possession of social and other forms of capital, but because of 'merit', in terms of their achievements and competencies.
>
> (Brennan 2011: 8–9)

As Brennan goes on to note, the whole—increasingly global—framework of rankings can obscure as much as it reveals, by being a very simplistic, inaccurate and unproven yet self-perpetuating instrument:

> [W]hereas quality assurance 20 years ago was about ensuring and demonstrating that quality and standards were broadly equivalent across

higher education, today the emphasis is much more about demonstrating and emphasizing difference (Brennan and Singh 2011). [. . .] However, the extent to which reputational differentiation really reflects differences in the experiences and achievements of students in different universities remains an important and largely unanswered research question.

(ibid.: 10)

Despite this lack of accuracy (or appropriate granularity) for judging the educational quality of a particular course, rankings can have a significant impact on a student's choice of a university. Yet, reputations built on the prestige of an institution's faculty, for example, may not have the assumed results in terms of educational quality, value for money or effectiveness of learning:

> As Clayton Christensen and Henry Eyring point out in *The Innovative University*, this remorseless increase in cost is predominantly driven by the 'bigger-and-better tendency'. They may exaggerate in suggesting that, over time, each university is striving to become Harvard, but the basic point is surely undeniable. The problem from the point of view of the undergraduate student is that much of the cost base of a traditional university is irrelevant to their experience and sometimes—as highly-paid expert research professors avoid undergraduate teaching responsibilities, for example—detrimental.
>
> (Barber et al. 2012: 13)

Rankings also work to promote the 'brand,' and are self-reinforcing in that elite universities are already better placed to attract funding, faculty, and nonacademic partners than are institutions 'lower' down the hierarchy and can more easily maintain their position as leaders, predominantly through and because of their long heritage. As Barber et al. go on to say, "in this market, perhaps more than any other, history counts—a degree from Oxford, Cambridge or Harvard counts in part because it always has" (ibid.: 21). Thus, well-endowed institutions continue to attract more funds from multiple sources (businesses, research councils, charities, alumni, philanthropists and other sponsors) and are able to be research intensive, a key factor in existing higher education ranking systems. This is because all three of the major university league tables—the Academic Ranking of World Universities (ARWU), the QS World University Rankings, and the Times Higher Education (THE) World University Rankings—weigh research-related activity as more than 50 percent of the criteria for deciding on university quality, even though research may have little direct effect on an undergraduate student's study. It also means that new private providers, many of whom are purely teaching institutions, cannot compete, at least not in the short term, and that very good courses within universities lower down the league become invisible. As Altbach (2010) says, in response to his own rhetorical question, "Where is teaching in international rankings?" the answer is

> [n]owhere. One of the main functions of any university is largely ignored in all of the rankings. Why? Because the quality and impact of teaching is virtually impossible to measure and quantify. Further, measuring and comparing the quality and impact of teaching across countries and academic systems are even more difficult factors. Thus, the rankings have largely ignored teaching. The new *Times Higher Education* rankings have recognized the importance of teaching and have assigned several proxies to measure teaching. These topics include reputational questions about teaching, teacher-student ratios, number of PhDs awarded per staff member, and several others. The problem is that these criteria do not actually measure teaching, and none even come close to assessing quality of impact.

Many authors then—from across the political spectrum—have both challenged the limitations of contemporary ranking systems, and asked why universities tend to want to emulate the 'top' Ivy League institutions. For some, such as Barber et al. (2012) and Christensen and Eyring (2011), rankings are problematic because they prevent new entrants (particularly newer for-profit universities that do not do research) from gaining a reputational foothold, whereas Brennan et al. (2004) are more concerned that high-quality programs and departments within the more 'middle-ground' universities and colleges cannot compete fairly against these subjects in the elite universities. Nonetheless, the framework of higher education rankings is increasingly governing (globally) how managers and administrators decide on 'strategies' and 'missions'.

Ultimately—and crucially—is the issue that emulation of the 'best' universities is in fact both irrelevant and impossible to achieve. When Christensen and Eyring (2011) looked in detail at the comparative history of Harvard and Brigham Young University, Idaho, they show that the Ivy League universities in the US (and their equivalents worldwide) are very specific historic developments, not easily reproducible by universities and colleges more generally, because the business model for these long-term elite institutions so strongly depends on alumni funding and sponsorship. As Shirky (2012) argues, this produces a real problem when the elite universities continue to be seen as both the 'ideal' model of higher education and its norm. As he notes, writing about the US,

> Harvard [. . .] is our agreed-upon Best Institution, and it is indeed an extraordinary place. But this very transcendence should make us suspicious.

> Harvard's endowment, 31 billion dollars, is over three hundred times the median, and only one college in five has an endowment in the first place. Harvard also educates only about a tenth of a percent of the 18 million or so students enrolled in higher education in any given year. [. . .]
>
> Outside the elite institutions, though, the other 75% of students—over 13 million of them—are enrolled in the four thousand institutions you *haven't* heard of. [. . .] These are where most students are, and their experience is what college education is mostly like.
>
> (Shirky 2012)

Thus, the vast majority of existing students' higher educational experience is ignored or is set negatively against a few elite universities, and much debate about the increasing for-profit provision (which is looked at in greater detail in Chapter 2) is also compared not to the great majority of higher education but again to this elite group.

Of course, university and college managements may not feel they have a lot of room to maneuver here. They are dealing both with the complexities of their own internal legacies and dynamics and with the policy and regulatory frameworks of their governments (that are also tending to push for this hierarchical structure of 'merit' and league table or other ranking practices on a global basis). But they *could*—and there are examples in this book—take a more critical and proactive stand on both internal and external demands. I myself have worked at a number of 'mid-range' UK universities that seem only able to follow fads, by competing against each other in attempting to copy the academic reputations of the top universities (without the resources or strategies to do so effectively). This is resulting in management obsessions with jockeying for position in the academic league tables, which in all to many cases seem disconnected from any kind of real educational vision or set of principles.

This brings me to my third point. For despite regularly researching other entities, universities and colleges are relatively poor at using evidence-based research in their own operations. Brennan (2011) argues that much higher education research is framed—and therefore limited by—existing policy issues. In his UK examples, this is both because of the ubiquity of on-trend government-supported terminology (already highlighted here) and because of the search for suitable performance metrics:

> Currently, a lot of higher education research tends to be a mixture of some 'grand narratives' (for example, 'knowledge society', 'globalization') and what Ball has described as 'empirical analysis' or 'political arithmetic', i.e. largely quantitative studies shaped by pressing policy concerns.
>
> (Brennan 2011: 11)

Brennan also suggests that current higher education research is too influenced by government policy agendas:

> Most higher education researchers are interested parties in the topics of
> their research. Where links to policy processes are involved, the research-
> ers are likely to be affected by the policy outcomes. Thus, the potential
> for openly critical research may be limited. For example, the notion that
> higher education is a 'public good' which should be more equitably shared
> across all groups in society is a sentiment which is quite commonly held.
> Much less so, among researchers, would be the view that higher education
> is a public 'bad' which needs control and reform, and perhaps contraction.
>
> (ibid.:10)

At the same time, research into higher education remains both relatively
specialized and underrepresented in processes of recognition and reward for
academics and in institutional reputation building. This has meant that university and college faculty outside the specific field of education are often not
supported in researching their own learning and teaching activities:

> [S]ocial scientists beyond the higher education specialists generally
> showed little interest in higher education as a research topic. Yet it could
> be these social scientists beyond the membership of the specialist higher
> education research tribe who might bring fresh and critical perspectives
> to bear and who might more readily escape the dogmas and assumptions
> of the current policy debates.
>
> (ibid.: 11)

If universities and colleges are to be less influenced by external pressures, and
more able to respond effectively to their own internal dynamics, then they need
to 'learn' more effectively from what they already do, to factor in both the cost
and time requirements for ongoing review and evaluation of new strategies and
initiatives, to develop methods for generating and analyzing relevant data, and
to embed this research and data analysis into institutional decision-making processes. Again, there are examples in this book that suggest future directions here.

Using this Book

Overall, *Building Better Universities* is organized into themes and subthemes, with
each of the six chapters taking a key issue affecting higher education today—innovative educational models, the effects of increasing for-profit and not-for profit
hybridization, internationalization, changes in learning spaces, new learning
technologies and their impacts on learning, teaching, and critical inquiry—and

then draws out some of the ways educational institutions are responding, both critically and creatively. It gives many illustrations of how universities and colleges are working through the unbundling and rebundling of existing higher education functions at a variety of different scales, with goals that stretch across and between profitability, educational quality and effectiveness, meeting societal challenges, civic engagement, increasing accessibility, and developing open education models. And it considers what questions are raised, and what we can learn from these examples, to support the building of better universities.

Chapter 1, "Reshaping Universities and Colleges," explores some of the new higher education entrants who are rethinking how learning, teaching, research, and business and civic engagement can be done differently, by reordering what goes together and what is left out. Chapter 2, "New Patterns of Public and Private Competition and Collaboration" takes this further, by looking particularly at some of the new kinds of hybrids being produced as for-profit and nonprofit higher education providers work increasingly together, as well as in competition. Chapter 3, "Responding to Internationalization" considers how universities and colleges are and could respond to the increasingly global environment in which they operate. Chapter 4, "Changing Learning Spaces" examines the new typologies of campus environments being generated out of changing ideas about formal and informal learning and by the increasing interconnectivity between higher education and its locality or region. Chapter 5, "Beyond Virtual Learning Environments" looks at recent innovations in eLearning, starting from Massive Open Online Courses (MOOCs), to see how far higher education is expanding beyond university-defined and controlled virtual learning systems. Finally, Chapter 6, "The Implications of New Technologies for Learning" examines how the ubiquity of the web, cloud-based computing, the increasing ease of interoperability and access to online information and services through mobile devices, and innovative forms of embodied learning (through, e.g., the Internet of Things) are impacting on higher education. In conclusion, the last chapter suggests some central cross-theme-cutting issues that universities and colleges need to examine, as they develop higher education in the twenty-first century.

It is important to note that the themes, subthemes, and examples offered here are in no way intended to be comprehensive or to provide a 'one solution fits all.' By bringing together a multitude of cases, described in outline, *Building Better Universities* can only skim the surface of current initiatives. As I mentioned at the beginning, the book looks at educational strategies and initiatives, not at governance, management or financing, which are well dealt with elsewhere (Clark 2004; Shattock 2010), and although the focus starts from learning and teaching, in the current period this cannot be—and should not be—disaggregated from either research or business and civic engagement. Some of the examples used are well known, almost to the point of cliché, from having been repeated documented in a variety of forms. At the same time, many important examples are oversimplified, or overlap across themes, so may seem oddly placed. Important case studies may well have been left out. Others may be out of date even before the book is published, will be interpreted differently as new information becomes public, or will have been superseded by other approaches. Some may not take adequate account of the variations across nations, regions, or institutions, or in relation to different regulatory contexts. Although most of the examples here are from the English-speaking world, *Building Better Universities* aims to recognize and critically investigate some of the enormous amount of creative educational developments going on worldwide. Again this means there will be absences, particularly where information has not been translated into English. Finally, it is important to note that there are many organizations worldwide that regularly update examples of university and college initiatives through websites and publications (see, e.g., Oblinger 2012; Johnson et al. 2013; Organsiation for Economic Co-operation and Development 2013; Sharples et al. 2013).

The book is organized in this way because of an overall aim to explore across as wide a terrain as possible, and to bring together in one publication aspects of higher educational provision that are often dealt with separately, so as to allow cross-reference and cross-fertilization. As I said earlier, these themes, subthemes, and examples have been selected and reviewed here not as 'good practice' but to open possibilities and to enable critical thinking and debate, and they will thus be of varying value and relevance to different institutions, managers, and faculty. As I have also said, the ultimate intention is to support action and debate that does not fall into the simplistic divisions of public good versus private market; academic autonomy versus academic inefficiencies; or education as an individual transaction versus a cultural necessity. In resisting these simple oppositions between 'private' and 'public' educational provision, it aims to explore positive kinds of hybridity, and in challenging existing dominant discourse intends to bring to the fore concepts that are often less visible in policy debate, such as social enterprise, civic engagement, and open education. So, while *Building Better Universities* looks at a range of contemporary strategies, spaces, and technologies, it unashamedly focuses on education as about something more than either profit or the economy. Many examples here are deliberately chosen because they offer ways of going beyond simply enhancing employability (e.g., a pressure felt particularly at this moment in the US and the UK) by making more central the public value of universities.

Conclusion: Quality and Equality?

In 2011, Clayton Christensen and colleagues produced a paper for the Center for American Progress titled *Disrupting College*, based on his already well-known work on creative disruption in the education sector (Christensen et al.

2011; Christensen and Eyring 2011). In it he argues that universities and colleges no longer seem able to offer a good "product" to the increasing percentage of the population they are meant to serve, at an affordable price, and at low cost. Instead, as already noted here, "universities' prestige came not from being the best at educating, but from being the best at research and from being selective and accepting the best and brightest—which all institutions have mimicked" (Christensen et al. 2011: 1). He suggests that the conventional university is increasingly unsustainable because it tends to have large administrative overhead, again as argued earlier, the result of a business model that is trying to do too many things at once:

> [F]or decades now they have offered multiple value propositions around knowledge creation (research), knowledge proliferation and learning (teaching), and preparation for life and careers. They have as a result become conflations of the three generic types of business models—solution shops, value-adding process businesses, and facilitated user networks. This has resulted in extraordinarily complex—some might say confused—institutions where there are significant coordinative overhead costs that take resources away from research and teaching.
>
> (ibid.: 3)

He also proposes that—stuck in their existing mode—conventional universities are not taking advantage of the opportunities of new technologies for online learning or changing their business models radically enough. They are thus vulnerable to new entrants, who can operate differently, both to open up new student markets and to move increasingly into direct competition with what such 'conventional' universities offer.

This book has been informed by, and accepts much strength in, Christensen's analysis and those writers and thinkers who have taken it forward—particularly in showing how the currently structuring of higher education through emulation and 'bandwagon' jumping is having detrimental effects on higher education provision overall:

> [W]hilst society has focused on how higher education can serve a wider range of purposes, particularly the creation of a highly skilled workforce, higher education itself has its focus elsewhere, namely how to raise institutional prestige. So at the very time when society needs a wider array of institutions to serve a more diverse set of students, particularly students from less advantaged groups, higher education is moving towards homogenization and a focus on supposedly better students.
>
> (Brown, n.d.: 5)

However *Building Better Universities* also starts from the belief that Christensen's argument oversimplifies how universities and colleges have been developing and changing over the last decades—and could improve in the future—as they respond to both internal dynamics and external pressures. They may be much more hybrid entities than before, with multiple income streams and customers, but this is not necessarily a failing. Universities are combining with business to enable direct application of research; are collaborating regionally, nationally and globally to offer different kinds of services; are offering innovative forms of community engagement and investment; are developing new hybrid interdisciplinary networks; and are outsourcing many of their previous functions. If, according to Christensen and Eyring (2011), these are sustaining rather than disruptive innovations, it does not reduce their potential value, impact, or resource effectiveness. However, it does make them harder to manage, potentially more expensive to run, and overly complex. So the unbundling and rebundling of universities and colleges many operations is certainly overdue.

At the same time, such an unbundling and rebundling process does not automatically lead to Christensen's conclusion—that the key innovative new model for education (based on the disruptive potential of new technology) is the for-profit online higher education provider aiming at a mass-scale, cheaper, and more instrumental form of education for the sectors of the market previously poorly catered for by universities. Rather, it suggests that there can be many new and innovative educational models in a variety of forms, because there are many creative and resource-effective ways to re-pattern the existing complex and hybrid 'shape' of higher education. This can lead to a variety of alternative approaches rather than merely a binary differentiation between elite and mass sectors of the educational market. This might be, for example, by developing new kinds of hybrid discipline groupings; by offering cross-cutting educational themes such as global educational citizenship, social enterprise, creativity, entrepreneurship, or inclusive pedagogies; or by forming new kinds of embedded business or community engagement in which the conventional 'boundaries' of the university are reformed into completely new kinds of entities. And, while there may be pressures from the for-profit sector, specializing in vocational and career-oriented study, there are many examples to learn from of universities and colleges that remain committed to a public and social dimension for higher education.

Throughout this Introduction, I have signposted the importance of going beyond current educational discourses and concepts, as essential to building better universities. Before going on to explore many different and interesting examples of contemporary university and college initiatives in the rest of this book, I end here with just one piece of work to illustrate how higher education might begin to more critically examine its own internal dynamics, engage proactively with external pressures, and develop research that informs its educational decision-making. In a recent Economic and Social Research Council–funded project, titled *Quality and Inequality in University First Degrees* (Ashwin et al. 2012), the research team members from Nottingham, Lancaster, and Teeside Universities in the UK have challenged some of the underlying assumptions of university and college ranking systems, critiqued earlier. They have examined how quality and 'excellence' might be redefined in ways that capture both the individual and social dimension of higher education for students and that can communicate the effectiveness of different courses and universities in other ways. And they have produced an explicit and practical example of how this can be implemented. They first show how standardized public information (such as the National Student Satisfaction Survey and the league tables in the UK) is inaccurate in how it differentiates quality:

> This is because such tables misleadingly oversimplify the complexity of a high quality undergraduate education and because they offer no indication of students' engagement with academic knowledge. By using measures that largely reflect historical reputation and financial advantage, national higher education league tables are likely to reinforce social inequality by suggesting incorrectly that students who have been to higher status institutions have received a higher quality education and are likely to have developed greater knowledge and skills.
>
> (ibid.: 6)

As they write, focusing particularly on the social sciences,

> [t]he research proposed here is designed both to question the assumption that teaching and learning are self-evidently better in higher status universities; and, to develop a definition of the quality of teaching and learning which is fair and which takes account of the idea that a university education is for personal growth and the good of society, as well as for economic growth of the nation and prosperity for the individual.
>
> (www.pedagogicequality.ac.uk)

In their final report Ashwin et al. (2012: 2) propose alternative criteria for judging quality in higher education, based on defining high-quality undergraduate courses as "those which lead students to engage with academic knowledge in transformative ways." They see this transformative impact as having three threads—access to and understanding of academic knowledge that is interesting and relevant to students' lives, changes in the way that students understand themselves and their place in the world, and a deeper understanding of people and society. This in turn, was developed as a set of questions that could be used to evaluate student achievements.

In their research, the team members identified indicators of high-quality learning outcomes and processes that they argue are not captured by the measures currently used in higher education league tables. They were also able to define suggested graduate outcomes for social science education (the subject area they particularly focused on), which incorporated both individual and social benefits. These were the following:

- enhanced academic and employability skills
- understanding of and empathy for a wider range of people
- a change in personal identity and an intention to change society for the better.

> The extent to which students experienced each of these individual and social benefits was positively and significantly related to their levels of engagement with academic knowledge or mastery of their subject.
>
> (ibid.: 6)

Research such as this offers just one example of how universities and colleges can 'talk back' about what they believe are the key and distinctive characteristics of a university or college education – important issues that are getting lost in current debates and policy changes. Throughout the rest of *Building Better Universities* there are many more examples. The ultimate aim is that these will help senior managers and faculty to critically and creatively review their own institutions and to enable a more nuanced and learning-centered public debate about the state of higher education more widely.

1
Reshaping Universities and Colleges

'Higher education' is an educational process that may or may not be found in universities: it is a critical concept that provides standards such that educational processes in universities (or institutions of higher education for that matter) can be assessed as to the extent to which they fulfil the criteria implied in the idea of higher education.
—Barnett (2011: 2–3)

Contemporary public universities, as the major providers of higher education, have developed a common shape—with, of course, many variations—out of their local and national traditions and practices. The history and contemporary state of the typical western university has been written about many times. As outlined in the Introduction, universities tend to offer a variety of subjects, usually covering a comprehensive range across the sciences, social sciences, arts, and humanities. They offer learning as a structured experience over several years, organized through levels, and with entry controls and exit accreditation at each stage. They (mainly) break learning into components such as modules that are then built sequentially by students into a coherent set. They have powers of accreditation that benchmark levels of achievement and quality against national and international norms. They combine knowledge creation with its dissemination and application. They develop different subject and vocational expertise that is then 'passed on' to others, both for their own personal and career development and for developing the academic discipline area and university itself. Although there are many differences in how subjects are bundled, taught, researched, governed, and funded across various educational institutions, this underlying educational model remains recognizable yet also has inherent tensions and difficulties, which are returned to throughout this book.

I explore in more depth how this typical university shape is being challenged by for-profit educational providers and new kinds of public–private partnering in Chapter 2. First, however, I want to explore some of the new forms of higher education—sometimes calling themselves universities and sometimes not—that are currently emerging. Are there hints of alternative kinds of educational models, offering different ways of learning, teaching, and researching? Can (or should) universities restructure the conventional model, and if so, why and in what different kinds of bundles? How and why might the student experience be different—and even better—to the 'norm'? And can we support students more effectively in their studies? Examples of efforts in each of these areas are examined, both to open up debate about what universities are *for* in the early twenty-first century and to investigate how this is affecting their actual reshaping 'on the ground.'

More or Less the Same?

The current view of contemporary universities from its disaffected critics in the English-speaking world is well summed up by Rolfe, is his comments on the ubiquitous mission statement:

> Most university mission statements tend to express more or less the same aims, observations, aspirations and assumptions [. . .] and which 'all claim that theirs is a unique educational institution.' They 'all go on to describe this uniqueness in exactly the same way'. (Readings 1997: 133) One possible reason for this conformity is perhaps, because, as William Melody observes, 'the primary measure of the modern university is simply to do what its funders want it to do.' (1997: 82)
>
> (2013: 54)

University mission statements often exemplify the complexification of our educational models and the tensions and dilemmas involved (Pinheiro et al. 2012; Pinheiro and Stensaker 2014). As higher education accumulates more and more—potentially contradictory—activities, it still maintains a preference for a comprehensive 'all things to all people' version of the university, in too many cases just adding more items to its mission list. Beyond the elite institutions (that can continue to build on their national and international prestige) this is having the effect of many educational institutions competing for the same territory. They promote themselves as multipurpose organizations, providing 'excellent' or 'quality' education to attract the 'brightest and the best'—copying and reproducing the existing system rather than innovating in new directions. Within a context predominantly about developing differentiation generated by the market, this is unwittingly supporting a simplistic bifurcation between vocationally oriented colleges (together with many new for-profit providers) and universities ranked by status and reputation. It is potentially leading to a world in which colleges and their equivalents only do 'one' thing—locally relevant or massively scaled-up vocational courses, whereas universities offer a full array of learning, teaching and research and scrabble not to drop to the bottom of the league table or—if the worse comes to the worse—find themselves 'merely' teaching universities. However, there are in fact many alternatives to such a self-perpetuating system. Here I explore some examples that have taken different views on how to reshape these conventional components—both at the level of the whole university and within it. This chapter thus considers some of the emerging educational models of new providers, being developed across the public, private, and open sectors. Three themes are drawn out. The first is an increasing lack of relevance of formal accreditation, even that provided by a recognized 'prestigious' university. In fact, reputation and status are potentially disaggregating from certification; new entities are selling themselves on the quality of their academics alone or on the value of the learning, not on the heritage of the institution. Many of these new organizations are thus positioning themselves as apart from, and therefore better than, conventional universities and colleges. The second theme concerns the radical restructuring of current degree delivery. Here, the challenge is to the assumptions behind what constitutes a 'standard' university course and what types and combinations of courses universities should be offering. The final theme explores some examples of rethinking relationships between university and student, such that the learner is not merely a passive 'receiver' of services.

Theme 1.1: Alternative Universities?

1.1.a Singularity University, Silicon Valley, USA

The Singularity University (SU) starts not from a model of the typical all-purpose university but from a specific, focused, and unifying *theme*, as expressed in the strap line on their homepage: to "assemble, educate and inspire a new generation of leaders who strive to understand and utilize exponentially advancing technologies to address humanity's grand challenges" (http://singularityu. org/). Such a thematic view cuts across separate subject areas. It is a direct response to the contemporary moment, in which the rate and the hybrid nature of technological change creates a demand for education across many academic and applied disciplines. As cofounder Peter Diamandis says, he "realised there was no place I could go and learn this stuff without getting a PhD in multiple fields. I said to myself, I bet there's a great market for an international interdisciplinary university teaching all the exponential technologies" (Rowan 2013).

Cofounded with Ray Kurtzweil in 2008—and linked to his work in *The Singularity is Near* (2006)—the university is based at NASA's Ames site. It began as a summer school and is now expanding into a much larger operation, with an intended global reach. Its business model comes from the conventional logic of achieving a high ranking, status, and reputation. Its market is an elite audience, paying large fees for a variety of events and courses, and benefiting from working with world-famous guest speakers, specialist faculty, and having access to high-quality equipment and resources:

> The four- and seven-day executive programmes—six this year—help to fund the ten-week graduate-studies programme, in which 80 carefully chosen international students split their time between lessons and "creating projects that will impact humanity". After about 160 lectures and several days of intensive workshops, they work on business ideas that could potentially affect a billion people. Last year there were 4,000 applicants from 120 countries for the 80 slots. [. . .]
>
> The project is also scaling up. The university recently acquired the Singularity Summit conferences and the Singularity Hub web portal; and it will launch two-day Singularity Summits in various cities. Online education will be "a huge initiative for 2013", according to Gabriel Baldinucci, in charge of development and strategy. "It will be a paid course. We see ourselves as very complementary to graduate schools."
>
> (Rowan 2013)

The university has also moved from nonprofit to a for-profit benefit corporation, because a central aim is to create business incubators and take stakes in spun-out companies. Crucially, SU is not accredited and does not plan to become so: "You need to fix your curriculum for that," says Salim Ismail. "We change ours five times a year! One of the deans at Stanford proudly told me they update theirs every six years. But if you're doing a master's degree today in neuroscience or advanced robotics or biotech, by the time you finish you're out of date" (quoted in ibid.).

So, here is a university that does not give awards but still promotes itself as a high-quality and innovative educational institution, albeit via the conventional norms of the sector: based on the reputation of its academics and on the excellence of the provision. It is also likely to be successful in competing for, and attracting, high-achieving students who, in turn, will cement its reputation. For Diamandis, "we're building a university here, a community, a family of people who are thinking about the future. And we're iterating. This is just the beginning. In a world where the biggest problems on the planet are the biggest market opportunities, why wouldn't you be focusing on them?" (ibid.). SU, then, competes with the most elite universities worldwide, with a unique selling point (USP) that challenges a reliance on history and tradition to guarantee quality. But unlike the Massachusetts Institute of Technology (MIT) Media Lab, say, that also combines courses with start-up opportunities, SU can be very flexible and adaptable, offering a variety of courses at market prices with fewer overheads or external oversight demands. It cross-subsidizes single semester courses with commercially priced one-off events (in the summer of 2013 $12,000/£7,650 for a seven-day program) and aims to 'sweat' all its assets, including offering its faculty up as guest speakers (Figure 1.1).

The underlying tendency—toward an emphasis on current technologies and interdisciplinary development—is, of course, being reflected elsewhere, often linked as with SU to direct entry into the elite global educational market. In Saudi Arabia, for example, the King Abdullah University of Science and Technology opened in 2010 and is already the world's sixth-richest university, with a $10 billion endowment. Like SU, it does away with academic departments,

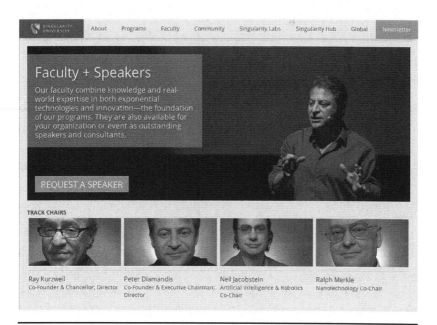

Figure 1.1 Singularity University's 'request a speaker' webpage
Source: http://singularityu.org/faculty/. Reprinted with permission from Susan Moran.

instead having four interdisciplinary research institutes focusing on biosciences, materials science, energy and the environment, and computer science and math.

1.1.b The New College of the Humanities, London, UK

The philosopher A.C. Grayling's new London-based educational institution, the New College of the Humanities (NCH), also aims for an elite clientele, but this time not so much looking 'forward' as 'backward' based on precisely the idea of tradition and heritage as a marker of quality. It offers a traditional liberal arts education, reclaimed from what Grayling considers the latest fads and unnecessary bureaucratic requirements of existing universities, to focus on the "study of the humanities [which] provides personal enrichment, intellectual training, breadth of vision, and the well-informed, sharply questioning cast of mind needed for success in life in our complex and rapidly changing world" (NCH 2013: 4). It is framed around the Oxbridge model of small-group teaching, very regular writing tasks and individual tutorials with faculty. Begun in 2012, NCH is still a tiny organization, but has received a lot of media attention, particularly in the UK (Figure 1.2).

Figure 1.2 The Georgian townhouse in which the New College of the Humanities is based in Bedford Square, London, UK

Source: Photo by Jos Boys.

NCH does not have its own award-giving powers—it is not a university—obtaining its formal accreditation by preparing its students for an already existing and validated University of London undergraduate Honours degree, designed for international students. Applicants choose from programs in economics, English, law, philosophy, and politics and international relations. To differentiate itself from these programs (because these are also offered by the University of London), the NCH program adds additional modules. Its students take twelve modules through the University of London (with exams set and assessed through that university as awards giver) and then an additional eight others. These are a contextual course (of four modules), three core modules (in Applied Ethics, Logic and Critical Thinking, and Science Literacy) and a professional program. Success in these 'other' eight modules is then recognized through an additional NCH diploma:

> This is a novel and highly important feature of the education at the College. These modules give intellectual breadth, a genuine understanding of the complex world we face, and the capacities to deal with it.
>   (www.nchum.org/about-nch/welcome)

According to the organization, NCH students experience "one of the best student-to-staff ratios in UK higher education, with extra contact hours each week and personal guidance in all aspects of study and work, including weekly one-to-one and small group tutorials." Facilities such as libraries and student accommodation are provided by the University of London. However, students also pay for this concentrated amount of guidance, with fees currently at £18,000 a year, "twice the maximum that even the most famous British universities are currently allowed to charge" (Collini 2013). This also means that its students do not qualify for publicly backed loans, nor has it obtained 'trusted sponsor' status from the visa authorities (and so it cannot bring in students from beyond the EU), although the college does award scholarships.

The NCH is funded as a not-for-profit college, a subsidiary of the private provider Tertiary Education Services Limited, which can distribute its own profits—when there are any—to directors and shareholders (McGettigan 2013). As Collini notes, with just fifty-six students enrolled in the first year and sixty-five in the second, "in McGettigan's view, NCH 'is unviable but for the deep pockets of its private equity backers,' principally a Swiss family who run a venture-capital company based in Lucerne" (2013). In time, the college hopes to admit 300 to 350 students every year (the size of a large Oxbridge college) but, as with many of the elite universities, may become reliant on additional private funding, despite the level of fees.

More recently, the NCH has decided not to use success in secondary school exams as the only form of gatekeeping applicants' academic standards. This is "because of an 'increased mistrust' in the traditional sixth-form exam. [. . .] The change, applying to students starting courses this autumn, follows a similar move towards unconditional offers at several other leading universities" (Patton 2014). Although this move can be read as a shift away from the limitations of 'standard' admissions procedures, and their effects on restricting entry, it is obviously also a means to increase student numbers.

The NCH, then, is a very contemporary hybrid. It promotes itself as "a liberal arts institution that offers intensive teaching of the humanities in an intimate setting" (Gentleman 2013) based on a conventional 'top' university education model—the best way, according to Grayling, to learn. But it has done this through offering a niche USP, adapting existing validated programs rather than developing its own, externalizing costs by using existing facilities from its 'host' university, bringing in big names for a few guest lectures, not doing research, 'adding' on extra educational components to intensify and deepen study, and getting backing funding through private investors. SU and the NCH, then, locate themselves in very different ways at the elite end of the higher education marketplace, but both aim to compete on status and reputation. They have both divested themselves of obtaining their own accreditation—with its associated costs and inflexibility—and to some extent of other costs and management overheads. Both obtain research and educational expertise by bringing it in. Both have done what Christensen recommends in his many writings on educational disruption, which is to simplify their functions and thus their business model.

In many ways, SU is much more radical (and can afford to be so, given the investment potential already embedded in its USP). It does not bother with formal accreditation at all. It does not see degree attainment as the only criterion for success and is not interested in a standard model with sequential levels of achievement and certification as a goal. It defies the current criteria for educational ranking systems. This move away from a degree structure and formal certification seems to be an important driver toward alternative kinds of university-level education more generally. Barber et al. suggest, for example, that some fellowship schemes have more prestige than top university qualifications:

> The Thiel Fellowship is unlike anything you've ever experienced. The Fellowship brings together some of the world's most creative and motivated young people, and helps them bring their most ambitious ideas and projects to life. Thiel Fellows are given a no-strings-attached grant of $100,000 to skip college and focus on their work, their research, and their self-education. They are mentored by our network of visionary thinkers, investors, scientists, and entrepreneurs, who provide guidance and

business connections that can't be replicated in any classroom. Rather than just studying, you're *doing*.

(2012: 6)

As with SU, learning takes place through the translation of ideas into practice, preferably in the real world. Informed by business methods and training processes, this is a kind of work-based learning based on peer mentoring, practice simulations and live projects. Another example given by Barber et al. is the [E]nstitute, a recent New York start-up with the tagline 'learn by doing' (2012:20). Here, courses are based on expert mentoring and an apprenticeship, so students learn from practitioners rather than from academics. The implication is that students who undertake these kinds of high-achieving educational programs can compete just as easily with, if not better, than someone who has studied at Harvard or Cambridge.

If the previous examples tend to an elite market, others are looking to extend the adult education, lifelong learning, and open education sectors. The School of Life (see Text Box 1.1 and Figure 1.3), also in London, was similarly set up by a philosopher, Alain de Botton, and colleagues. Here, however, the intended customer is very different, based on learners taking additional classes to their everyday work and/or student life. Adult education in the UK, which has had a variety of relationships to the university and college sector, has struggled with reduced public funding in recent years. This has generated some interesting new entrants—such as the School for Life—that has extended conventional adult educational courses into guest lectures and events, therapy courses, short business courses, a shop, branded publications, room hire, and international programs. It is also beginning to franchise out its name globally (with outlets in Melbourne and San Paolo). Another example is *The Guardian* newspaper, which is leveraging the expertise of its own staff (as well as invited experts), and its prestigious facilities in central London, to offer short courses in creative subjects validated by the University of East Anglia.

TEXT BOX 1.1   THE SCHOOL OF LIFE, LONDON, UK

The School of Life has the professed aim of putting "learning and ideas back to where they should always have been—right in the middle of our lives":

The School has a passionate belief in making learning relevant—and so runs courses in the important questions of everyday life. Whereas

> most colleges and universities chop up learning into abstract categories
> ('agrarian history' 'the 18th century English novel'), The School of Life
> titles its courses according to things we all tend to care about: careers,
> relationships, politics, travels, families. An evening or weekend on one
> of its courses is likely to be spent reflecting on such matters as your
> moral responsibilities to an ex partner or how to resolve a career crisis.
>
> (http://alaindebotton.com/the-school-of-life/,
> accessed January 25, 2014)

The school's selling point is that it takes ideas from the humanities—from philosophy to literature and psychology to the visual arts—not to so much to develop expertise in a subject as to inform everyday life, aligning perhaps more with the museum and gallery education sector to offer 'ideas that will exercise, stimulate and expand your mind.' It does this through a range of educational services, centered on classes and therapies at the school itself, both for individuals and for consulting and training for businesses. It also publishes books, films in-house events, and sells a range of 'objects and tools that will assist you in the quest for a more fulfilled life.' These are provided within a domestic environment:

> The School offers communal meals, holidays and a beautiful shop with
> fascinating gift vouchers and other items. It also has a division offering
> psychotherapy for individuals, couples or families—and it does so in a
> completely stigma-free way. For the normally reserved British, it must
> be a first to have an institution that offers therapy from an ordinary
> high street location and moreover, treats the idea of having therapy as
> no more or less strange than having a haircut or pedicure, and perhaps
> a good deal more useful.
>
> *Reference*
>
> http://alaindebotton.com/the-school-of-life/
> (accessed January 25, 2014).

1.1.c Alternative Art and Architecture Schools, UK

If most of the previous examples have explicitly developed as new business opportunities aimed at the fee-paying end of the education market, there are other—grassroots-up—initiatives, responding to the difficulties caused for potential learners by increasing tuition fees and perceived inadequacies in existing university provision. These build on an alternative tradition, particularly in Europe, of student-led and self-directed universities in opposition to the

Figure 1.3 Exterior of the School of Life, London, UK
Source: Photo by Jos Boys.

establishment. Recently, across the UK, for example, groups of artists have been
developing alternative models of post-degree education based on crowdsourcing and peer-sharing (techniques transferred from the web that are explored in
greater depth in Chapter 6):

> A former library in Hackney may seem an unlikely venue for London's
> most talked-about new art school. [. . .] The year-long programme boasts
> visiting lecturers, including the curator of contemporary art and perfor-
> mance at Tate Modern, Catherine Wood, and artists such as Pablo Bron-
> stein and Ed Atkins. And, at a time when art MAs in the capital cost
> up to £9,000 a year, the students pay no tuition fees. The project, which
> opened in September, is the latest alternative art school to be established
> in the UK. Open School East co-founder Sam Thorne, an associate editor
> of Frieze magazine, says their recent proliferation has been driven by the
> rise in fees and a growing disillusionment with university art education.
>
> (Batty 2013)

Open School East works on a barter system. Its selected thirteen associate
artists per year receive free tuition and studio space, in return for working with

local community groups one day a month. This might be through their own art practice, by involving local people, or by giving lessons in subjects such as dance or furniture design. Educational aims for the student artists are thus integrated with regenerating a building and neighborhood through wider social, cultural, and learning activities. Some lectures and workshops are also offered publicly for local people. The school also has a placement project with young people and rents out the building for community use. Started in 2013, the initial year has been funded by £110,000 from the Barbican and Create London, with the aim of developing longer term into a nonprofit but self-supporting social and cultural enterprise. Although this kind of study is visualized as operating at a postgraduate level, there is no interest in accrediting it.

Another example, also in London, is The School Of The Damned—an "underground Fine Art MA course run by its students and overseen by a board of captured academic advisors" (http://theschoolofthedamned.com/). This is offered free, based on informal labor exchange that allocates three days across the course of students' time to their visiting lecturers. Its aim is to offer a place where artists who cannot afford to study on an accredited program and/or have problems with the existing educational system can engage critically with their subject and with their own art practice. Similarly, the founders of do-it-yourself (DIY) art school in Manchester say their initiative is 'a survival tactic.' Set up last year by Manchester Metropolitan University graduates, the school provides a support network for recent graduates. Cofounder Katy Morrison says, "I would adore to do an MA but I can't afford it. This is about trying to create a professional pathway for ourselves" (Batty 2013). The proposed London School of Architecture (Text Box 1.2) plans the same for architectural students, creating a system of peer mentoring for the professional elements of their course.

TEXT BOX 1.2   PROPOSED LONDON SCHOOL OF ARCHITECTURE

The London School of Architecture (LSA) was created by architectural journalist Will Hunter and was developed through a research group called Alternative Routes for Architecture (ARFA) set up in 2012:

> Our starting point was a simple one: how can you make architectural education lower cost and better value? The first so that the profession is an affordable career for talented students to enter; and the second so that graduates are well equipped with the intellectual creative capital

and the core competencies to shape the built environment in the 21st
century. [. . .]

Rather than get trapped in the false dichotomy between 'academia'
and 'practice'—where one is where 'thinking' happens and the other
is about 'buildings'—we thought instead about 'design' and 'research'
as activities that both students and practitioners would engage in
throughout their careers. The question was how can you make a bridge
to unite these two groups around those twin pursuits?

(Hunter 2013)

The school argues that architectural practice in the UK has changed and
that conventional university education has struggled to keep up with its
multidisciplinary, networked, and flexible forms. Hunter asks if universities
"often ossified structures allow enough flexibility to respond to the speed and
scale of the changes in the outside world?" (2012) The LSA also aims to be
cheaper, by savings on overhead and by working directly with practitioners.
It plans to charge fees at half the price of a London post-degree architectural
diploma course (i.e., £4,500 rather than £9,000 per year as of 2014). The
LSA proposed model is one of self-directed learning, supported by place-
ments in architectural practices. Students will be expected to self-organize
into research clusters and to work together to produce leading-edge work
and debate that can be shared with the wider profession. Year on year, projects will concentrate on a particular locality, and students will have a budget
to spend on renting space relevant to their needs. The architectural practices
where they work will be involved in teaching, and given a budget to bring in
relevant professional expertise, as required.

For more information see: www.the-lsa.org/

References

Hunter, W. (2012) "Alternative Routes for Architecture: The Urgent Case
for a New School of Architecture," *Architectural Review*, December 28.
Available at: www.architectural-review.com/essays/alternative-routes-for-
architecture/8636207.article (accessed January 2, 2014).

Hunter, W. (2013) "New School of Architecture Launched," *Architectural
Review*, October Available at: www.architectural-review.com/view/overview/
new-school-of-architecture-launched/8653692.article (accessed January 2,
2014).

Other examples are aiming more specifically to widen access to higher education. The well-known artist Ryan Gander intends to set up a postgraduate art
academy that would give preferential consideration to poorer applicants:

He says the school, called Fairfield International, would level the play-ing field between students from disadvantaged backgrounds and the "trustafarian rich kids" whom he fears increasingly dominate the major art schools. Based in a former Victorian school in Saxmundham in Suf-folk [UK], where Gander lives, it will offer free studio space and accom-modation for 12 students a year and offer tuition from renowned artists.

(Batty 2013)

These cost-free, labor-sharing, and non-accredited models all currently operate at a very small scale. Nonetheless, they compete with conventional university–based education, both in challenging standard undergraduate and postgraduate degree structures and costs and in redefining the assumed rela-tionships between students, tutors, practitioners, and the wider community. When Batty asked established university providers of art education to com-ment, respondents were well aware of current difficulties for potential students, particularly in the arts and humanities:

Simon Ofield-Kerr, vice-chancellor of the University for the Creative Arts in Kent, believes the trend poses a challenge at a time when there is a "real danger of postgraduate study being devastated". [. . .]

Susan Collins, director of London's Slade School of Fine Art, adds that recent cost-cutting measures in some art departments, such as scrap-ping dedicated studio space, have reduced the attractiveness of university study. "Presenting hot-desking as an idea for art education is not the way forward," she says. "I can completely understand why some artists want to pursue other models of learning."

(ibid.)

There are many different hybrids of this kind extending beyond art edu-cation, which may combine fees with labor exchange and volunteer elements or may offer alternative learning practices to the university (such as the Uni-versity of the People, covered in Chapter 5). The Silent University (http://thesilentuniversity.org/), an alternative school for refugees and asylum seekers, set up by Turkish artist Ahmet Öğüt during his residency at the Tate Mod-ern last year, now runs courses in several European countries. Although such educational offerings are not based on the three- or four-year structure of the conventional undergraduate degree—offering instead intensive, short courses or different ways of accumulating learning—they could have the potential to become direct competitors to university-style education, as people decide to embed different types of learning throughout their lives and careers, rather than take the linear sequence of school–university–employment. It should also be noted here that this increased opening up of many different kinds of educational opportunities is making the problem of finding out what is available much harder, as well as how educational value and relevance can be judged or compared (both by potential applicants and by potential employers), issues that are followed up on in Chapter 5.

What then, is the potential of these developing models? They all, in different ways, reflect the unbundling/rebundling and hybridization processes going on across the higher education sector. Each focuses on a clear—more specialist—mission than the conventional university and then aims to leverage its assets in creative and sometimes unexpected ways, across educational, financial, and social intentions. And, as I have already said, in most cases formal accreditation has become much less relevant, replaced instead by an alternative kind of prestige or different goals of personal learning development and/or social engagement.

Theme 1.2: Radical Restructuring

Existing universities have also been revisiting their current 'shape.' Many are attempting various forms of rationalization or consolidation of courses, and restructuring or closing departments and schools. Here I first outline perhaps two the best-known approaches, that taken at Melbourne University to deliberately re-pattern the proportion of undergraduate to postgraduate programs and then the various moves to build a competencies rather than course-based educational framework, such as, for example, at Western Governors University. I then note how the kinds of rebundling into new cross-disciplinary groupings, already considered earlier, is being articulated through a shifting in internal academic organization—here, at Arizona State University.

1.2.a *The Melbourne Model, New South Wales, Australia*
In 2008 Melbourne University in Australia put in place a ten-year project for radically restructuring the University's curriculum offer, aiming to shift the focus from undergraduate to postgraduate education. What had been a large number of undergraduate courses were replaced with just six degree programs, so that students could obtain a broad background knowledge, before moving on to studying a subject in depth. To develop greater 'cultural literacy' among undergraduates, students also take six of twenty-four subjects from a range outside their core course (and can obtain an additional diploma qualification in this subject area). The restructuring also aimed to build in study abroad and student exchange programs. This shift came together with a planned reduction in the number of undergraduate enrolments and a cut in overall student

numbers from 50,000 to 35,000. The emphasis, then, is now on postgraduate research, professional entry, and professional development degrees:

> There was a vision of what excellent education should be—young people gaining a broad, general education before specialising. But the Melbourne Model was also based on a recognition that in a highly regulated yet underfunded sector, the area that was both least regulated and potentially most lucrative was postgraduate programs. There the university had more freedom to charge fees, and hence more freedom to pursue an independent vision of excellence.
>
> (Simons 2010)

Not surprisingly, this change to more generalist undergraduate degrees, followed by specialization at master's level (which has been partially informed by the European Bologna Declaration) has provoked some controversy in Australia, in terms of its relevance to students, in its impact on staffing, and as to whether it was mainly an excuse for cost cutting. Here, the key point is the challenge it offers to other universities who have not been prepared to take this kind of risk and to consider reducing student numbers, rather than increasing them.

1.2.b Competencies-Based Education
When LinkedIn asked Jeff Selingo (2013a) for a 'big idea' for 2014, he wrote that

> [m]ore colleges will shift from measuring learning based on how much time students spend in a classroom to a system that is based on how much they actually know. The official term for this is "competency-based education," and this past year, three universities—Northern Arizona University, the University of Wisconsin, and Southern New Hampshire—experimented with offering degrees in this way.
>
> Here's how it basically works: Students demonstrate mastery of a subject through a series of assessment tests or assignments, instead of following a prescribed set of courses. Faculty mentors work closely with students throughout a degree program to design a schedule and access the learning materials they need to demonstrate mastery and then another group of course evaluators grades those exams, research papers, or performance assessments.

Competency-based education organizes entry through learner profiling—through showing what you already know, rather than having it implied through some previous accreditation certificate. After that, students work at their own pace. If they understand the material they can move on more quickly; if they struggle, then they can take more time. Assessment comes at the point that the *student* decides they have learnt enough and are ready to be tested. Western Governors University (WGU) has followed just such a competency-based model since it was founded in the late 1990s (Text Box 1.3). Twenty-five thousand students pay just under US$3,000 a semester for as many courses as they can complete in a six-month period. The average student at Western Governors completes a bachelor's degree in about two and half years, at a cost of about US$15,000 (Selingo 2013a). This pattern of pricing and costing is based on a rationalization and segregation of different learning, teaching, and management components:

> [WGU] organize the delivery of instruction separately, through standardized processes using specially trained instructors and mentors. They support both functions through centralized infrastructure management systems that provide additional economies of scale.
>
> (Sheets et al. 2012: 9)

TEXT BOX 1.3 WESTERN GOVERNORS UNIVERSITY

Western Governors University (WGU) is a private nonprofit university, founded in 1997, with seedbed funding from nineteen western state governors. Its aim was to expand access to affordable college education for working adults as 'a new kind of university' based on online learning and on the knowledge students possess rather than the number of hours they spend in a classroom.

It is made up of four colleges, each offering bachelor's and master's degree programs: Business, Information Technology, Teacher Education, and Health Professions (including Nursing). As of January 2013, it delivered fifty-five bachelor's, master's, and postbaccalaureate degrees, as well as teacher endorsement preparation programs, offered across four colleges and with additional affiliated sites in Indiana, Tennessee, Texas, and Washington. The university does not develop its own courses but, instead, licenses course modules from commercial providers such as Pearson and McGraw-Hill.

Crucially, WGU has a competency-based framework, allowing students to take different amounts of time to achieve certificates or degree awards:

> Competency-based programs allow students to demonstrate through assessments that they have acquired the set of competencies (levels of knowledge, skill, or ability) required for a particular degree or certificate, allowing students to build on what they already know, and just

concentrate on what they need to learn. For example, the university states that the business management bachelor's degree requires "132 Competency Units (credit equivalents)" and can be completed in four to five years for students with little or no prior college, but that "successful students who commit 20 hours or more per week to their studies are often able to complete their programs more quickly."

(http://en.wikipedia.org/wiki/
Western_Governors_University)

Students at WGU are each given a working mentor who works with them throughout their studies. Each mentor/student team creates a personal academic action plan (AAP) that helps the student track his or her progress through each six-month term. Students at WGU have some control over how much course work they complete per term but are required to complete a minimum each term to maintain full-time status. There are no regulations concerning study loads, but students must have the mentor approval to add courses during a term. Students may also take certain exams without study for some courses if they show competency via pre-assessments. Other courses require weeks-long participation in online courses and in written submissions that are graded by independent contract evaluators.

For further information see:
www.wgu.edu

The major USP here is the flexibility offered to students in the amount and speed of learning, and the possibility of having a variety of types of learning recognized beyond conventional credentialing. The University of Wisconsin, for example, clearly articulates what is special about its offering its 'flexible option' programs:

Earn credit for what you know:
You may draw upon your existing knowledge to complete assessments and make progress toward your degree. It does not matter where you gained your knowledge—from prior courses, work experience, military training, or other learning experiences. If you know it and can show it, you can use it to earn credit.

Advance at your own pace:
Progress toward your degree is based on assessments of key competencies determined by UW faculty, not seat time in a classroom. Take assessments whenever you are ready. Pass one and move on to the next.

Receive personalized support:

A dedicated Academic Success Coach will work with you to create your learning plan and a timeline tailored to fit your goals and knowledge. Your coach will help you prepare for assessments and point you to the learning resources you need to succeed.

Start when you want, at the beginning of any month:

Your progress is not limited by a traditional semester or term-based schedule, and you can take breaks in between subscription periods if and when you need to.

Learn skills employers value:

By passing assessments of critical competencies, you will prove your mastery of the skills and knowledge that are important to employers.

(http://ecampus.wisconsin.edu/online-degree-programs/flex-option.aspx)

The market for these degrees is also very clearly framed—mature and working students aiming to improve their vocational and employability skills. However, it is not inherent in the competencies-based model that these are the only learners it suits.

1.2.c Arizona State—A New American University?

Like many universities, Arizona State University (ASU) has been reducing the number of its academic departments to save money, in this case by forming larger multidisciplinary groupings seen as being better matched to the cross-fertilization and hybridity of contemporary academic and business knowledge. For example, academics with a variety of specialist expertise are now clustered in the School of Earth and Space Exploration, through the combination of the Departments of Geology and Astronomy, the School of Human Evolution and Social Change, some faculty from the Department of Anthropology, and some from the Department of Sociology. It has also unbundled the administrative functions often replicated across different departments. This results in academics being differently 'located' in other ways:

The implementation of the university-wide ASU graduate faculty model in 2007 had several immediate effects. First, because faculty could be members of several graduate faculty groups at once, there was a 72 percent increase in the listings of faculty in doctoral programs across the university. Second, whereas only a few faculty members had served on multiple doctoral committees previously, the reorganization led to over 620 faculty members' officially being recognized as members of multiple graduate programs—over half the doctoral faculty. Third, as ASU launched new interdisciplinary PhDs, the graduate faculty model became central to their structure and success. [. . .] This model has broadened faculty thinking about degree programs and has also increased the intellectual capacity and experience available to our students.

(Capaldi 2009: 128)

Capaldi goes on to argue that most universities are 'stuck' in both their existing academic and administrative structures because of the way academic departments work as separate silos and that this is now an outmoded form (ibid.: 134). This strategic rebundling, together with a series of other developments, has led Michael M. Crow, the university's president, to promote Arizona State as a 'new American university' (2011) model for the future.

Theme 1.3: Enhancing the Student Offer

The previous examples have been concerned to reshape what is offered to students for promotional, pedagogic and resource-effective motives. The final theme is about adding value, through rethinking the student experience beyond the simple 'accumulation' of a subject-specific education, therefore reframing the relationship of the student to their studies, to the university, and to the wider world. As already shown, the alternative courses increasingly on offer make students central—not just as consumers of services but also as members of an extended learning community and as co-creators. This, then, has the potential to generate innovative forms of enhanced learning opportunities, valuable knowledge exchange, and learning that easily turns into applied and action research. Here, I want to expand on this issue by considering how making students central beyond the 'degree' transaction, can have implications for learning, teaching, and research, for the role of student services and for governance. Whereas in the UK, for example, the Higher Education Academy (HEA) 'students as partners' agenda (see www.heacademy.ac.uk/students-as-partners) is having some impact on how students are perceived by their institutions, the extent to which students are envisaged as actors beyond their particular courses of study remains limited. Klemencic argues that students' learning can be deeply enhanced by their involvement in the university beyond studying:

> [H]igher education governance in general and student participation in particular is of particular relevance for students' civic learning, as one of the purposes or social roles of higher education. First, student participation in institutional governance opens practical learning opportunities for the student representatives directly engaged. As Biesta (2007, p.4) suggests, 'the most significant "lessons" in citizenship actually are the

result of what people learn from their participation (or for that matter: non-participation) in the communities and practices that make up their everyday life'. [. . .]

Second, and more far reaching, involving students in institutional decision-making as partners emphasises the value of individuals' engagement in the public sphere (to which public higher education institutions undoubtedly belong).

(2011: 75)

Thus, enhancing the student offer has potential to add value in a number of ways, for individual students, for universities and colleges, and for society. Involving students as representatives in formal institutional decision-making processes enables them both to be more engaged with their learning and to develop useful personal skills. Enabling students to engage with wider activities that are concerned with social value across the whole university can help them to identify with their institution and supports the social and public dimension of higher education as well as its self-interests. There are many ways of extending learning opportunities beyond an individual's course such as through cross-course projects and volunteering, some of which will be explored here.

1.3.a Beyond Disciplinary Boundaries

Some of these 'added-value' initiatives are also informed by the new subject hybridity outlined earlier and are therefore about enabling students to develop cross-disciplinary knowledge and skills. For example, Stanford University d.school (Text Box 1.4) sits "above and across" existing graduate programs at, so that "students and faculty in engineering, medicine, business, law, the humanities, sciences, and education [can] find their way here to take on the world's messy problems together" (http://dschool.stanford.edu/our-point-of-view/). It thus extends the conventional curriculum, integrates the university with the wider world, and brings students, staff and others together in new kinds of 'mash-up,' both face-to-face and online.

Text Box 1.4   d.school Institute of Design, Stanford University

The Hasso Plattner Institute of Design at Stanford University, known as the d.school, is a hub for innovators offering a wide variety of flexible learning spaces and resources, including studios, workshop spaces, furniture, and learning resources, to encourage exploration and innovation. The d.school focuses on creating transformative learning experiences for students of engineering, medicine, business, law, the humanities, sciences, and education. It is unique within the university in that all students from Stanford's seven schools are eligible to enroll in the d.school regardless of level or course they are undertaking. The aim of the d.school is to develop students who are capable of addressing the complex challenges of today's world by working on projects with partners in academia as well as corporate, nonprofit, and government-sector organizations. These partners often make financial contributions to support the d.school.

Students at Stanford are encouraged to augment their initial degree programme with supplementary classes in the d.school, where they work collaboratively on projects with students from different disciplines across the campus, drawing on methods from engineering and design and combining them with ideas from the arts, tools from the social sciences, and insights from the business world. Using a design thinking approach and design-led methods, students are required to define problems and take creative and analytical approaches to solving them through a variety of challenging projects that can last from a few hours to months, or even years. Solutions are tested iteratively in real life solutions, enabling students to reflect and learn at each stage and develop a variety of solutions to problems. By working together at each stage of the project, students are able to find ways of addressing problems that are more creative and innovative than if they had worked only with students from their own discipline.

For further information see:

d.school. Hasso Plattner. Institute of Design, Stanford University (2014) Available at: http://dschool.stanford.edu/ (accessed April 3, 2014).

"Pushing the Edges: The d.school" (2010) *360°*, no. 60 (Fall): 14–15. Available at: http://360.steelcase.com/articles/pushing-the-edges-the-d-school/ (accessed April 3, 2014).

In another variation, building skills beyond one's own disciplinary area is linked to the notion of the citizen-scholar. The Office of Sustainability at the University of Vermont (UVM), aims to foster sustainable development and promote environmental responsibility, not just through its approaches to campus planning and management but also "by strategically bridging the academic activities of teaching, research, and outreach with the operations of the University" (www.uvm.edu/sustain/). Students and staff are engaged through a series of initiatives, which develop them as innovators in this area. Over the years, students, faculty, and staff have collaborated to create systems

Figure 1.4 University of Vermont Clean Energy Fund: Call for ideas and example projects
Source: http://vimeo.com/channels/289293 (accessed May 01, 2014). Reprinted with permission from Mieko A Ozeki.

and projects that reduce the university's environmental 'footprint.' In 2012, for example, UVM became one of the first institutions nationwide to end the sale of bottled water on campus and agree that one-third of vending machine drinks should be a healthy. In addition, the university runs a green ideas competition for students. It asks for ideas and feedback for improving sustainability efforts on campus and has a Clean Energy Fund to support renewable-energy-related ideas—sustained by a self-imposed student fee of $10 per student per semester (Figure 1.4). Many other universities have developed similar sustainability and green campus initiatives, as well as networks such as University Leaders for a Sustainable Future (ULSF) and the Association for the Advancement of Sustainability in Higher Education (AASHE).

1.3.b Lincoln University, UK—Student as Producer

At the University of Lincoln rethinking the 'place' of the student had led to an explicit definition of higher education study that does not separate out learning from research (a point I will return to in the conclusion). If higher education is envisaged as a community of practice (Lave and Wenger 1991; Wenger 1998) centered around both specific subject areas and the university itself as a knowledge producer and disseminator (Boys 2010), then learning becomes part of a continuum toward developing both research capabilities and disciplinary knowledge. At Lincoln this has become articulated through a specific concept:

> Student as Producer emerged out of work that was already ongoing at the University in the area of research-engaged teaching. Academic staff and colleagues supporting teaching and learning as well as students were, from the outset, involved in the development and design of Student as Producer, ensuring a high degree of ownership across the University. This work evolved over a period of time, beginning in 2007, before being adopted as the University's Teaching and Learning Strategy in 2010.
>
> (QAA Good Practice Knowledgebase Case Study 2013: 1)

By explicitly linking academic research activities to undergraduate learning and by engaging students explicitly in research and critical inquiry, the project aims to articulate their students as increasingly expert collaborators, rather than just consumers of knowledge:

> Research-engaged teaching and learning is defined as: 'A fundamental principle of curriculum design whereby students learn primarily by engagement in real research projects, or projects which replicate the process of research in their discipline. Engagement is created through active collaboration amongst and between students and academics'.
>
> (http://studentasproducer.lincoln.ac.uk/project-proposal/)

This, then, is a whole institutional strategy for learning and teaching, embedded in the university's research culture. Implementation has been developed through a set of what are called 'infrastructural platforms,' named as bureaucracy, student engagement, teacher education, and learning landscapes. The approach also aims to generate opportunities for debate around the meaning and purpose of higher education across staff and students. This has been done through a series of principles (Text Box 1.5) that are then embedded into course monitoring procedures, as well as academic debate. The process is also supported through a Student Engagement Officer, and induction and student representation processes. For example, "academics are [. . .] asked to demonstrate the extent to which students are involved in the design and delivery of programs and courses, and show how the course enables students to see themselves having a role in creating their own future, in terms of employment, and to make a progressive contribution to society" (QAA Good Practice Knowledgebase Case Study 2013: 2).

Text Box 1.5 University of Lincoln, UK: Key Features of the Student as Producer Framework

Discovery

The programme or module should be presented in a *discovery* mode, which in HE [higher education] is usually characterised as one of the following:

Problem-based learning (PBL)
A student-centered approach where students collaboratively solve problems and reflect on their experiences [. . .]

Enquiry-based learning (EBL)
EBL describes an environment in which learning is driven by a process of enquiry owned by the student [. . .]

Research-based learning (RBL)
Research-based learning is an approach to programme design and implementation in which students have the opportunity to make intellectual and practical connections between the content and skills that characterise their programmes, and the research approaches and frontiers of the underlying disciplines. [. . .]

Technology in Teaching: Digital Scholarship
Research engaged teaching implies a change in the relationship between tutor and student. This changed relationship is facilitated by web 2, and is evident in various web-based activities, for example, commons-based peer-production [. . .] and Personal Learning Environments based on user choice of available tools to complete educational tasks. [. . .]

Space and Spatiality: Learning Landscapes in Higher Education
The use of space and spatiality in teaching is recognised as an important aspect of the new learning landscape (Dugdale 2009; Neary et al. 2010). In programme and module planning, tutors can show how they intend to use space in their teaching practice [. . .]

Assessment and Feedback: Active Learning in Communities of Practice
Tutors should show the ways in which their assessments reflect the discovery mode of teaching and learning [. . .]

Research and Evaluation: Scholarship of Teaching and Learning
Evaluation of teaching practices includes student feedback, but can go beyond the collection of feedback by involving staff and students in a programme of pedagogical research into their own learning and teaching experiences. [. . .]

Student Voice: Diversity, Difference, and Dissensus
The issue of student leadership is becoming increasingly important in the HE sector. The issue is related to the government's intention to develop a new style of politics and citizen engagement within which the student voice is not only heard, but amplified (Higher Education Funding Council for England 2009). The emphasis on the Student Voice reflects the ways in which Student as Producer is dedicated to developing a community of learners and teachers which is respectful of diversity and difference, allowing for the space of dissensus and disagreement, driven by engaged and participatory pedagogies.

Support for Research-Based Teaching and Learning through Expert Engagement with Information Resources
Programmes should seek to engage with the University Library service to integrate the development of skills in, and the use of information resources in their programmes. Academic Subject Librarians are trained and equipped to work with academics to support this process.

Creating the Future: Employability, Enterprise, Postgraduate, Beyond Employability
[. . .] Student as Producer supports the career preparation and aspirations of students, in the form of a traditional route into the professions, working within an Small and Medium Enterprise (SME), creating a new start business, employment within the growing third sector or going on to further study.

Student as Producer maintains that research-engaged teaching and learning is more likely to result in graduates who are better prepared to cope with a globalised labour market which is characterised by ever-changing technology and working practices [. . .]

Reference
http://studentasproducer.lincoln.ac.uk/documents/key-features/ (accessed March 24, 2014).

Turning around the Tanker?

According to ASU president Michael M. Crow, existing universities sometimes seem like massive tankers: very difficult and slow to turn around (2011: 12). This is perhaps why change to these institutions is so often undertaken as an addition, or as an offshoot, rather than through root-and-branch remodeling. The examples outlined here offer some of the rethinking and restructuring currently being undertaken—whether to open up new markets, to offer economies of scale, to improve resource effectiveness, to better leverage assets, to offer a distinctive USP, or some combination of all of these. At the same time I have given examples of many innovative and alternative forms of knowledge, labor and resources exchange; and of the rebundling of relationships among learning, teaching, and research and among academics, students, and others.

All of these versions of university, college and 'other' learning organization start from an *idea* of higher education, and then attempt to implement it concretely in a particular context. What is most important here—and will be returned to again and again—is that these examples offer possibilities beyond the either/or stereotypes of for-profit training versus nonprofit academic elitism, outlined in the introduction. In their myriad ways they negotiate educational models that both add value for learners and aim to be resource effective (however that is defined). What constitutes value combines varying degrees of both individual and societal improvement and what constitutes resource effectiveness roves across actual costs and benefits and what might be called social or public costs and benefits. Judgments as to where added value should lie in higher education, and how it should be paid for, are not made here. These issues are for individuals to discuss and decide, for senior managers to embed in university and college decision making, and for stakeholders across the educational landscape to open up for wider debate, so as to ultimately have an impact on policy and regulation. This chapter, then, has set the scene for, and an approach to, the many examples given throughout this book. In the next chapter, I further explore the relationships between for-profit and nonprofit educational provision and how these are intersecting in new and interesting ways.

2

NEW PATTERNS OF PUBLIC AND PRIVATE COMPETITION AND COLLABORATION

[A] new phase of competitive intensity is emerging as the concept of the traditional university itself comes under pressure and the various functions it serves are unbundled and increasingly supplied, perhaps better, by providers that are not universities at all.
—*Laurence Summers, Foreword, in Barber et al. (2012 : 1)*

So far I have been arguing that we should not get caught up in debates over nonprofit versus for-profit educational providers. But this does not mean ignoring the changes being wrought by the growth in corporate and for-profit universities and colleges. For, as these newer players enter the market, a variety of new patterns of competition and collaboration are emerging, some state-led and some developed through market or public-sector initiatives. This chapter explores how higher education is shifting its boundaries across and between public and private sectors, leading to different patterns of organization from mergers to alliances and other hybrid arrangements. As Fielden et al. put it,

> [a] classic way of looking at providers has been to distinguish between providers with a profit motive and ones operating on a not-for-profit basis. This no longer seems to be a relevant distinction, since almost all UK not-for-profit universities now work on a businesslike basis and are expected by their funding bodies to accumulate surpluses in order to finance expansion and capital investment. [. . .]

Internationally, UK universities are expected to trade profitably and not to draw on the funds allocated to them for UK students or research. In addition, all universities have trading activities which generate income that is fed back into academic activities. Universities are becoming large consumers of investment funds and some universities undergo financial scrutiny by credit rating agencies such as Standard and Poors or Moody's in order to assist their capital- raising activity.

(2010: 13)

We now have public university with-profit arms, collaborative private–public entities and strategic collaborations for specific projects, as well as new kinds of outsourcing patterns. Although the corporate universities such as HamburgerU, Deloitte, and Motorola have been around some time, and new private education providers such as Apollo, Kaplan, and Pearson Education are beginning to compete for an increasingly large share in the higher education market, this chapter concentrates in its examples on hybrids—on public–private overlaps. This is both where a considerable amount of current development is happening and where we can best review alternative educational models and practices.

This means first exploring the extent to which the for-profit sector—in predominantly operating in a market manner, centered on developing individuals' career goals—has interacted with university and college traditions that include a social and public purpose. Is it, as Brown suggests, that "the underlying challenge [of for-profit institutions] is to the public purposes of higher education or, to be quite precise, how (and indeed whether) the public and private purposes can be reconciled" (n.d.: 1)? Has the increasing dominance of neo-liberalist ideas meant that the more civic aspects of the university are retreat? Rolfe, for example, suggests that

universities are now being organised and run as major business players in the increasingly lucrative 'knowledge economy'. [. . .] Supporters of these developments regard them as necessary responses to changes in how universities are funded (particularly the need to attract more 'paying customers'); to the emergence of new academic disciplines (and the demise of long-established ones) in response to the demands of those paying customers for vocational courses; and to the growing need for management, administration and accountancy in an every larger and more complex organisation.

Academics and students alike are being told that the university can no longer afford them the time for unproductive speculative thinking, that they must engage with the 'real world' of finance and industry, and, increasingly, that academics must justify their existence in terms of research grants from external funding organisations.

(2013: 3)

To Rolfe, the public purpose of universities *is* under attack. But the solution is not that we 'go back' to some imagined ivory tower of learning; instead, we must take the opportunity of a situation where "the wider social role of the University as an institution is 'now up for grabs'" (Readings 1997: 2). This also means that the public sector must face up to the underlying challenge from the for-profits that it is not able to provide *mass* higher education effectively. As I concluded in the previous chapter, across for-profit, nonprofit, and hybrid educational forms, the issues of added value and resource effectiveness need to be addressed, whilst underpinned by a commitment to meeting the public and social as well as private and individual goals of university and college education.

The Privatization of Higher Education

In much of the developed world, higher education has been increasingly privatized and marketized, meaning, first, that costs fall predominantly on education's 'customers' rather than being subsidized by the state and, second, that private-sector companies are accessing the university and college market in high numbers. As Fielden et al. have written,

> The growth of the private higher education sector is a global phenomenon. Levy (2009) estimates that private sector provision has grown to approximately 30 per cent of total global enrolments and that most of this is through non-profit private provision. By contrast, in the United States (which already has a large non-profit private sector), the fastest growing segment of higher education is the for-profit sector which has now reached almost 10 per cent of all enrolments in higher education.
>
> (2010: 10)

This is part of a longer-term process, taking place differently from country to country but with an underlying global trend over the last thirty years, as neoliberalist attitudes have taken hold:

> In the United States, state support peaked in 1972 at 62 percent and has declined steadily ever since. At the beginning of its most recent spiral in 1991, it was 40 percent. [. . .] Currently in the United States, both private and public institutions draw the majority of their support from non-state sources, including tuitions, research grants, and gifts (Duderstadt 2000) [. . .] there is evidence that the trends clearly visible in the United States towards privatisation are visible elsewhere [. . .] but given differences in the situations of American, European, Latin American, Australian and Asian colleges and universities (with differences among

these as well) the public university is currently the dominant form of higher education globally.

(Odin and Manica 2004: xv–xvi)

A similar process has been underway in Australia:

Australia's higher education system became a deregulated and commercially oriented system within a decade of major reforms. A number of initiatives came into play from the mid-1980s through the 1990s, all working to privatize the costs of education. [. . .] In 1989 certain postgraduate courses were made liable to fees; in 1994 the restrictions surrounding these courses were almost entirely removed, effectively leaving postgraduate coursework a fee-paying domain. Then from 1998 the Coalition (Liberal Party and National Party) government permitted universities to enrol a proportion of private Australian undergraduate students. [. . .] In the three years since 1998, government funding continued to fall, so that it now represents 50 percent of all funding for universities.

(Currie 2004: 54–55)

And in the UK,

[t]his government's whole strategy for higher education is, in the cliché it so loves to use, to create a level playing field that will enable private providers to compete on equal terms with public universities. The crucial step was taken in the autumn of 2010 with the unprecedented (and till then unannounced) decision to abolish the block grant made to universities to support the costs of teaching [. . .]. From the point of view of private providers, that change removed a subsidy to established universities which had hitherto rendered private undergraduate fees uncompetitive in the home market.

(Collini 2013)

TEXT BOX 2.1 UNIVERSITY OF PHOENIX

The University of Phoenix is a US for-profit institution of higher education that has been providing online education for more than twenty years. Its stated goal is to meet the needs of working and under-served students. It offers degree programs at associate, bachelor's, master's, and doctoral levels as well as certificate programs for career development, individual courses in a wide range of subject areas, and continuing teacher education. In addition to online learning the university provides on-campus education at more than 100 locations in the US and worldwide, including many forms of flexible ways of learning such as evening classes, flexible scheduling, and continuous enrolment.

The University of Phoenix also offers a range of financial plans for students including a federal financial aid plan, scholarships, institutional grants, cash plans, tuition deferral, third-party billing, military or government billing, tribal funding, and private student loans. The university also has the Phoenix Scholarship Reward Program for undergraduate students, which they can apply for if they complete the first twenty-four credit hours of their degree program within fifty-two weeks. Students, who are accepted from the age of sixteen, are not required to provide standardized college entrance exam scores or essay submissions for admission to the university but do need to have access to a working environment in which they can apply the theories and methods they learn in the classroom.

However, the University of Phoenix has faced several years of declining enrolment, with overall and new enrolment in 2014 being approximately 16 percent lower than in the previous year, as well as issues over recruiting practices. The university has stated that it plans to expand internationally in the future.

For further information see:

Blumenstyk. G. (2014) "U. of Phoenix Chooses Michigan's CFO as its New President," *The Chronicle of Higher Education*. April 2. Available at: http://chronicle.com/article/U-of-Phoenix-Chooses/145663/ (accessed April 6, 2014).

Marcus, J. (2013) "US For-Profits Must Up their Game to Regain Lost Ground," *Times Higher Education,* October 3. Available at: www.timeshighereducation.co.uk/news/us-for-profits-must-up-their-game-to-regain-lost-ground/2007743.article (accessed April 7, 2014).

Stratford, M. (2012) "Judge Says Lawsuit Over U. of Phoenix's Recruiting Practices May Proceed," *The Chronicle of Higher Education,* July 9. Available at: http://chronicle.com/article/Judge-Says-Lawsuit-Over-U-of/132791/ (accessed April 6, 2014).

University of Phoenix (2014) Available at: www.phoenix.edu/ (accessed April 6, 2014).

In the US, the predominant response from the private sector has been in online education; most famously the University of Phoenix (Text Box 2.1), and more recently with the advent of MOOCs (which are discussed in Chapter 5). In the UK, the most immediate growth has been in private campus provision. In 2009 BPP College—the first publicly owned private company in the UK to have award-giving powers—was taken over by Apollo Group and become

BPP University with study centers developing across the UK and Europe. BPP specializes in professional education; it has schools of business, law, health, and English-language studies (Text Box 2.2). These newer providers generally seem to fit the model predicted by Collis more than ten years ago:

> Examination of the course offerings of the corporations entering higher education reveals a striking predominance of business related material. Seventy-five percent of the companies are focused on areas such as management, performance improvement, and specific corporate skills, such as information technology. Of the remaining 25 percent, a large fraction offer courses to doctors and lawyers, focusing on continuing education for those professions. [. . .]
>
> These facts reflect a natural progression in an entrepreneurial entry strategy. The most lucrative and receptive market is for business courses. As firms build brand names and establish presence in the market, one can predict an evolution in course offerings from short management certificates and continuing education for the professions, through more general and softer leadership skills and performance improvement, to an MBA or other professional degree, and only finally into undergraduate liberal arts degrees.
>
> (2002: 12)

TEXT BOX 2.2   BPP

BPP is Europe's largest specialist professional education, training and publishing provider comprising of

- *BPP Learning Media*—a specialist publishing company.
- *BPP Professional Education*—which offers preparation for professional examinations, as well as apprenticeships and short course for professional development.
- *BPP University*—a UK degree-awarding body providing its own awards and operating through four schools: BPP Law School, BPP Business School, BPP School of Health, and BPP School of Foundation and English Language Studies.

BPP University is an independent UK university within the wider BPP Professional Education group. BPP University, which is based in London, does not receive Higher Education Funding Council funding but can set its own level of tuition fees and students on undergraduate courses qualify for loans. The aim of the university is to be a specialist provider of professional and business education by offering a wide range of degrees at both under- and postgraduate levels in its four schools, located in various city centers throughout the UK. Degrees are also offered in Amsterdam, the Netherlands. Approximately 80 percent of BPP University's students are from the UK or the EU, and the university awards a number of scholarships each year.

Undergraduate students have the choice of three start dates per year, and the degrees offered provide at least one accreditation or exemption from professional body qualifications. The master's courses include personal development coaching and a work placement option. Pre-master's courses are offered to enable students to gain additional study or language skills prior to starting their degree. Facilities offered by BPP University include up-to-date eLearning and technology facilities in classrooms, study rooms, and libraries; specialist libraries with extended opening hours; and mock courtrooms at most of the law schools.

For further information see:

BBP (2014) Available at: www.bpp.com/ (accessed April 5, 2014).

The Guardian (2013) "University guide 2014: BPP University, 4 June 2013" (2013) *The Guardian*, June 3. Available at: www.theguardian.com/education/2012/may/22/university-guide-bpp-university-college (accessed on April 5, 2014).

As many authors have shown (Brennan and Shah 2011; Collini 2012; Brown and Carasso 2013; McGettigan 2013), to enable this increasing privatization and marketization of higher education, a series of conditions have had to be put in place by state institutions, dependent on political will and existing contexts. These include pay-as-you-go pricing systems, a diversification of offers to meet different market needs and increase 'choice,' and the improvement of comprehensive information available to consumers in order to improve competition. The costs of providing higher education are shifted to its consumers and away from the state. Grants for student support are being replaced or supplemented by loans or voucher systems. This, in turn, focuses education on its private and self-interest components, not just as a mode of neo-liberalist thought but also in the actual ways it comes to be perceived by its participants. In addition, many authors have also taken this to imply a shifting pattern in the overall shape of higher education:

Three predictions may be made with some degree of confidence:

1. there will be a greater variety of providers;
2. there will be a further rationalisation of existing providers;
3. there will be a sharper degree of differentiation between them.

(Brown 2011: 19)

Barber et al. (2012: 55–60) have taken this further by suggesting that universities and colleges will increasingly subdivide, beyond a public–private bifurcation, to cover different parts of the higher education market. They propose that the elite universities will remain in much the same form, whilst a decreasing number of 'mass' universities will aim for a growing global middle class (currently the most-competed-over sector of the higher education market). These will be supplemented by 'niche' institutions that promote themselves as specialist in particular areas, local universities and colleges that are explicitly located to service a city or region, and 'lifelong learning' services that can be completed without having to physically attend a university.

Whether this outline is correct or not, the implications are—at least in some countries—of expansions and contractions across higher education, through mergers, takeovers, and even closures. For example, Brown predicts the taking over of some public universities by the private sector in the UK:

> In 2009–10 a quarter of universities were underperforming financially on at least one of the Funding Council's measures and 9 per cent had run a deficit for at least three years (National Audit Office, 2011). Many of these are bound to be absorbed into larger, multi-faculty institutions and/or be taken over by private providers. Even though the transactions costs (staff redundancies, absorption of senior management time, costs of rebranding, etc. are formidable, it is difficult to see any other scenario for these institutions.
>
> (2011: 20)

Successes and Failures of Higher Education Providers

At the same time, the private sector is not having a smooth time. As already hinted, the biggest player in the for-profit online market—University of Phoenix—with about 600,000 students at its peak in 2010 and annual revenue in excess of US$4 billion, announced plans to close 115 campuses at the end of 2012 as its profit margins collapsed. Meanwhile, a US Senate investigation showed that 60 percent of Apollo students dropped out within two years, while of those who completed their course, 21 percent defaulted on paying back their loans within three years of finishing. It also revealed that 89 percent of Apollo's revenue comes from federal student loans and that it spends twice as much on marketing as on teaching (Collini 2013). And an investigation by the *Huffington Post* into another private provider, Educational Management Corporation, found that after it was taken over by Goldman Sachs, its recruiters were issued scripts "which instructed them to find potential applicants' 'pain' so as to convince them that college might be a solution to their struggles" (Collini 2013).

We are thus in a situation where both public and private universities are under critical review—not just because of what are best called ideological differences but also because both face challenges as to the effectiveness of their performance as educators. In the US, a two-year investigation into 'for-profit' higher education institutions found issues with profit margins, retention and achievement, differential success rates, and student debt. In addition, there was some aggressive marketing. There is thus an increasing problem with students from less-privileged backgrounds enrolling on courses and then dropping out, leaving then with large debts. This relative lack of retention of, or achievement by, students in higher education is of course also a problem for many nonprofit universities and colleges, one that becomes crucial when more and more students are bearing direct and increasing costs for their studies:

> The cost of college [in the US] has skyrocketed during the last two decades, rising by 429 percent, a rate that's even higher than the rate for health care. To cover these costs students have borrowed ever-larger amounts resulting in an average debt at graduation now exceeding $27,000. Yet only 50 per cent of students pursuing a bachelor's degree— and 21 per cent of those pursuing an associate's degree—complete their college programs.
>
> (Sheets et al. 2012: 1)

Thus, we are in a situation where the higher education provided for most students (rather than the top few) is very uneven. The tensions between a definition of quality based solely on institutional 'elite' reputation and attempts at other means of judging educational standards (such as quality assurance) are really beginning to reveal themselves, as are the gaps between either of these approaches and the urgent need for more coherent and rich ways to evaluate both educational value and institutional teaching competencies (as illustrated by the example in this book's introduction).

The neo-liberalist view is of course that competition and (a version of) the free market in higher education will be able to push up quality while driving down costs. Here the key point is that, in innovating different educational models, the for-profit sector is also exploiting the resource-saving aspects of free-market business models—both focusing only on the most profitable courses and externalizing many of the costs that nonprofit universities and colleges have to cover (including those that have historically been subsidized through public funds):

> One of the concerns that traditional providers in America have is that the new competitors, particularly the for-profits, will cherry-pick the

more "profitable" areas of study, leaving them with the financial "dogs", which have hitherto been protected through cross-subsidy. This could lead to the unbundling of the curriculum and a reduction in the number or attractiveness of comprehensive institutions.

(Brown, n.d.: 4)

As already mentioned, this is having a noticeable impact on the viability of programs in the non-science areas (that are seen both as less relevant by governments focusing on business-oriented research and as not profitable enough for the private providers). More broadly, this concerns the bigger issue of who pays for both societal and individual costs and benefits of higher education. How will research continue to be undertaken if typical private colleges (campus-based, online, or hybrid), who employ teaching-only staff, become the dominant model? How will the 'less-profitable' courses in arts and humanities survive in a completely free-market system? How will the resources and facilities of a traditional university (libraries, sports facilities, social clubs) be funded or continue to be part of the life of all students whatever kind of educational institution they attend? We have already seen in Chapter 1 a version of this in the New College of the Humanities. Here (as with other hybrid public–private partnerships that I address next), the private sector can leverage the publicly funded assets, not just of libraries and other existing university and college facilities but also of the research and teaching expertise of academic staff previously employed in the nonprofit sector. What is more, by focusing on being teaching institutions, for-profit and nonprofit private educational providers keep away from many of the demands being made on the public universities in terms of research innovation and of business and community partnership development.

How, then, are public universities and colleges to respond to these new entrants into the market as both potential competitors and collaborators? What kinds of new strategies are private providers bringing that more traditional universities and colleges can learn from? How can universities leverage their assets better, to build new kinds of alliances and to improve their performance, but still be integrated with maintaining a commitment to the public good? What kinds of outsourcing opportunities are developing? And how can the whole high education sector improve access to its services and better support all learners? First, I outline some of the new hybrid public–private partnering forms already well embedded in higher education, then go onto some of the possible ways of combining both market- and public purpose–oriented initiatives, informed by models beyond conventional business practices such as social enterprise and the open education movement. Finally, I explore examples of widening participation and of enhancing student performance as central themes for both private and public provision, in order to improve the quality and effectiveness of higher education for everyone.

Theme 2.1: Hybrid Nonprofit and For-Profit Entities

2.1.a Outsourcing Educational Services

The increasing hybridity of nonprofit and for-profit entities has been around for many years, as universities and colleges have developed a 'third stream' income in collaboration with business and other organizations. In addition, for many years, the private sector has provided services across the noncore areas of higher education from catering, facilities management, and group purchasing through to database services and staffing agencies. More recently it has found gaps and opportunities to provide specialist learning and teaching services across the whole higher education sector. Examples include Kaplan and INTO colleges based on university campuses, delivering pre-degree English-as-a-second-language courses, and public–private co-partnering with universities to provide online and distance learning versions of their existing programs (Text Box 2.3); organizations such as Vitae delivering resources and workshops for training academic researchers; the outsourcing of examinations across many higher education institutions through assessment companies such as College Board, Educational Testing Service, and Pearson Vue; personal development planning services; course selection and careers information provision; open badging frameworks (see Chapter 5); and educational technology and instructional design services, such as EmbanetCompass, 2U, and Knewton, all educational technology companies that partner with universities to co-design online degree programs.

TEXT BOX 2.3 KAPLAN OPEN LEARNING AND THE UNIVERSITY OF ESSEX

In 2007, when the University of Essex went into partnership with Kaplan Open Learning, a private, for-profit US global provider of educational services, it established a collaboration of public and private institutions with the aim of offering flexible, part-time, online foundation degree courses for working adults in the UK to improve competencies and skills in the UK workforce. Kaplan Open Learning is financially supported by the Higher Education Funding Council for England.

The first Kaplan Open Learning (Essex) Limited courses to be validated were Business Studies foundation degrees, followed by courses in criminal justice and financial services. Certificates in Continuing Education, honors, and master's degrees in business and in health have been added in recent years. These programs are designed to make higher education more accessible to students who might not be able to attend traditionally delivered courses and to provide them with practical work-based skills while 'badging' their studies with the status and reputation of a traditional university.

For further information see:

Higher Education Funding Council for England (n.d.) *Collaborate to Compete. Seizing the Opportunity of Online Learning for UK Higher Education.* Available at: www.hefce.ac.uk/whatwedo/lt/enh/oltf/casestudies/essexka-plan/ (accessed April 11, 2014).

Kaplan International English (n.d.) *Information on Kaplan Open Learning.* Available at: www.kaplaninternational.com/about/kaplan-online-learning. aspx (accessed April 11, 2014).

Student Finance England (2013) *Kaplan Open Learning—University of Essex Online Programmes.* Available at: www.practitioners.slc.co.uk/ policy-information/designated-courses/kaplan-open-learning-university-of-essex-online-programmes.aspx (Accessed April 11, 2014).

Sheets et al. suggest that these kinds of public–private business models can be expanded even further by

> outsourcing curriculum development through partnerships with other universities and colleges, content aggregators, and academic and professional publishers who are moving to provide "curriculum as a service." This outsourcing could draw from public and private learning exchanges similar to the Learning Registry, launched by the U.S. Departments of Education and Defense in November 2011. Outsourcing could provide institutions with nationally branded curricula (using the brand of a leading university) or institutionally branded curriculum (using a "private label") that could be delivered through the institution's own delivery channels.
>
> (2012: 9)

Pearson Education is an example of a private provider aiming to expand and diversify into a much wider range of higher education services, from a background in educational textbooks. Together with other higher education publishers it developed CourseSmart (where students can buy and rent college textbooks in e-format and store these on a common platform) as well as other technology products, including a digital repository system called

Equella, and assessment services through EmbanetCompass. Meanwhile Pearson College offers online business and degrees in the UK, and in the US the group partners with more than 200 colleges and universities to provide online services and classes (Singer 2014). The longer-term business model seems to be to offer a comprehensive course design service to existing universities and colleges worldwide, supported by a palette of online tools and delivery mechanisms. However, as of 2014, progress has been uncertain in what is an emerging and uneven market and as Pearson has invested in shifting from print to digital services:

> Pearson has been making a big push to expand its education, digital services, and testing programs in the United States and in Third World countries, but the problem may be that the company is way over-extended and cannot deliver on its promises. In February 2014, Pearson was selected by the University of Florida to maintain and promote its online undergraduate degree programs, but the partnership got off to a rough start when the director of the project resigned after three months. Pearson and the university were also criticized when it became public that Pearson required the university to pay cash up front on the project. Pearson stands to make $186 million over the eleven-year life of the contract.
>
> (ibid.)

Thus, the effectiveness and value of for-profit organizations as they move into providing higher education services continues to be contested.

2.1.b Hybrid Nonprofit and For-Profit Partnerships

For private–public partnerships developed between business and higher education, the tendency is moving away from opportunistic connections to more considered arrangements. Although historically, many collaborations have grown out of individual and departmental interests and contacts, universities are now becoming better at taking partnership decisions more strategically with "a noticeable trend towards coordination of partnership activity at the centre and vetting and rationalising partnerships so that they are adequately risk-assessed, manageable and fit academic and other objectives" (Fielden et al. 2010: 41).

As already noted, in many countries there has been a considerable push for academic research and development, and new partnerships, to more directly meet the needs of business:

> Universities are an integral part of the supply chain to business, a supply chain that has the capability to support business health and therefore

economic prosperity. A thriving knowledge economy depends upon its universities in three critical dimensions: the application and exploitation of research capability; the enterprise and entrepreneurial culture that is developed amongst its students; and the applicability of the knowledge and skills of all its graduates.

(Wilson 2012: 13)

As part of his 2012 report examining how British universities and businesses can work together more effectively, Wilson mapped out a 'collaboration landscape' of the wide-ranging kinds of alliances in this area:

- From future-oriented research in advanced technologies, to in-house upskilling of employees;
- From university science park developments, to support for entrepreneurial research students finding their way in the business world;
- From providing progression routes to higher-level apprenticeships, to enhancing the skills of post doctoral staff for their transition into the business world;
- From improving enterprise skills amongst our undergraduates, to enabling small companies to recognise the value of employing a first graduate;
- From supporting spin-out companies from research teams, to helping government agencies attract major employers to invest in the UK.

(ibid.: 23–24)

Of course, universities are also making other kinds of alliances, to develop and extend their knowledge sharing; as already said, there is pressure for interrelationships with the world beyond the academy to be part of their core business. This may be with the commercial sector, with the cultural industries or through community engagement. The University of Twente, the Netherlands, for example, calls itself an 'entrepreneurial' university, and has built strategic networks both with other technical universities in Holland (3TU Federation) and with businesses at the regional, national, and international levels. The campus is also host to about 100 businesses, including student-led businesses, and has its own business park. For this chapter, however, what is most interesting in the extent to which *learning* in higher education is being offered through private–public partnerships.

2.1.c For-Profit Educational Entities in Public Universities

A common strategy for public universities is to make alliances with a private provider as an 'offshoot,' separate from its core services. This can leverage a university's reputation, but with the least risk in terms of time and money to the institutions and often with minimal objection from faculty:

> One of the more fascinating developments in higher education at the turn of the twentieth-first century is the creation of for-profit arms in several universities including Columbia, Cornell, Stanford, New York University, and the University of Maryland, with others soon to follow. Why, one might ask, would a non-profit university want to establish a for-profit venture—which would not qualify for tax-exempt status—as part of its operations? The answer is twofold and further attests to the blurring of lines between non-profit and for-profit institutions. First, these for profit arms provide access to private investment capital, which functions as a kind of endowment in for-profit institutions. Universities with international brand identity, as well as institutions with strong regional or even local presence, are beginning to realise that their names and reputations can be used to attract potentially large sums of investment capital. [. . .]
>
> Secondly, relatively little financial risk is involved in setting up these ventures. Even if they fail, the university itself will not go bankrupt or suffer financial exigency; it will simply continue to rely on its main business.
>
> (Ruch 2004: 96)

At both Harvard and Columbia Universities, for example, a for-profit arm has been developed—Harvard Business School Interactive (HBSi) and Morningside Ventures, respectively. At Columbia, this has enabled offerings directly to businesses, supported by open enrolment programs:

> Morningside's activities fall into three areas: online course/content development (Columbia Online); technology transfer within new media (Columbia Technology); and incubation of new businesses (Columbia Enterprises).
>
> Columbia Online will create courses with staff members and market and distribute them; this may involve a licence arrangement with a third party. It will also collaborate with groups within the university to develop marketing opportunities for content, rather than courses.
>
> Columbia Technology will match commercial opportunities with the steady stream of inventions and software created by the staff. Work is under way on projects such as internet telephony and video search and retrieval. This may take the form of licences to third parties or may generate ideas for independent businesses.

Columbia Enterprises will provide seed capital and strategic planning for these businesses. The most promising will be spun off as separate companies, with the university retaining a stake.

(Kirschner 1999)

This longer-term investment in online learning public-private partnerships, has also enabled some of the 'top-end' universities in the US to move more easily into open courseware (OCW) and Massive Open Online Courses (MOOCs), which are dealt with at greater length in Chapter 5.

In other cases, such collaborations bring together a complex mix of business, research and educational crossovers between universities and other organizations. The Digital Peninsula (also linked to CISCO's National Virtual Incubator initiative) is a partnering between CISCO, London Borough of Greenwich, and Ravensbourne College of Art, aimed at leveraging collaboration across learning, business, community engagement, and regeneration (Text Box 2.4).

TEXT BOX 2.4   CISCO NATIONAL VIRTUAL INCUBATOR AND THE DIGITAL PENINSULA, GREENWICH, LONDON, UK

The CISCO National Virtual Incubator (NVI) is an initiative of CISCO's British Innovation Gateway (BIG) program, which awards innovative UK businesses prize packages, including marketing, public relations, and legal support through its BIG Awards competition. At Greenwich in London, the Digital Peninsula project collaborates with CISCO in aiming to become a leading digital zone, by bringing together higher education (Ravensbourne College of Art and the University of Greenwich) with local government, private-sector businesses, and a development corporation. The creation of a mixture of opportunities in one place can offer a multitude of overlaps and innovations through partnerships working across learning, business, community engagement, and regeneration institutions.

Communication is an important part of working in hubs such as the Digital Peninsula. Regular events are held to help the various companies network with each other and to encourage the sharing of ideas, while peer-to-peer mentoring helps users of the hub inspire each other. Many of the start-up companies also provide internships for Ravensbourne students so that they can work on particular projects, or employ them on a consultancy basis, thereby providing encouragement to graduates of the future who may wish to set up their own business.

More widely, the CISCO NVI aims to bring together business incubators, science parks, and universities through interlinking hubs, called 'NVI Nodes,' to enable them to work collaboratively on digitally creative projects throughout the UK, thereby increasing UK research and innovation, as well as promoting the creation and growth of start-up companies and small to medium enterprises. There are plans to have more than 100 NVI Nodes within the next few years. Each of the NVI Nodes specializes in a different form of technology but shares expertise through a common platform of advanced technologies supported by the JANET (UK) education and research network. This provides the latest technical equipment, computer software and shared workspaces, together with networking opportunities and professional business support for the development of creative digital, media, and technology businesses.

For further information see:

Baldwin, C. (2013) "Cisco Incubator to Connect UK Startup Clusters," *Computer Weekly.* Available at: www.computerweekly.com/news/2240203365/Ciscos-incubator-will-connect-startup-innovation-clusters-across-the-UK (accessed April 18, 2014).

Cisco (n.d.) *Cisco British Innovation Gateway National Virtual Incubator Alliance Charter of Membership.* Available at: http://nvinetwork.com/nvicharter.pdf (Accessed on 18 April 2014).

National Virtual Incubator (2014) Available at: http://nvinetwork.com/ (accessed April 18, 2014).

Theme 2.2: Social Enterprise and Civic Engagement

Universities and colleges have also been building partnerships with other non-profit entities such as museums, libraries, cultural and community groups, and charitable and professional organizations, to enable learning and knowledge exchange linked to social inclusion and civic engagement. In the UK, government-funded programs of Knowledge Transfer Partnerships (KTPs) and Beacons for Public Engagement have aimed to increase and consolidate these kinds of relationships. More widely, concepts around the creative economy, cultural regeneration, and the making of cultural quarters to support city and regional development (United Nations Conference on Trade and Development 2010; Roodhouse 2013) have led to universities and colleges partnering with local government and the cultural industries (a theme covered in Chapter 4). The rest of this chapter is concerned to explore how some universities and colleges are working in partnerships that enhance their *public* purpose as learning institutions.

2.2.a University of Northampton, UK

Within the university sector in the UK, social and public good has been frequently linked to employability through the concept of social entrepreneurship,
for example, by supporting individual students in social enterprise start-ups,
through groups such as UnLtd (http://unltd.org.uk/). At the University of
Northampton in the UK the idea of social enterprise has been taken up at a more
strategic level, integrating it across teaching, research, business, and local community collaborations—even procurement—through an overall strategy (Text
Box 2.5) and supported through a series of interconnected initiatives across the
university. Through embedding social enterprise strategically, the university has
changed a wide range of its practices. In postgraduate education, for example, an
incubator program, the Social Venture Builder (SVB), has aimed to develop and
provide a balanced mix of support and skills development for social innovators:

> We are now looking for individuals or organisations to submit ideas that
> have the potential to change the way public services are provided. The
> latest round of its Social Venture Builder (SVB) incubation programme is
> looking for ventures which address social problems in new and innova-
> tive ways and are looking to grow, open up new markets, or change their
> trading delivery model to increase their impact.
>
> The SVB is an exciting and innovative new opportunity which not
> only serves to improve the marketability of the social venture, but also
> addresses the investment potential of the organisation, as well as develop-
> ing the skills of the innovators and entrepreneurs on the programme by
> linking the ventures development to an accredited postgraduate qualifica-
> tion, the MA Social Innovation.
>
> (www.northampton.ac.uk/business-and-enterprise/business-support/
> social-venture-builder)

Text Box 2.5 University of Northampton Social Enterprise Strategy

We define social enterprise as using market disciplines to achieve a social
outcome-driven by social values. The University of Northampton's social
enterprise work is underpinned by three very clear values:

- We will provide a unique student experience of the very highest quality,
  developing both theoretical and practical competence in social enterprise that prepares the leading social entrepreneurs of the future.

- We will encourage, support and develop entrepreneurial skills and enter-
  prising attitudes among our students, our staff, and the members of the
  communities we work with.
- We will deliver a fairer and more inclusive society.

As a university we are 'living' these values through seven key social enterprise initiatives:

- a unique student experience that builds on our Changemaker Campus commitment; enabling all students to develop the skills required to
  stand out in the employment market and to be the change leaders of the
  future
- the integration of social enterprise with teaching and research—all of
  our courses, research opportunities, and extracurricular activities build
  social enterprise and innovation competence within our students as well
  as offer competitive degree qualifications
- nationwide support for social enterprise—our Inspire2Entereprise service
  provides comprehensive customer focused and market driven support to
  new and existing social entrepreneurs and enterprises
- investment in social enterprises—where we identify social enterprise activities that provide both exceptional placement opportunities for students and
  make life better and fairer, we will invest in them
- evolution of university support functions to social enterprises—we will
  examine each of our support services, and where possible run them as
  social enterprises, providing services to the university community on a
  commercial basis while also fulfilling a clear social purpose
- creating a fairer society for all—working with a wide range of partners
  we develop socially innovative ways of transforming the lives of everyone
  for the better; whether that is through influencing the private sector,
  transforming public sector service delivery or building capacity in the
  social enterprise sector
- influencing policy and practice—using our knowledge and experience we
  will influence the policy and practice of social enterprise in the UK and
  beyond

Source: Adapted from www.northampton.ac.uk/business-and-enterprise/enterprise
(accessed April 4, 2014).

Other examples include a recent project, funded by the Higher Education
Funding Councils, Research Councils UK, and the Wellcome Trust. In this
case two universities (Bristol and West of England) have set up a national

coordinating center for public engagement, including a manifesto and toolkit (see www.publicengagement.ac.uk/).

2.2.b Baltic 39

A smaller scale and more localized example of social and cultural enterprise is the collaboration between the BALTIC art gallery in Newcastle upon Tyne and Northumbria University's Faculty of Art, Design and Social Sciences, also involving Arts Council England and Newcastle City Council. The building, called Baltic 39, brings together a city-center gallery space, programmed by the gallery, with thirty-two affordable artists' studios and fine art student teaching spaces (Figure 2.1). Through a coordinating organization—the BxNU Institute of Contemporary Art—university students have the opportunity to develop their fine art practice in a hybrid environment bringing together research, internationally renowned artists, and the professional artists based in the studios, as well as having regular access to the exhibition space and to a series of public events, curated by a professor funded by the project, who says, "[T]he Institute will be a very special place where conventional barriers between disciplines, artists and researchers, between the public and the institution, need not apply" (www.balticmill.com/39/bxnu-instatute).

Figure 2.1 BALTIC 39, University of Northumbria, Newcastle upon Tyne, UK
Source: Photo by Jos Boys.

In the US, established networks such as Campus Compact also aim to embed public purpose across their members:

> Campus Compact is a national coalition of more than 1,100 college and university presidents who are committed to fulfilling the civic purposes of higher education. As the only national higher education association dedicated solely to campus-based civic engagement, Campus Compact promotes public and community service that develops students' citizenship skills, helps campuses forge effective community partnerships, and provides resources and training for faculty seeking to integrate civic and community-based learning into the curriculum. Campus Compact's membership includes public, private, two- and four-year institutions across the spectrum of higher education.
>
> (www.compact.org/about/history-mission-vision/)

For example, a 2012 initiative aims to see community colleges strategically operating to help localities hit by the financial recession through aligning civic engagement with economic development—calling this an engaged learning economy (Wittman and Crews 2012).

Theme 2.3: Widening Participation

One of the central arguments for the development of private higher educational provision is because of its perceived ability to widen participation by reaching sections of the population who do not access conventional universities for a variety of reasons:

> In the United States, where community colleges already provide an important segment of higher education, private "for profit" providers have essentially acted as demand absorbers, catering for market segments that conventional "not for profit" institutions cannot or will not service: typically, courses of varying length in applied curriculum areas offered at times most convenient to the customer.
>
> (Brown 2011: 20)

In some developing countries, private providers are enabling a massification of higher education very quickly. We need to address the relevance, quality, and effectiveness of that education and at the same time recognize that, in terms of widening access and enhancing the performance of students from poorer backgrounds, the whole higher education sector—including mainstream public universities—needs to look at improving its performance.

2.3.a Anhanguera Educacional Participações

In the developing world, World Bank strategies and funding are supporting this kind of private sector growth. For example, Anhanguera Educacional Participações S.A. (AESA) is currently the largest postsecondary education institution in Brazil; at the time of this writing, it was second only to the American Apollo group in size (and planning a merger with the other major private provider in Brazil, Kroton). At the end of 2012, it had 412,000 students on 278 campuses and in 133 learning centers (Busch 2013):

> These centres are not full-blown colleges; they only offer a few courses and, to a considerable extent, rely on video tutorials, e-learning and other forms of long-distance teaching. Anhanguera, however, did not only grow by buying other companies. It also kept on setting up new campuses and learning centres, replicating its successful approach to teaching. Its market is adults of middle and low-income working during the day and study at night, a segment not fully served by institutions of higher education in Brazil. To this end, the Company offers a wide range of courses including: vocational, undergraduate, postgraduate and continuing education.
> (http://en.wikipedia.org/wiki/Anhanguera_Educacional)

The courses are relatively cheap, and the company uses economies of scale to, for example, reduce the cost of textbooks, by printing these in plainer formats. As with other large-scale private providers, AESA focuses on employability:

> Anhanguera's programmes are geared to what employers need. That is evident in the courses on offer: business administration, information technology, architecture, electrical engineering et cetera, as well as subjects like social work or physiotherapy. In our eyes, Anhanguera is more like a polytechnic or a professional college than a full-fledged university. The emphasis is always on teaching; research is hardly noteworthy. An Anhanguera degree definitely improves a person's opportunities in the labour market. Brazil's economy has been growing fast in the past years, and skilled staff is in great demand.
> (Busch 2013)

However, it should be noted that in Brazil, government-run higher education is free, and the nevertheless large market for for-profit private education could be seen as a result of differential access to publically funded education:

> The Universidade de Sao Paulo—USP for short—is run by the government and has an excellent international reputation. USP does not charge

tuition fees. The entrance exams are really tough however. Government-run high schools don't prepare their graduates for this challenge. Even the graduates of expensive private-sector high schools normally need one year of tutorials to pass, and those tutorials cost yet more money. With very few exceptions, only the children of the better off manage to pass USP's entrance exams. Basically, this system serves the elite.

(ibid.: 2013)

There is thus something of a symbiotic relationship between conventional public universities in Brazil and their private counterparts, which is echoed elsewhere. Despite moves to widening participation in many countries there remains an unmet demand from poor-income and nontraditional learners for higher education. Whether this is only a demand for goal-oriented 'training' remains unclear (distorted both by availability and by the dominance of neo-liberal discourse). A recent change in Brazilian law is requiring state-funded universities to begin accepting at least half of their intake from public-sector secondary schools and low-income families, which may affect the penetration of AESA. But it also suggests the importance of critically exploring innovative private business models such as these for both opening up some of the assumptions behind publicly funded education and in exploring how widening participation might have an impact on thinking about a different kind of high-quality education.

2.3.b University Extension Programs in Denmark

Widening participation is not just about getting more students to sign up for conventional educational courses, whether on campus or online. In Denmark, university extension programs have been running since the nineteenth century, aiming to make higher learning available to everyone through specially prepared lectures:

The Danish Government confirmed its formal recognition of University Extension from the very outset by providing a grant in the spring of 1899 towards establishing its courses. Ever since (except for one year) the Government has allocated a sum of money in the Budget every year for what was called "popular university education" *(folkelig universitetsundervisning)*. For the first 70 years, University Extension was annually obliged to submit a substantiated and documented application for a grant, but from 1969 it was placed in the group of general education institutions that are entitled to receive State subsidies. This came about with the passing of an Act covering leisure-time education *(Lov om fritidsundervisning)* in which a separate chapter was devoted to University Extension. After this,

University Extension was automatically entitled to receive State subsidies in accordance with fixed criteria.

(Persson 2000)

University extension in Denmark not only concerns state-subsidized leisure-time education but also emphasizes improving public knowledge of the results of scientific research, of scientific methods and of other relevant subjects. The idea is that scholars should present their research work to a wider public in a straightforward, uncomplicated form:

> The aim is to ensure that the educational courses offered continuously cover the entire spectrum of scientific subjects, ranging from theology, the humanities, the social sciences and health science to various subjects in the natural sciences. The most widely attended courses are those within the humanities: art history and subjects connected with psychology, philosophy and history. The short courses are the most popular: lectures and lecture series comprising from two to ten double periods. The university courses, in which the classes are smaller and presuppose active participation in tuition based on discussion (and also incorporate the reading of scholarly or scientific literature) comprise between six and 24 double periods. In Copenhagen such university courses are organized in a system of single courses that provide the possibility of assimilating whole subject areas. In all, about 24,000 double periods are available annually.
>
> (www.folkeuniversitetet.dk/default.aspx?
> pagetype=6&custID=8)

These courses, then, are not accredited nor 'separated' out into adult education provision. Rather they act as a public 'bridge,' linking university-based research and learning activities with what is usually called lifelong learning.

2.3.c *Idea Stores—Community College and Library Collaboration, Tower Hamlets, London, UK*

Another 'bridging' approach is to make the move from school to college feel an easier one. The five Idea Stores, developed by the London Borough of Tower Hamlets in collaboration with the local Further Education (FE) College did this through a collaboration based on extending the idea of local libraries. Research showed that local people were not using the existing libraries, which were often difficult to get to and had become quite dated. The Idea Store has therefore combined traditional library and information services, with classrooms for adult education (supported by courses supplied on site by Tower Hamlets FE College), a local history archive, and a variety of reading and study spaces. Study rooms are

Figure 2.2 Interior of Ideas Store, Whitechapel, East London, UK
Source: Photo by Jos Boys.

part of the library itself, so that school pupils can use them to do their homework, as well as seeing these rooms in use for formal FE classes. Through its Idea Stores project, Tower Hamlets aimed to double the use of library and adult education facilities across the local area within five years and, in fact, exceeded this target. In addition, the local further education college gained access to another facility to extend its 'offer' beyond the existing campus, this being particularly relevant to potential students who might not otherwise consider studying 'at' college. The Idea Store, then, is neither a college nor just a local library, but an interesting intersection between both (Figure 2.2).

Theme 2.4: Improving Student Performance

When Roger Brown reflected on the similarities and differences for UK and US higher education in facing contemporary challenges, he noted that

> the two systems are clearly not the same. The American system is not only much larger but also far more diverse as well as being much better funded. It also has a much longer, and stronger, tradition of public accessibility as well as, paradoxically, a greater openness to market forces.

(n.d.: 1)

This support in the US for improving access to, and performance at, higher education institutions is exemplified by the many large-scale initiatives funded through its major charitable foundations. There has been considerable investment from philanthropic groups, particularly in the community college sector, explicitly concerned to address increasing participation by lower-income groups, to improve the effectiveness of learning, and to enable better retention and achievement rates (Text Box 2.6). This has meant working directly with potential and actual students, with teachers and institutions and with new kinds of educational intra-structure (e.g., via the Open Learning Initiative considered in Chapter 5).

Here, I can only give a few examples of the kinds of activities going on. The Bill & Melinda Gates Foundation's educational focus, for example, is on improving US high school and higher education to support students from disadvantaged backgrounds by using technology and working in collaborative partnerships with colleges and universities. Two programs have been created to address this: 'College-Ready Education,' whose goal is to ensure that students who graduate from high school are able to succeed in college and in their future careers, and 'Postsecondary Success,' which aims to increase the number of students who gain a postsecondary degree or certificate that will help them in their chosen career.

The William and Flora Hewlett Foundation also has an education program that provides funding to improve education for K–12 schools and community colleges in a number of ways. In addition, a California Education Policy Fund has been set up to raise student retention and achievement, again particularly for students from disadvantaged backgrounds. The Deeper Learning strategy of 2010 was developed to help students succeed in college and in their future careers. It encourages students to master key academic skills such as mastering academic content, critical thinking and problem solving, effective communication, directing their own learning, and believing in themselves (William and Flora Hewlett Foundation 2012).

TEXT BOX 2.6 THE CARNEGIE FOUNDATION FOR THE ADVANCEMENT OF TEACHING

The Carnegie Foundation for the Advancement of Teaching is an independent policy and research center, that considers itself a community builder and boundary spanner whose mission is to bring together networks of ideas, individuals, and institutions to deal with complex and difficult issues, with the aim of improving teaching and learning. By working with 'Networked Improvement Communities' consisting of researchers, teachers, designers, practitioners, students and policy makers, who together create and develop innovative resources, procedures and information, they are able to communicate that knowledge to people who can make change happen within their own institutions. In 2014, new collaborations with other networks will see the Carnegie Foundation for the Advancement of Teaching addressing the failure rate of college students undertaking mathematics and 'gateway' courses, and explore how to engage with the high number of inexperienced teachers in public schools.

In addition, the Carnegie Foundation for the Advancement of Teaching has joined with the Bill & Melinda Gates Foundation and The William and Flora Hewlett Foundation, investing US$2.5 million to identify strategies to raise student achievement and improve retention in colleges. It has been found that for many students, particularly those from disadvantaged backgrounds, postsecondary education ended after undertaking an initial developmental course or they did not complete a follow-on course. These three foundations have joined up to invest in research that identifies solutions to this problem. These solutions are being tested in various educational contexts and are then rapidly refined as appropriate.

For further information see:

Bill & Melinda Gates Foundation (2014). Available at: www.gatesfound ation.org/ (accessed April 21, 2014).

Carnegie Foundation for the Advancement of Learning (2009) *Carnegie, Gates, Hewlett Foundations Unite to Tackle Roadblocks to Student Success.* Available at: www.carnegiefoundation.org/newsroom/carnegie-gates-hewlett-foundations-unite-tackle-roadblocks-student-success (accessed April 21, 2014).

Carnegie Foundation for the Advancement of Learning (2014a) *New Carnegie Report Examines Rise in Inexperienced Teachers in Public School Classrooms Highlights Causes, Consequences, and Promising Responses.* Available at: www.carnegiefoundation.org/newsroom/press-releases/new-carnegie-report-examines-rise-in-inexperienced-teachers-in-public-schools (accessed April 22, 2014).

Carnegie Foundation for the Advancement of Learning (2014b) *Three Organizations to Collaborate to Improve Student Success in Mathematics.* Available at: www.carnegiefoundation.org/newsroom/press-releases/three-organizations-collaborate-improve-student-success-in-mathematics (accessed April 22, 2014).

Carnegie Foundation for the Advancement of Learning (n.d.) Available at: www.carnegiefoundation.org (accessed April 21, 2014).

The William and Flora Hewlett Foundation (no date) Available at: www.hewlett.org/ (accessed April 21, 2014).

2.4.a   Higher Education Academy Retention and Achievement
'What Works' Initiative

In the UK, where both philanthropy and alumni-giving seems to have less hold in higher education, an example of some research and advice on enhancing performance is through a partnership between the Paul Hamlyn Foundation and the Higher Education Funding Council for England (HEFCE). This work provides clear evidence of the connection between feelings of engagement and belonging, and students' patterns of retention and achievement (Thomas 2012). The "What Works? Student Retention and Success" project was a three-year program run between 2008 and 2011, through seven projects involving twenty-two higher education institutions, that all aimed to identify, evaluate, and disseminate effective practice to improve student retention. Detailed findings are set out in the seven individual project reports, and a compendium of effective practices in higher education produced to provide more practical exemplars of successful interventions (see www.heacademy.ac.uk/what-works-retention). Among the key findings were how important relationships between staff and students and peers are, and how these need to be nurtured pre-entry, in the classroom and in the delivery of student support services. The research also showed that the most effective actions tended to take place in the academic sphere:

> Such interventions often develop peer networks and friendships, create links with academic members of staff, provide key information, shape realistic expectations, improve academic skills, develop students' confidence, demonstrate future relevance, and nurture belong.
>
> (Thomas 2012: 8)

As falling resources and increased numbers mean that many university and college courses are reducing staff–student contact time and the amount of formal teaching provision, other support is needed that can help students engage with their students better and be confident in self-directed study beyond the classroom (a point I will return to in Chapter 4). Finally, the research showed that some programs have better rates of retention than would be predicted based on entry grades, and some specific interventions have been shown to improve retention rates by up to ten percentage points.

Meeting Public and Individual Educational Needs?

> Higher education is simply not making substantial progress in addressing its most significant challenges: educating an increasingly diverse body of students while containing the cost that is putting postsecondary education beyond the reach of a growing percentage of the world's population.

Tweaking long-standing strategies to achieve incremental improvement is no longer enough. The need to seek new ideas in traditionally over-looked arenas is urgent.

(Thille and Smith 2011)

This chapter has continued to try to move beyond simplistic 'private versus public' education debates. Rather, universities and colleges need to learn from the innovative business models being developed by for-profits, to accept the problems it reveals with their traditional services, and—most crucially—to open up alternative gaps and opportunities by developing educational models that clarify their public purpose and can extend their services to a wider audience in resource-effective, accountable, and equitable ways (recognizing that some of this may best be achieved through various kinds of public–private partnership). In fact, the major challenge from the for-profits is, I suggest in how it highlights how much of the potential higher education market is not being met through the existing university system. The next chapter, then, extends this out to the current global context.

3

RESPONDING TO INTERNATIONALIZATION

Postsecondary education is now a massive globalising industry and it is perhaps impossible to overestimate its potential. [. . .] It is projected that by 2010 there will be 100 million people in the world, all fully qualified to proceed from secondary to tertiary education.
—*Odin and Manicas (2004: xiv)*

It is well known that higher education has become more and more internationalized. There is now a considerable movement of students between countries, and more universities are offering their services worldwide—not only increasing global competition but also offering new possibilities for collaboration. Although much of this concerns the economic imperatives of expansion and opportunities for increasing student numbers and fees, international collaborations are also being seen as enabling better research, educational, and cultural interactions and as a means of enhancing students' understanding of, and engagement with, the wider world. In this chapter I focus on how universities are responding to these shifting patterns of mobility and interaction (rather than any more comprehensive understanding of globalization economically, politically, or culturally). This is not only about higher education institutions in the developed world teaching more international students but also about how a maturing global education sector, beyond the Western 'leaders,' is likely to have an impact in the years ahead, as these emerging states and institutions also compete for students beyond their national borders.

The Contemporary Background

Across the developed world, many universities and colleges have been sub-sidizing the education of their home students through international student fees. In the UK, for example, over the last ten years, the number of full-time overseas students at UK universities has increased from 175,000 to nearly 300,000. This means that one in six students at UK universities now comes from outside the European Union (Collini 2013). However, in both the UK and the US, this has also brought tensions in relation to a political tendency toward more conservative immigration policies. Barber et al. note what is hap-pening in America, before going on to remind us of the value of immigrants to a national economy:

> In 2011 there were 720,000 foreign students studying in American insti-tutions. Many of these students competed within their countries for an opportunity to come to the US—representing some of the best talent in the world. This is illustrated by the fact that from 1990–2005 immi-grants founded over 50 per cent of start-ups in Silicon Valley and from 1990–2000 they won 26 per cent of US-based Nobel Prizes, despite rep-resenting just 13 per cent of the population in 2005.
>
> By contrast, the US Citizens and Immigration Service issues work visas to only 85,000 of these immigrants per year through a lottery sys-tem. Businesses have to follow suit—the number of foreign analysts at the McKinsey New York office fell from nearly 50 per cent in 2007 to less than 5 per cent in 2008, illustrating a huge loss in diversity and talent.
> (2012: 25)

They also argue that well-educated graduate students are increasingly being attracted by places such as Singapore and Hong Kong to the benefit of those countries instead.

There are, of course, differences across countries in the financing, character and goals of the existing variety of higher education institutions, and as out-lined in earlier chapters, an increasing variety of providers, including "public/private, research universities/liberal arts colleges, four year colleges/community colleges, non-profit/for profit, proprietary schools, online universities, corporate universities and finally 'diploma mills' digital or otherwise" (Odin and Manicas 2004: xv). Many of these universities and colleges already have international links. This may be by, for example, 'importing' international students, having study abroad and exchange schemes, undertaking franchising and articulation agreements, offering double degree or joint degree programs, setting up branch or satellite campuses, generating distance learning programs, and develop-ing international campuses in collaboration with other countries. Of course, international interactions are also research based—such as collaborations, joint

Extent of International Reach	Corresponding International Initiatives		
	Curriculum and programs	Student body	Faculty and research
Importers	1. Offer special courses on the international dimension of the subject taught (when relevant) 2. Infuse an international dimension in all the courses (when relevant)	1. Enroll foreign students in the institution's programs 2. Attract international students enrolled in study-abroad programs offered by foreign institutions	1. Invite visiting foreign faculty 2. Host international seminars and conferences 3. Recruit foreign faculty 4. Recruit local faculty trained abroad
Exporters	1. Help foreign institutions design and deliver a program to its students 2. Offer online courses and programs to students from around the world (virtual exporters)	1. Offer study-abroad, work-abroad, and exchange programs 2. Involve students in international consultancy and development assistance projects	1. Encourage sabbaticals abroad 2. Train foreign faculty 3. Involve faculty in international consultancy and development assistance projects 4. Set-up research centers abroad
Academic Joint Ventures	1. Offer *dual*-degree programs with a foreign institution 2. Offer *joint*-degree programs with a foreign institution	1. Each institution recruits students separately 2. Students are recruited through a common admission process	1. Set-up joint research projects 2. Join international research agreements 3. Set-up joint research centers
Academic Partnerships, Alliances and Consortia	1. Offer partner's students access to your courses and programs 2. Offer partner's students your degrees	1. Students admitted by one institution are automatically qualified to attend courses in the partner's institution with credit mutually recognized	1. Faculty can teach their load in either one of the institutions 2. Faculty have access to common research budget 3. Set up partnership research centers
Campuses Abroad	1. Offer the *same* curricula, programs and degrees on the foreign and home campuses 2. Offer *different* curricula, programs and degrees on the foreign and home campuses 3. Students allowed to move freely between campuses to benefit from integrated curricula and programs	1. The admission process is either the same as in the home campus or different from the home campus 2. Students are recruited locally or regionally with little mobility 3. Students are recruited internationally and can move between campuses	1. Fly-in/fly-out of faculty (from the home campus or visiting) 2. Use permanent or temporary faculty recruited to work exclusively on the foreign campus 3. Use permanent or temporary faculty that originates from the home campus

Figure 3.1 Global universities' extent of international reach and corresponding internationalization initiatives
Source: Reprinted from Hawawini (2011: 39) with permission from INSEAD.

research, and publications, international fellowships and research awards, cross-country institutional research bids and projects, knowledge-exchange processes, and international university–business collaborations. Hawawini (2011) has usefully captured different levels of involvement in diagram form (Figure 3.1).

Developing branch campuses in other countries, some in partnership with local institutions and some freestanding, is a fast-developing trend:

> The number of branch campuses has risen steadily over the last decade and stood at 183 in March 2011. Half of these branch campuses belong to American HEIs. In the eighties and nineties most of these campuses were located in Europe and Japan. During the past decade the Gulf countries (Qatar and the United Arab Emirates) and Asia (Singapore and China) have experienced the highest number of openings.
>
> (ibid.: 18)

While Hawawini notes that most of these have been successful, there have also been some failures. For example, the University of East London campus, set up in Cyprus in 2012, was closed only two years later after recruiting just seventeen students (Collini 2013). Similarly, in 2012–2013 the University of Central

Lancashire (UCLan) lost money on a failed joint venture in Thailand and suffered some adverse press in relation to its ongoing engagements with Sri Lanka and Cyprus (Morgan 2014). Satellite campuses closer to home, such as London campuses for UK regional universities, have also witnessed some uneven success and closures.

A Global Convergence?

Many authors have argued that there is an increasing tendency for the internationalization of higher education, led by Western universities, to produce a convergence of approaches, based on their historical cultural dominance. As already outlined in the introduction, the increasing importance of both national and global world ranking tables, prioritizing the elite and research-intensive institutions, is further embedding and 'normalizing' the emulation of a reputation-driven model. This is underpinned by a process through which elite—particularly research led—institutions are joining together to strengthen brand identities and to increase global reputations and connections:

> [V]oluntary convergence is apparent in the reform of higher education institutions in many nations to bring them closer to the dominant template, that of the comprehensive, science-based university on Anglo-American lines. This form of institution, which could be called the Global Research University, is powerfully valorized by university ranking systems. [. . .] At bottom they do so because they have been drawn together into the single interdependent system of the global knowledge economy in which isolation is punished and there is no choice but to engage . . . the spontaneous synchronies of individual scholars with each other, researchers with each other, and institutions with each other are matched by mimetic approaches in government.
>
> (King 2011:26)

Thus, some authors argue that we are also moving toward an internationalization of the underlying *assumptions* about what higher education is, because of the number and types of evolving global networks:

> Social interaction is now more intense, extensive, and elaborated between the individuals, institutions and states that constitute global higher education than two decades ago. Moreover, policy internationalization and diffusion, leading to isomorphism and similar forms of policy 'synchrony' between higher education states, appear widespread [. . .] International organizations such as the OECD, the WTO, the EU, and UNESCO have become more prominent and influential in higher education; and

global rankings of universities have begun to exert powerful forces on both national states and many of their higher education organizations.

(ibid.: 24)

This is running together with both federalizing and neo-liberal pressures toward the opening up of the education market to enable freer transferability of services across national borders, thus needing clear frameworks for agreeing comparability and transferability. The main objective of the Bologna Process since it's beginning in 1999 has been to ensure more coherent and integrated systems of higher education in Europe, resulting in the creation of a European Higher Education Area (EHEA) in 2010. And although negotiations continue to stall, international developments in higher education are also potentially affected by World Trade Organization (WTO) plans to liberalize world trade as a free market through the General Agreement on Trades in Services (GATS):

> One of the reasons for the complexity of GATS is related to the technical difficulties associated with the commercialization of services. We should take into account that services are usually consumed where they are produced and are both produced and consumed simultaneously. So, how is it possible to 'export' services? To solve these dilemmas, the agreement contemplates four modes of commercializing services (instead of the unique mode of trade in goods). These are:
>
> • cross-border supply: provision of a service at a distance. In the case of education, this mode materializes in e-learning or, in general, in distance learning programs;
> • consumption abroad: the consumer (in our case the student) travels to another country to access to the service;
> • commercial presence: the service company sets up a subsidiary abroad. For example, a university sets up a branch campus in another country;
> • presence of natural persons: a professional travels to a foreign country to provide a service.
>
> (Verger and Robertson 2008)

Each of these definitions of services matches the kinds of international operations already being carried out by the higher education sector. All WTO member countries are supposed to adopt liberalization commitments through ongoing negotiations, with the underlying principle that no foreign supplier of higher education services can be treated less favorably than service suppliers of any other WTO member country. Beyond the concerns (desirable or not) of free trade, this also raises the wider issue of how to engage with different patterns of national and local governance, curriculum content, and learning and teaching methods and the extent to which models of, for example, democracy, individualism, or neo-liberalism should or can be 'exported' from the West to other countries.

How, then, are universities dealing with the complexities, risks, and political, economic, and cultural interactions that come from the internationalization of higher education? The aim here is not to list the many already successful collaborative ventures and their variations but to explore what kinds of strategic initiatives are likely to have an impact in the years ahead and what opportunities exist in the gaps—in what is being left out—as higher education competes and collaborates for shares of the global market.

Theme 3.1: International Collaborations

3.1.a Ningbo Campus, Nottingham University

In 2004, the University of Nottingham was one of the first foreign universities to set up in China (in Ningbo, Zhejiang), with a campus modeled on their UK facilities and curriculum, in cooperation with Zhejiang's Wanli Education Group—a key player in the education sector in China. Since then, it has developed a range of initiatives, including the development of Chinese studies in the UK (Text Box 3.1).

TEXT BOX 3.1 UNIVERSITY OF NOTTINGHAM NINGBO CAMPUS

In 2004 The University of Nottingham Ningbo (UNNC) was the first Sino-foreign university to open in China at the Ningbo campus. UNNC is run by the University of Nottingham in collaboration with Zhejiang Wanli Education Group. There are three faculties within UNNC: Arts and Education, Social Sciences, and Science and Engineering, as well as eleven academic departments. The teaching approach adopted by the university reflects that of Nottingham. UNNC offers undergraduate, postgraduate, and research degrees and degrees at both campuses run in parallel and are subject to the same quality assurance processes. Regardless of which campus students attend, all students graduate with degrees from the University of Nottingham.

At UNNC, all teaching is undertaken in English by staff on secondment from University of Nottingham or by staff who meet the agreed standards of the university. Course work, exams, and assignments are in English and students are taught in a range of both large and small groups. English-language support is offered to all students through the Centre for English Language Education, although students are expected to have a minimum level of English before they are accepted on degree programs. UNNC offers a mentoring scheme for undergraduates whereby they are mentored by outstanding alumni and other successful individuals.

The university's 6,000 students, who come from more than sixty countries worldwide, can opt to study at The University of Nottingham in the UK or can take advantage of a number of options to study overseas. UNNC offers a wide range of international study options, including the Study Abroad Programme, which enables international students from any university to go to China for either a semester or a year of study to gain credit toward their degrees provided they have completed at least one year of study at their home university. Other options are for students in partner institutions to take part in the international exchange program, and UNNC students can join the intercampus exchange program or the international summer school.

UNNC undertakes extensive collaborative research with The University of Nottingham and within China and internationally. Nine Research and Knowledge Transfer Priority Groups have been established to address global issues and a further five have the objective of leveraging external funding. It is anticipated that these groups will have a maximum life span of five years to allow priorities to evolve as necessary.

For further information see:

Ningbo China (n.d.) Available at: www.nottingham.edu.cn/en/index.aspx (accessed April 23, 2014).

3.1.b Global Schoolhouse, Singapore

As noted earlier, internationalization is no longer a one-way process, where Western expertise is exported to the developing world. As with other emerging economies such as Qatar and the United Arab Emirates, Singapore has a project to create a world-class educational hub and has become a major provider of international study. Long seen as a market for international students, particularly by British and Australian universities, Singapore now intends to be a center of university education for the Asian market:

> The global demand for international higher education will exceed 7 million students by 2025. Asia will dominate, accounting for 70 per cent of this future demand [. . .] A large part of this demand will be met in Asia itself in advanced cities like Singapore. Our objective is to make Singapore a 'Global Schoolhouse'. (Yeo, 2003) The key idea is the creation of a virtuous circle: draw in the 'best universities' with global talent, this talent

then creates knowledge and knowledgeable subjects, through their actions and networks, then creates the professional jobs that drive a vibrant [knowledge-based economy].

(Sidhu 2005: 16)

To do this, the government is aiming to attract world-class universities to set up campuses in Singapore, marketed predominantly to Asian students. These are intended to raise the intellectual and education standards of Singapore itself, and to support the development of new businesses and technologies there. The goal is to increase the recruitment of international students into Singapore by 'double or triple' the current numbers of 50,000 (Yeo 2003; Olds and Thrift 2004). In addition, the Global Schoolhouse Project wants to develop local creativity and risk taking and to strengthen the local, private higher education for-profit sector (Sidhu 2005: 17). Sidhu goes on:

Given that education is the largest consumer expenditure in China after housing, Singaporean companies have moved rapidly to participate in education ventures in partnership with the Chinese state and with Chinese private corporations. One of the most successful Singaporean education companies is Informatics, a private provider which has established 65 centres in 35 Chinese cities to teach business management and information technology.

(ibid.: 17)

Crucially, for Sidhu, such developments need to be explored for the ways in which the predominant concepts and language of globalization are negotiated across "networks of bureaucrats, consultants, journalists, technocrats and academics, [and so] do not merely report on or describe globalization, but actively constitute the object of their study" (ibid.: 4). So concepts increasingly circulating worldwide, such the 'knowledge-based economy,' become reframed in different contexts, and by different actors—whether by the universities entering into various agreements with Singapore, or the government and its agencies:

In the competitive international education market, Singapore is taking a safe stance by emulating the marketing strategies of the Anglo-American education industry. Like the United Kingdom and Australia, the Singaporean government has embarked on building an education brand identity—the Singapore education brand. The brand's identity is premised on selling the country's educational excellence, its quality infrastructure and its cosmopolitanism, all of which serve to construct its marketing slogan, 'Springboard to a better future'.

(ibid.: 22)

The Global Schoolhouse Project has thus deliberately enabled the transfer of Western-style educational patterns into Asia, for Singapore's own strategic purposes, while supporting and perpetuating an increasing similarity of higher education across the world.

Theme 3.2: International Networks

3.2.a Networking Groups

As higher education and research have become increasingly international, so have the supporting networks. Universitas 21, for example, tags itself "the leading global network of research universities in the 21st century" (www.universitas21.com/). Two other examples of international research-led university networks are Worldwide Universities Network (WUN) (www.wun.ac.uk/) and the International Alliance of Research Universities (IARU) (www.iaruni.org/). WUN is made up of eighteen member universities from across five continents, whereas IARU has ten members. Networks such as these bring together a mixture of initiatives, concerned to facilitate varieties of joint collaborative working (e.g., through staff and student exchange) and projects concerned with some of the 'grand challenges facing humanity.' At IARU, for example,

> [t]he Alliance has identified sustainable solutions on climate change as one of its key initiatives. As a demonstration of its commitment to promote sustainability, IARU has sought to lead by example through the establishment of the Campus Sustainability Programs aimed at reducing the environmental impact of our campus activities. IARU has also successfully organized an International Scientific Congress on Climate Change in 2009 and plans a Sustainability Congress that will take place in October 2014 in Copenhagen. Some of its members have also cooperated on major research projects pertaining to aging, longevity and health, global security and sustainable cities.
> (www.iaruni.org/about-us/iaru/about-iaru/iaru)

These groups, then, can both strengthen individual partners through collaborative activity and share a commitment to working together on world problems.

3.2.b Talloires Network

The Talloires Network is an international association with (as of June 2013) 300 college and university members in seventy-one countries, the largest global grouping focused on strengthening the civic roles and social responsibilities of higher education. It was established by a group of twenty-nine vice-chancellors, rectors, and presidents in September 2005, in Talloires, France, and still focuses on senior leadership. Out of initial meetings, a Declaration on the

Civic Roles and Social Responsibilities of Higher Education was drafted, and the network launched to enable ongoing collaboration and debate. The network, based at Tufts University, promotes the civic engagement activities of its members, providing expertise, undertaking conferences, and publishing activities. It aims to build regional capacity by partnering with existing colleges around the world, and cosponsors events, such as faculty training institutes and student workshops. It also provides institutional assessment and planning tools. Interestingly, the network has struggled in two areas (Hollister et al. 2012). First, where it has tried to have a common global project "to unite the membership by working together on a concrete initiative" (ibid.: 96) based on global literacy—including reading, numeracy, digital literacy, and financial literacy—there was little shared commitment to such a goal. The group had to agree that civic engagement be driven by local priorities and programs, rather than across the whole network. Second, implementing evaluation processes has also not been effective. Talloires has therefore not been able to exploit any 'scaling-up' or standardization of its activities. However, as participants in the 2011 Madrid conference noted, the civic engagement role for universities has been increasing over the years:

> The world is a very different place than it was when the Talloires Declaration was signed. Across the globe, the societies in which our institutions are situated are facing increased economic, social, and civic challenges. At the same time, in universities on every continent, something extraordinary is underway. Mobilizing their human and intellectual resources, institutions of higher education are increasingly providing opportunity and directly tackling community problems—combating poverty, improving public health, promoting environ- mental sustainability, and enhancing the quality of life. Many universities across the globe are embedding civic engagement as a core mission along with teaching and research. Around the world, the engaged university is replacing the ivory tower.
>
> (Hollister et al. 2012: 82)

Talloires is an example of building social responsibility and community engagement into university planning. It also links to concerns for common frameworks for developing civic engagement within higher education worldwide (Watson et al. 2011; Hoyt and Hollister 2014); with enabling engaged scholarship by academics (www.compact.org/initiatives/trucen/ trucen-toolkit/): and in building in metrics for measuring activities such as the Carnegie Community Engagement Classification (Carnegie Foundation for the Advancement of Teaching n.d.), all of which will be returned to in later chapters.

3.2.c *World International Summit on Education*

As I have already noted, although in its early stages the internationalization of higher education tended to mean attracting foreign students to Western universities, and exporting Western models of education to developing countries, the balance is now shifting with dialogue around appropriate educational models being shared more equally. The World International Summit on Education (WISE), for instance, is an example of the shifting 'centers' of world educational debate (Text Box 3.2). But if Qatar, like Singapore, is aiming to develop into a knowledge-based economy, it is also interested in opening up education to many voices, offering sizable sponsorship, and prize giving, underpinned by its oil and gas wealth:

> Unlike other notable foundations with an education focus, such as the Bill & Melinda Gates Foundation, the Qatar Foundation does not only target specific outcomes or specific projects. Their investment, especially with WISE, is in long term conceptual areas such as "innovation in education" and "education for all". Creating a forum to share innovations, outside of prescribed criteria established in advance, is urgently needed. In times of rapid change and uncertainty, experimentation, action, and discourse are needed, rather than following status quo solutions. After a decade of attending and presenting at learning, technology, education, and innovation conferences, WISE is the best forum that I have encountered for having the most important global education conversations.
>
> (Siemens 2013b)

Text Box 3.2 The WISE Initiative

The World Innovation Summit for Education (WISE) was established by Qatar Foundation in 2009, and is an international, multisectoral platform for creative thinking, debate, and purposeful action with the aim of building the future of education through innovation. WISE is a global, ongoing initiative that, through an annual summit and different programs, promotes collaboration and builds the future of education.

The various initiatives include the following:

- The annual WISE Summit, which since 2009 has brought together decision makers, influential experts, and practitioners to discuss worldwide issues, explore new innovations, and take concrete action in education
- The WISE Prize for Education—an individual or a team of up to six people is given recognition for their outstanding, world-class contribution to

education. To date, these awards have been made for initiatives, which have improved the lives of millions through education across three continents, have provided education and literacy to millions at minimum cost, and have improved the quality of basic education in low-income schools.

- The annual WISE Awards identify and promote six innovative projects that have had a transformative impact on societies. The projects come from a wide variety of sectors and winners receive a prize of US$20,000, as well as worldwide visibility.
- WISE Learners' Voice selects a group of young learners between the ages of eighteen and twenty-five to take an active role in the WISE Summit and other activities throughout the year with the aim of supporting them to develop communication, entrepreneurship and leadership skills to prepare them for leading roles in education.
- WISE Books—WISE have published a number of books to encourage innovative thinking and sound practices in education.
- The WISE Haiti Task Force has brought together innovators and successful projects that are contributing to rebuilding Haiti's educational system, which was devastated in the earthquake of January 2010.
- Since September 2010, Euronews has been broadcasting *Learning World*, a magazine dedicated to education (www.euronews.com/programs/learning-world/).
- The WISE Community Platform is an interactive knowledge base that offers a wide range of tools to people working in education-related sectors. It includes a social networking feature that enables the WISE community to connect, interact, and share knowledge and best practices.

For more information see:
WISE Initiative (n.d.) Available at: www.wise-qatar.org/content/wise-initiative (accessed April 24, 2014).

Theme 3.3: Developing Global Citizens

3.3.a Global Educational Opportunities

As New York University in Abu Dhabi (and soon to open in Shanghai) explains it, the global network university (GNU) is a new paradigm in higher education—what Hawawini (2011) would call a transnational university:

> Designed to draw the most talented and creative students and faculty from around the world, it enables those students and faculty to circulate seamlessly throughout the network without leaving the University's

intellectual community and resources. Research and learning at each of the network's sites are connected to and enhanced by the whole, and students become global citizens.

(http://nyuad.nyu.edu/about/global-network.html)

Here globalization is framed as supporting all students' mobility between and across different locations, through its 'anchor' campuses, which "are deeply related to each other, each using and building on one another's assets. There is no longer a 'hub' institution with 'satellites' (Text Box 3.3).

TEXT BOX 3.3   NEW YORK UNIVERSITY, ABU DHABI

New York University and the Emirate of Abu Dhabi had a shared understanding of the roles and challenges facing higher education in the twenty-first century, including a belief in the value of a liberal arts education, the value of a research university to society, the importance of interaction with new ideas and people, and a commitment to educating students to be worldwide citizens. Through these shared beliefs New York University Abu Dhabi (NYUAD) was created in 2010. NYUAD, which is funded by the Abu Dhabi government, is the first comprehensive liberal arts campus to be operated abroad by a major American research university. It has five campuses in Abu Dhabi, which are all linked and designed to create interaction between students and staff and has also opened "portal campuses" or academic centers in a dozen cities, including Accra, Berlin, Buenos Aires, Shanghai, Tel Aviv, and Washington, D.C.

NYUAD offers courses in the Arts and Humanities, Social Sciences, Science, Engineering and Mathematics. As part of their course, students are required to participate in a series of global exchange programs through the NYU's 'Global Network University' (GNU). The first of these, the 'January Term,' involves students taking one full-time course in January lasting approximately three weeks. Three of these courses are taken over the course of a student's degree and are designed to intensify students' focus beyond the classroom and incorporate experiential learning, allowing students to connect with the place where they study. These courses can be taken at any of NYU's GNU sites around the world.

'Study Away' is an essential part of study at NYUAD. It incorporates the January Term as well as further international study for students to spend up to two semesters of their degree studying overseas at any of GNU's academic centers. Students can also apply to spend two semesters at other universities

if this would be beneficial to them. Study trips are also offered to students to enable them to discover more about the history and culture of the location in which they are studying. These trips are normally taken during spring and autumn breaks, but can also be part of the January Term and are of varying duration. Locations that have been included in the program to date include the seven emirates of the United Arab Emirates, Cyprus, Ethiopia, India, Morocco, Nepal, Oman, Qatar, Saudi Arabia, Sri Lanka, Turkey, and Zanzibar.
For more information see:
New York University Abu Dhabi (n.d.) Available at: http://nyuad.nyu.edu/about.html (accessed April 23, 2014).

At Rochester Institute of Technology (RIT), this idea is localized through the design of a integrated living, studying and entrepreneurial study environment:

> four continents have been together in one nine-acre, 414-bed living and learning campus community. [. . .] RIT's Global Village provides a unique living/ learning experience, and is a "one-stop" complex that provides students and faculty with support for pursuing multicultural and global education opportunities.
>
> (www.rit.edu/fa/globalvillage/housing)

The Global Village "prepares students to enter the global community and culturally-diverse workforce through educational programming, unique activities, and a worldly living environment" (ibid.). It includes a study abroad cluster that houses students intending to follow these programs as a means of preparing them for international experience.

In another example of enabling global educational opportunities, Penn State Global Learning Laboratory allows students and faculty to have access to colleagues, partners, and corporate sponsors worldwide. This is through a modern, 1,000-square-foot teleconferencing suite offering an infrastructure specifically designed for global project collaboration. The facility has a state of the art room equipped with Polycom technology and consists of five key components: a main teleconferencing room, a benchmarking area, a mobile Polycom unit, a feed to an auditorium, and an International Language station (www.ie.psu.edu/AboutUs/Facilities/InstructionalLabs/GlobalLab.html).

3.3.b *Working with Others*
The preceding examples operate from within a higher education paradigm, but there are also initiatives concerned with developing global citizenship that

go beyond university boundaries. Enactus, for example, envisions students as global entrepreneurs (http://enactus.org). Previously known as Students in Free Enterprise, Enactus's program works from the principle that entrepreneurial action can be used for worldwide community empowerment:

> "Our organization was created almost 40 years ago—long before concepts like micro-loans and social enterprises even existed—in order to prove the transformative power the entrepreneurial spirit can have in people's lives," said Alvin Rohrs, Enactus' CEO. "Our core belief has always been that the same kind of creativity and rigor and accountability that fuels businesses around the world is not only transferrable but actually essential to human progress."
>
> The organization has pioneered a groundbreaking model that deploys student teams, with the advice and support of academic and business leaders, to design and implement community empowerment projects in 39 countries.
>
> (http://enactus.org/sife-changes-their-
> name-to-highlight-a-deep-commitment-to-
> entrepreneurial-action/#.U2O0I61dVhM)

The nonprofit organization brings together students, academics, and business leaders to undertake community empowerment projects worldwide, through 'innovation labs' that explore ways to address specific challenges in different places.

Open Spaces for Dialogue and Enquiry (OSDE) faces up to the issue of not only global problems but also difference and conflict, by enabling students from various countries to work together in potentially problematic situations. It has designed a methodology for introducing global issues across all levels of education (developed by a group of educators and researchers in eight countries) and is hosted by the Centre for the Study of Social and Global Justice at the University of Nottingham (www.globalfootprints.org/osde). OSDE is a dialogue-based process for enabling students to engage with difficult and controversial international subjects. Here, getting involved in globalization becomes an explicit means for improving critical literacy, independent thinking, and active citizenship skills.

3.3.c *The University of the Third Horizon*

Plans for the University of the Third Horizon (H3Uni) have grown out of the International Futures Forum (www.internationalfuturesforum.com/), and a series of projects by its founding members (who have mixed business consultancy and educational backgrounds). These projects have focused on what are called "messy complex challenges that seem impervious to old solutions and existing ways of thinking—what we have called 'conceptual emergencies'" (O'Hara and Leicester 2009) and that, like OSDE, have worked through bringing together diverse participants using tools that engages with differences in opinion, understanding competing perspectives and dilemma resolution, for example, through the IFF World Game (www.internationalfuturesforum.com/world-game). Clients have included Scottish cities looking to reinvent themselves for the future, national public health services attempting to deal with rising health care costs and US universities. However, unlike OSDE, these activities have led to the intended creation of a completely new type of university. Rather than seeing educational internationalization as an agglomerative process, the argument behind 3HUni is that learning in the contemporary world demands a new methodology. Its developers start from the belief that we are now in times where we can no longer follow business as usual in higher education:

> The world changes. Forty years later it is again in turmoil, threatened by financial collapse, high unemployment, exponential advances in technology, population migrations, geopolitics in Europe, the rise of China and India, globalization, and hanging over all, the threats posed by global climate change. These are powerful times when entire cultures—from the individual behavior of citizens to the processes of society—must adapt to an altogether different world. So once again education is being challenged to respond with new ideas, new forms of teaching and learning, and new curriculum content adequate to the cultural tasks before us.
>
> (O'Hara, n.d.: 1)

Such global problems do not merely require international university networks, or specific international initiatives. Rather, they demand a whole new way of teaching and learning, that goes beyond the current state of higher education where "people find themselves working ever harder to improve their institutions using the usual measurement, standards, and quality assurance methods, but with ever decreasing returns" (ibid.: 2). This is articulated as a third horizon beyond either merely repeating the status quo, or just tinkering with existing systems:

> In order to face the social, economic and environmental challenges arising around the world, we need to shift our approach of *how we learn* and *what we learn*. We need to let go of seeing education as merely a means to getting better employment and to drop the notion that specialization is the answer. Learning *is* so much more than memorization. Our perspective of education needs to expand, expand to include the interconnection of life

itself, to unlock our capacity to communicate—knowing what information to share, when to share it, how to work together in partnership, and how to understand people's diverse perspectives.

(http://h3uni.net/h3uni/vision/)

This leads to a developing understanding of the curriculum as enabling a particular set of methods and skills. For the H3Uni developers these are listed as resolving horizon dilemmas, designing resilient systems, facilitating cognitive intelligence, gaming global challenges, organizing social enterprises, agile and creative thinking, and seeing and being a new future (http://h3uni.net/h3uni/). The most interesting aspect of this, then, is the implication that really thinking through internationalization could have much bigger impact - and more powerful potential-on learning at the tertiary levels than is currently being considered.

More than Satellites?

In his critical review of the internationalization of higher education Hawawini shows that many universities are developing international campuses and collaborations without fully recognizing the implications or the consequences; with global 'additions' to their existing facilities and practices only have marginal effects (2011: 3). He argues that this is because universities are too grounded in their own historical and geographical contexts, and—hampered both by internal inertia and by national regulations—are not well placed to act radically when entering the global education market. For him, a properly global university has probably got to be born out of an already international organization, or needs to be developed from scratch. It should be noted that Hawawini writes as a professor of finance and former dean of INSEAD International Business School, a private-sector provider with campuses in Abu Dhabi, Singapore, and France. His ideal global university has two or three campuses located in key international locations, with a truly cosmopolitan student body and faculty on each site and without any being the 'home' campus (not unlike the way INSEAD is developing). But his underlying concern is important—that the internationalization of higher education has not been informed enough by an equality in engagement between international participants, or an explicit investigation of the implications of cultural difference, or the valuing and embedding of cultural richness and global citizenship into the resulting education provision. We urgently need more explicit definitions of what internationalizing higher education involves and a stronger commitment to global educational and societal goals:

> [This] calls for a change in existing structures, operating modes, and mindsets in order for the institution to join and contribute to the shaping

of the emerging global knowledge and learning network. [. . .] [A] truly
global academic institution [aims] not to teach the world but to learn
from the world in order to enhance the institution's capacity to create
new knowledge and develop truly global citizens.

(Hawawini 2011: 5–6)

Some of the examples given here show how universities and other organizations are beginning to deal explicitly with these issues, at a variety of levels. In
the conclusion, I return to the importance of learning to become a global citizen and the roles universities and colleges are and should be playing in this. In
the next chapter, however, I explore how the local and regional environments
of universities and colleges are themselves also changing, as the location,
type and nature of learning spaces in higher education are increasingly being
questioned.

4

CHANGING LEARNING SPACES

The learning environment is not alone in having to deal with this [. . .] wider pattern in which the whole landscape of space use is changing: the hybridizing of space, the dispersing of work, the annexing of non-traditional spaces or the freedoms and constrictions that comes with new technology and the blending and layering of physical and virtual work arenas. The learning environment is, though, we would contest, in the front line of these developments.
—*Harrison and Hutton (2013)*

The physical environments of universities and colleges are increasingly coming under scrutiny. This is for several reasons. The development of innovative types of learning—more interactive, informal, and social—is challenging a conventional lecture theatre, seminar room and specialist lab arrangement. New technologies are interacting with physical space to suggest different kinds of blended and hybrid relationships. And institutions are looking to use their estates' resources more effectively and sustainably. A considerable number of landmark educational buildings are being constructed worldwide (Figure 4.1) as new campuses are erected, existing campuses consolidated and extended, and legacy buildings adapted and demolished. However, although the debate about these new learning environments tends to be framed oppositionally, that is, as 'conventional' versus 'next-generation' learning approaches, the realities are more layered and complex (Boys 2010). This suggests that what is needed

Figure 4.1 Interior, Swanston Academic Building RMIT, Melbourne, Australia
Source: Photo by Gill Zettle.

is both a better understanding of what matters about space for learning and the development of a more diverse range of actual spaces in higher education, which produce an efficient and flexible match across formal, informal, social, and specialist requirements.

At the same time, a new typology of higher education buildings has already been developing, and is affecting campus design internationally (Boys and Smith 2011). The 'look' often overlaps with corporate office environments with, for example, a large foyer atrium using minimalist, modern materials or can be much more highly colored, with decorated features and sculpture (Figure 4.2). These new, large entrance spaces also often provide 'one-stop' shops for student recruitment and guidance, as well as informal learning spaces—usually linked to cafes—for students to work individually or in groups in a relatively relaxed setting (Figure 4.3). Such new learning spaces for self-directed study are usually described as hubs, zones, nooks, streets, or commons and often use brightly colored furniture and elements to express a more informal mood. As part of these shifts, an increasing range of furniture types—again, often overlapping with new office design—are becoming available (Figure 4.4).

It is worth noting that early innovations in learning space design (both physical and virtual) has tended to come from outside 'conventional' academic

Figure 4.2 Entrance atrium, Ross Business School, University of Michigan, USA
Source: Photo by Jos Boys.

Figure 4.3 Entrance foyer and student hub, Business School, Manchester Metropolitan University (MMU), UK
Source: Photo by Jos Boys.

Figure 4.4 Example of seating, entrance foyer, University of Westminster, London, UK.
Source: Photo by Jos Boys.

activities, that is, have been initiated by library and student support staff, on one hand, and by learning technologists, on the other. The shifts in formal teaching, learning and research spaces have also been changing, but more unevenly. Next-generation learning spaces (Jamieson 2008; Fraser 2014) aim to offer a more interactive, flexible, and technology-rich teaching environment. This is made increasingly complex as universities and colleges become more able to offer interactions between physical, virtual, face-to-face, and online learning spaces and as new technologies become ubiquitous (an issue I return to in Chapter 5). This, in turn, has led to the use of concepts such as learning landscapes (Dugdale 2009; Neary et al. 2010) or learning ecologies (Siemens 2003; Ellis and Goodyear 2010) that can better capture the interrelatedness of learning and the many different kinds of (physical and virtual) spaces in which it can take place:

> The Learning Landscape is the total context for students' learning experiences and the diverse landscape of learning settings available today—from specialized to multipurpose, from formal to informal, and from physical to virtual. The goal of the Learning Landscape approach is to acknowledge this richness and maximize encounters among people, places, and ideas, just as a vibrant urban environment does. [. . .]

Rather than developing a master plan from the traditional perspective of siting future building blocks that are often identified as generic space types (such as "classroom," "departmental," or "administrative" buildings), the Learning Landscape approach defines a future campus by envisioning overlapping networks of compelling places and hubs, which can offer choices to users and generate synergies through adjacencies and the clustering of facilities.

(Dugdale 2009: 52)

There are also potential ongoing tensions between moves toward these more interactive pedagogic approaches (known as, e.g., constructivist, problem-based, experiential and active learning) that demand small-group teaching and the pressures for increased student numbers and reduced formal contact hours. This has also led to projects for large-scale but flexible lecture theatres, and other space arrangements for large classes—such as SCALE-UP (student-centered active learning environments for undergraduate programs; Oblinger 2006) and TEAL (technology-enabled active learning; Dori and Bletcher 2004). London Metropolitan University's Superlab Science Centre, for example, has more than 280 workstations with state-of-the-art facilities and is offered as a model for specialist laboratories around the world.

At the same time, and as already noted in Chapter 1, research is becoming more hybrid as innovations in science and technology demand multidisciplinary cooperation. This, in turn, has led to new kinds of research buildings that aim to use physical space to better integrate academic departments. These often deliberately mix up different subject specialists and physically interlink disciplines through shared circulation and 'overlooking' and informal meeting areas, with the intention of generating and supporting informal encounters and collaborations (Figure 4.15). Universities are also increasingly building in collaboration with businesses, governments, and civic organizations. As Dugdale writes, this means that campus spaces are increasing becoming interwoven across function, time, and space:

Traditional categories of space are becoming less meaningful as activities blend, space becomes less specialized, boundaries between disciplines blur, and operating hours extend toward 24/7 access. In the future, space types are more likely to be designed around patterns of human interaction than around the specific needs of particular departments, disciplines, or technologies. With greater mobility, students have a choice in where they can work and tend to gravitate to spaces they enjoy—so quality of design matters more. New space models for educational institutions therefore need to focus on enhancing quality of life as well as supporting the learning experience.

(2009: 52)

Campus-based planning model	Learning Landscapes planning model
Based on space standards and norms, needs analyses and space occupancy rates	Based on holistic strategies, underpinned by action research of learning and teaching activities
Management-centered planning and design process	Engages with users to co-develop learning spaces through pilots, supported by on-going evaluation and process improvement
Relies on standard classroom types, with associated furniture and fittings	Develops appropriate range of learning spaces across active/passive, formal/informal and taught/self-directed
Separates virtual from physical provision	Enables integrated virtual and physical learning through a variety of hybrid modes
Single-function usage	Offers flexibility of learning activities from formal and taught to non-formal and self-directed

Figure 4.5 Differences in Conventional and Learning Landscape planning models
Source: Adapted from Dugdale (2009: 60).

In addition, as part of rethinking campus planning and facilities management, there have been moves towards changing the academic workplace (Harrison and Cairns 2008).

Finally it should be noted that developments in bio- and nanotechnologies and the internet of things (covered in more depth in Chapter 6) are likely to have longer-term effects, both on the kinds of buildings that universities will need to be developing and on the creation of 'smart' campuses more generally. As Kortuem et al. (2013) have shown, China is taking a lead in this area. (Text Box 4.1).

TEXT BOX 4.1 THE SMART CAMPUS

The Internet of Things is gaining global significance. China, for example, has initiated a strategic program to push the development of core technologies and applications in the Internet of Things area, with a special focus on agriculture, logistics, transport, electricity, public health and other key areas.

> [. . .] [A]cademics are investigating the potential of the Internet of Things for reforming vocational education and University education. The main focus here is not on pedagogy but on the application of Internet of Things technologies (such as RFID and sensor networks) to improve the teaching system—i.e. the campus environment and the management and organisation of educational institutes.
>
> (Kortuem et al 2013: 11–12)
>
> Although we already have smart ('digital') campuses, for example, through the use of card entry and tracking systems or interactive screens for room booking, the expanding possibilities of the Internet of Things (IoT) are still to be fully explored. This is about campuses based both on new kinds of interactive intersections between human–human, human–machine, and machine–machine and on the impacts of a combination of wireless networks, increasing cheap (and tiny) computer devices, and different remote sensing and information exchange capabilities. In 2009, Jiabao Wen, then China's Premier, visited the micro- and nano-sensing network technology research center in Wuxi, Jiangsu Province. He has since made 'Sensing China' a national strategy, focusing Chinese central and local governments on the development and application of Internet of Things technology.
>
> China has thus invested in Internet of Things development across both its university and its business sectors, including developing the concept of the smart campus. Examples already in process include Radio-frequency Identification (RFID) tagging of books linked to mobile phones for ease of location, automatic facilities management for energy saving, and unified and intelligent data management systems.
>
> *Reference*
>
> Kortuem, G., Bandara, A., Smith, N., Richards, M., and Petre, M. (2013) "Educating the Internet-of-Things Generation," *Computer* 46 (2): 53–61.

Underpinning these shifts has been an increasing expansion and professionalization of the learning spaces field, through specialist design and briefing consultants and manufacturers, government-funded and other national and international advisory bodies, and through academic groupings and research networks such as the Learning Environments Applied Research Network (LEaRN) at the University of Melbourne and the Learning Spaces Collaboratory (LSC) in the US. This has also led to a proliferation of toolkits to help universities and colleges in developing and evaluating new learning spaces and offering case study examples (such as Scott-Webber 2004, Joint Information

Systems Committee [JISC] 2006; Oblinger 2006; Alexi Marmot Associates 2006; Tertiary Education Facilities Management Association [TEFMA] 2006); and the development of methods for managing change on a case-by-case building project basis, through specific ways of working directly with management and faculty on design briefing and enabling new, technology-enriched learning and teaching methods.

Learning Spaces Research and Development

There is also now an increasing amount of work that critically reviews the current situation (Barnett and Temple 2006; Temple 2008, 2014; Painter et al. 2012), that explores how to better evaluate the effectiveness of new kinds of teaching and learning space in higher education (Scott-Webber 2004; Bligh and Pearshouse 2011; Scott-Webber et al. 2013; Boddington and Boys 2011), and considers how to connect these changes with strategies for campus planning (Space Management Group 2008, Learning Spaces Collaboratory 2013, Society for College and University Planning (SCUP) Academic Council 2014). Much of this work argues that current learning spaces evaluations are still mainly quite poor and that we urgently need better ways of understanding the relationships between space and the activities that go on in it, to improve both our ability to judge the effectiveness of learning in different kinds of environments, and actual learning space design.

At the same time, university campus planning and management teams are finding that conventional benchmarks such as space standards (based on formal teaching rooms) and space rates no longer fit for purpose (Ellis 2011) and that methods for predicting space requirements and usage patterns are no longer workable. Dugdale (2009) suggests how the new and different approaches required might be understood (Figure 4.5).

However, as outlined earlier, it seems that we do not yet have effective tools for accurately mapping the dynamic intersections of pedagogies, space, access, ownership, timetabling, and cost in our existing or planned campuses; are not effectively integrating an understanding of pedagogic and scholarly activities with space and technology in university strategies and implementation processes; and have not yet developed sophisticated planning methods that can make value decisions across learning space performance and other demands such as sustainability, business and community partnerships, and so on. Yet physical space is a large capital and running cost for universities, and its more effective planning and occupancy can save income that could instead be invested in, for example, staffing levels. Space utilization rates remain low across the sector—usually operating at about 25 to 30 percent in formal teaching spaces (SMG 2008). This makes better matching space and demand more effectively, and being able to use existing spaces more intensively, a key issue for the higher education sector as a whole.

In addition, some recent research suggests that the type and quality of informal learning spaces available on campuses can have an important effect on students feelings of engagement and belonging, and thus on their retention and achievement levels (Boys and Hazlett 2014; Boys et al. 2014). The design and development of appropriate informal, self-directed learning 'zones,' whether in physical or in virtual space, is thus also becoming a central concern for universities and colleges. Particularly in institutions where financial constraints are leading to a reduction of formal classes and instruction, students are spending a much higher proportion of their time in self-directed and informal learning. This makes the type, amount, and distribution strategies of informal learning space—its patterning from generic to specialist forms and from open-access to 'owned'—central to the student experience. In a recent study of a UK university campus (Boys et al. 2014), students described how they negotiated the availability of informal learning spaces (from their own home through the variety of provided campus-based spaces to other spaces beyond the campus such as public libraries) and linked the effectiveness of the match directly to their own sense of 'connectedness' with the university. The implications here (although more research needs to be done) are that universities need to more strategically orchestrate:

- Interrelationships between the students they serve—and/or want to attract—and the amounts and types of learning spaces provided (including student accommodation and other off-site provision and services)
- Interweavings between individual perceptions and experiences of 'being a student' and the 'sense of belonging' and identity that the campus environment expresses and enables
- Better matching between formal and informal learning, teaching, and research and the space types and their availability
- Evaluations of impact of space–time patterns on attendance, 'belonging,' engagement, retention, and achievement

There is a final point to be made. This is the question as to why so many universities and colleges have tended towards building design based on either what might be called a 'corporate' aesthetic—linked to shifts in contemporary office design—or to a continuity with primary and secondary school environments, through bright colors and 'novelty' features. Are these based more on fashion, rather than the development of a deeper understanding of the distinctive characteristics of higher education, and the design qualities that could effectively underpin these (Boys 2010; Boys and Smith 2011)? For example, when we asked students of an innovative new learning space based on beanbags and other flexible elements (Melhuish 2011a, 2011b) what they

Figure 4.6 Development workshop for student-led design of informal learning space, University of Ulster, Northern Ireland, UK

Source: Photo by Diane Hazlett, reprinted with permission.

felt about it, half thought it an informal and relaxed setting conducive to learning, whereas the other half found it childish and unsatisfactory. In these circumstances, we need to know more about what students bring to their learning in terms of interpreting different physical settings, as well as the interrelationships between their experiences of learning and the spaces in which it takes place. In another learning spaces project at the University of Ulster, Northern Ireland, a student design competition for a new (student-led) informal learning space resulted in a winning group that wanted a 'professional' environment, which they felt appropriate to the practice-based ethos of their campus, in an explicit refusal of the more 'playful' and colourful examples currently in vogue. (Figure 4.6).

Universities in Their Wider Context

Although in previous waves of city economic and cultural regeneration (Landry 2008), universities and colleges have been marginal players, the development of concepts such as the 'knowledge city,' 'creative economy,' and 'creative class' has mean that higher education institutions have become much more involved in how they extend beyond the campus and have been concerned to be integral to local, urban, and regional development (Florida 2002, 2012; Rodin 2007; Berglund 2009; Goddard and Vallance 2013):

> [The portfolio of university learning spaces] extends throughout the period of formal education [. . .] It also extends both beyond and outside of those time and place limitations, to libraries (school, general and academic), research laboratories, public buildings such as museums and galleries, ad hoc public and private spaces such as hotels and conference centres and work-based adult activities, delivering apprenticeships and professional qualifications in homes and offices.
>
> (Harrison and Hutton 2013)

In some cases this has become a strategic collaboration between an educational institution and its local governmental organizations, rather than a project-by-project process. For example,

> in Copenhagen, the municipality collaborates politically and in planning terms with the University of Copenhagen to support the realisation of the Knowledge District North Campus, which focuses on the connection and integration between education, business, housing and infrastructure. The close collaboration bolsters the university's ability to influence e.g. traffic planning and development of urban spaces that make allowance for the encounter between people from the knowledge institutions in the area, just as the municipality has the opportunity to unfold physical and social urban development efforts via the large projects.
>
> (Danish Property Agency 2013: 24)

In other cases, the university location itself suggests a particular type of academic presence. Merced University, for example, was built on the land between San Francisco and Los Angeles in 2005, when the state and the umbrella organization for all of California's ten state universities decided to establish a new public university in order to increase the research-based educational offer regionally and to attract students from nonacademic homes. The university's location near the Yosemite National Park frames the university's research and educational profile, centered on sustainable environments.

Elsewhere, higher education institutions are examining their relationships to the urban and other contexts in which they sit, as potential property developers in their own right (e.g., through building student accommodation, conference facilities, science parks, dispersed campuses, etc.), as potential drivers of a more hybrid interrelationship between education and other activities enabling new interconnections and opportunities to emerge, and as generators of employment, culture, and economic regeneration. Of course, the university's wider physical presence also acts as an attractor and 'show window' for its research and educational activities:

> Paying attention to this agenda will be increasingly important for the salvation of universities. Building relationships with cities, putting in place the virtuous circle of good university, close links with business and public authorities, collaborative research and development, spin-offs and start-ups, the attraction of talented students and faculty, the development of 'cool' places to live—with good coffee, wine and music, for example—and then the further development of the university and the city should now become central to any traditional university.
>
> (Barber et al. 2012: 54)

However, integration with, and expansion into a locality, region or other country has advantages and disadvantages in different contexts, and—as part of the complexification problem already mentioned—may result in universities extending themselves too far or without creating real resource-effective benefits, moving into areas where they do not have adequate in-house expertise or even potentially negatively affecting their reputation, as University College London found, when they aimed to develop a new campus as part of post-2012 London Olympic Games (Text Box 4.2).

Box 4.2 University College London, Newham Campus Development, UK

In November 2011, University College London (UCL) and the London Borough of Newham announced plans to consider developing a new campus for the university, on the edge of the London Olympics site in East London as part of its intended legacy of urban regeneration. The proposed scheme, on the edge of the Olympic Park, was intended to include teaching and research space as well as additional community, residential, and commercial space. The planned site included public housing, called the Carpenters Estate, which was to be demolished.

For the university and the council, such a new 'university quarter' was seen to offer employment and educational possibilities locally. The Mayor saw it as "an exciting and ambitious proposition which offers great opportunities for Newham [. . .] This development of world-class academic facilities in Stratford would create a wealth of benefits for the local area, the borough and East London as a whole" (www.ucl.ac.uk/news/news-articles/1111/111123-newham-additional-campus).

A year later, the project was agreed. However, it turned out that both council and university had misjudged the popular mood, not just from local residents but also from journalists—and perhaps most importantly—from the university's own students and staff. A support group was gathered, Campaigners Carpenters Against Regeneration (CARP), which fiercely opposed the council's decision to demolish and rehouse residents rather than pay for refurbishments A website was set up and a report produced by some UCL students, highlighting the perspectives of the Carpenters Estate residents against the demolition. In this interpretation UCL, one of the most prestigious universities in the country, was seen as destroying the homes of 318 people, getting a cheap site compared to its central London location, and being too exclusive to offer education for local people. What was worse was that the local council was agreeing to lose social housing stock at a time when it had a huge waiting list for people unable to afford market rents or mortgages.

In May 2013, the proposal was dropped, although both parties say they remain committed to building the campus elsewhere in that area of east London. But some reputational damage was done, as can be seen from the website response to the collapse of the deal:

> This a momentous victory by the residents of Carpenters Estate and also shows that together students and residents can save homes from gentrification and resist the reckless agendas of today's universities.
>
> (http://ucl4carpenters.tumblr.com/)

For more information see:
Apsan Frediani, A., Butcher, S., and Watt, P. (Eds.) (2013) *Regeneration and Well-Being in East London: Stories from Carpenters Estate*, MSc Social Development Practice Student Report, Bartlett Development Planning Unit UCL. Available at: www.bartlett.ucl.ac.uk/dpu/news/dpu/programmes/postgraduate/msc-social-development-practice/in-practice/london-based-fieldwork/carpentersreport

Hatherley, O. (2012) "Housing Policy, Newham Style: Let Residents Make Way for a UCL Campus," *The Guardian Online*, November 7. Available at: www.theguardian.com/commentisfree/2012/nov/07/housing-policy-newham-ucl-campus (accessed May 25, 2014).

"UCL Looks East towards Newham for Additional University Campus" (2011) *UCL News*, November 23. Available at: www.ucl.ac.uk/news/news-articles/1111/111123-newham-additional-campus (accessed May 25, 2014).

York, M. (2013) "UCL and Newham Council Axe £1bn Campus Deal for Carpenters Estate, Stratford," *Newham Recorder*, May 7. Available at: www.newhamrecorder.co.uk/news/ucl_and_newham_council_axe_1bn_campus_deal_for_carpenters_estate_stratford_1_2183978 (accessed May 25, 2014).

As more and more universities and colleges gain experience of extending beyond their own campuses, there is a need to learn and share lessons. Projects such as Lincoln Institute of Land Policy's "The City, Land and the University Program" (www.lincolninst.edu/subcenters/city-land-university/), for example, aim to operate as a research network for collecting and sharing data on the various ways in which universities as large urban land owners engage with their localities. In the rest of this chapter, I briefly explore other examples of how some higher education institutions are rethinking the design and development of their campuses to better match learning in the twenty-first century.

Theme 4.1: Comprehensive Campus Redesign

4.1.a University of Melbourne, New South Wales, Australia
I have suggested that much learning space development remains relatively piecemeal and additive; with universities building landmark projects and/or experimenting with a few innovative teaching spaces, and student support areas- libraries, resource centers, open access learning zones—where the perceived and actual resistance of faculty has less impact. Examples of complete strategic reviews, where campus design is explicitly integrated with business and pedagogic models are less easy to find. As part of implementing the Melbourne Model (see also Chapter 1)—to shift from a predominance of undergraduate courses to a balance between undergraduate and postgraduate provision—the University of Melbourne has also been restructuring its physical space, through an on-going investment in a redesign and refurbishment program. There are at least two components here: spaces that offer 'home bases' for students, one for each restructured school (Figure 4.7), and a variety of tutor-led and self-directed informal learning spaces offered across the campus (Figure 4.8). These are supported by a technicians' network, various staff development programs, and other initiatives. This has also enabled the university to build-in support such as bookable lecture video capture, media editing for academics, access

Figure 4.7 School 'hub,' University of Melbourne, Australia
Source: Photo by Jos Boys.

Figure 4.8 Informal learning space, University of Melbourne, Australia
Source: Photo by Jos Boys.

to interactive learning spaces and equipment, and MOOC delivery through Coursera (see Chapter 5).

These campus developments are managed from the most-senior level:

> The Office of the Provost supports the Provost in the delivery of these responsibilities through the provision of strategic advice and executive support, and the coordination of strategic and business planning, budget and resource allocation, project management, and performance evaluation processes for the division. [. . .] The Strategic Advisor on Learning Environments is also based in the Office and leads the development of learning spaces and a broader understanding of the campus as a learning environment.
>
> (http://msl.unimelb.edu.au/op)

In developing these new adaptations and additions, Professor Peter Jamieson, Strategic Advisor on Learning Environments, deliberately aimed for distinctiveness over generic, flexible spaces:

> The emphasis in this project was the creation of a suite of quality, diverse and engaging settings that would attract and retain students within the campus in order to promote greater collaboration in learning and a richer social experience for students. Unlike similar projects at other institutions, many of the specific settings were created deliberately to avoid the saturation of technology and computer use that can too easily dominate campus learning environments. A distinguishing feature of the project, which stands counter to the popular belief in 'flexible' spaces, is the emphasis on designing bespoke settings that are largely fixed and unable to be relocated. The furniture, therefore, is an integral element of the design and the overall setting. This was driven by our belief that so-called 'flexible spaces' often lack gravitas as a result of the intention to meet a wide list of potential uses.
>
> Instead, the Melbourne project sought to create settings that expressed a genuine respect for the student occupants. As a consequence, and despite the absence of staff in all of the settings shown, the facilities have been well-maintained by students and the learning hub is regarded as the most popular facility on campus by students.
>
> (personal communication, October 7, 2013)

The appearance and layout of these spaces also tend more to the 'scholarly' rather than exploiting bright colors and 'fun' features—often building on traditional settings for clubs, old university common rooms, and libraries. These examples (Figure 4.9) at Melbourne and elsewhere, such as the library at Musashino Art University in Japan, (Figure 4.10) offer a thought-provoking

Figure 4.9 Informal learning space as 'club,' University of Melbourne, Australia
Source: Photo by Jos Boys.

Figure 4.10 Interior, Musashino Art University Library, Tokyo, Japan
Source: Photo by Edmund Sumner.

alternative to what is potentially becoming the standard aesthetic for contemporary university learning spaces worldwide.

4.1.b Rethinking Campus Planning for Learning—University of Sydney, New South Wales, Australia

When the University of Sydney reviewed its next stage campus master planning in 2011, it was concerned to make integrated improvements across organizational structure, curriculum design, pedagogy, space, and technologies, using the student perspective and learning outcomes as the orientation (Ellis and Goodyear, 2010). The driver for this realignment was the idea of emphasizing the university campus as a place of learning, which embraced both the physical and virtual. Data were gathered from students and faculties that showed a demand for improvement in learning and teaching spaces at the university—"improvement that involves more than just fabric and routinely includes technology" (Ellis 2011: 1). Properly engaging with these changing expectations required several shifts in university processes. First, it needed an explicit conceptual framework for understanding the dynamic and integrated nature of higher education learning across physical and virtual spaces. Crucially, the learning spaces strategy defined undergraduate and postgraduate learning as "engaged inquiry" (Ellis 2011: 1) and its spaces and technologies not as discrete entities but as elements in a dynamic network (Figure 4.11, Text Box 4.3).

Second, there needed to be systems for comparable data measurement of the amount, equipment, and use of different kinds of learning spaces. As the report noted (in common with many other universities),

> [t]he ability of the University of Sydney to set its own targets is impeded by:
>
> - A lack of a complete picture of space provision and use University-wide
> - A lack of shared definitions about the structure of learning and teaching space inventory
> - Disconnected space management models and space management tools across faculties and the University timetable office
>
> (ibid.: 21)

In addition, existing space standards guidance did not offer the best data:

> National benchmarks for this planning are impoverished because they only count contact *teaching* hours. We know from research and experience

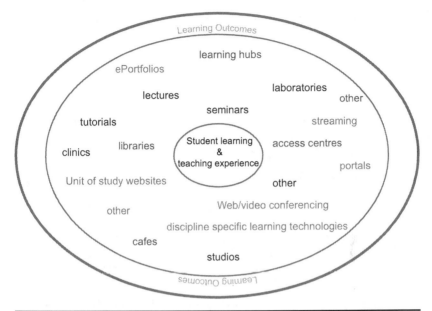

Figure 4.11 University of Sydney learning networks diagram, showing interconnections across formal, informal, and virtual spaces

Source: Reprinted from Ellis (2011: 65), with permission.

that total *learning* hours are a more accurate reflection of the on-campus and off-campus space required for students to achieve learning outcomes. This type of planning makes allowances for students to work in libraries, learning hubs and cafes on campus, as well as off campus at home or work online wherever they are through virtual means.

(ibid.: 20)

Third, there had to be transparency in sharing data and associated costs across faculty, to validate decision making about resource allocation, and, finally, there needed to be embedded management, monitoring and evaluation processes. As part of these developments at the University of Sydney, there has also been a strategic intention to shift the balance of space ownership from individual faculties to university-wide use and management to improve overall space design standards by focusing on a student perspective, and increasing space utilization and resource effectiveness.

This underlying framework has led to the development of learning space maps to inform campus planning developments and to a changed decision-making structure embedding learning spaces and technologies across senior management positions, changes in timetabling processes, the creation of built-in evaluation processes, and institutional advocacy for integrated learning space from the Office of the Deputy-Vice Chancellor (Education).

TEXT BOX 4.3   UNIVERSITY OF SYDNEY LEARNING SPACES STRATEGY: CONCEPTUAL FRAMEWORK

Much of student activity in networks of learning and teaching space (formal, informal, virtual) is driven by curricula objectives and learning outcomes. This fact enables a tangible, if difficult, objective in terms of campus planning for learning and teaching space. In principle, the provision of learning and teaching space at the university should largely be determined by the aggregated space requirements across curricula in our faculties [. . .] our provision, management and evaluation of those elements should strive to be as seamless as possible from the perspective of students as they move towards the learning outcomes identified in their units of study and programs.

The Student Experience of Engaged Inquiry

- Students spontaneously latch onto key ideas and iteratively pursue these ideas back and forward amongst the networks of modern learning and teaching space.
- These networks can be described as formal (lecture, seminar, laboratory, studio, clinic etc.,), informal (libraries, learning hubs, access centres, cafes, home, work, rural etc.,) and virtual (presentation, communication, interrogation, assessment technologies etc.).
- The student experience of learning should inform how the University should plan, provide, manage and evaluate learning and teaching space networks.
- The student survey and faculty responses together suggest that we should plan for capacity, flexibility, integration, innovation and sustainability across all our networks of space.

Key Questions for Learning Space Design at the Level of a University

Using the perspective of students and teaching staff as the orientation, the following questions emphasise key issues for integrated learning space planning.

Capacity

How aligned is total inventory of learning/teaching space to the current and projected curricula needs of faculties/teaching staff and students?

Flexibility

How does variation in the inventory of learning/teaching space align to variation in approaches to learning of our students and approaches to teaching adopted by teaching staff?

Integration

How seamless is the integration of access and support of virtual space in formal and informal space?

Innovation

To what extent is the development of learning and teaching space aligned to innovations in approaches to teaching from our teaching staff and changes to the way students are experiencing learning?

Sustainability

How do we sustain the quality and cost of evaluating, providing, supporting, refurbishing and renewing current and projected inventory of required learning and teaching space?

Source: Adapted from R. A. Ellis (2011) *Educational Planning Provision, Management and Evaluation of University Learning and Teaching Space—Learning Space Review Final Report.* University of Sydney, Camperdown.

4.1.c Steelcase University

Steelcase is a furniture designer and manufacturer that has increasingly moved into higher education learning space support, through research and consultancy activities into how new kinds of furniture and settings can better support learning. Its 'university' uses its own offices as prototypes to test detailed layouts and equipment designs (Figure 4.12).

It also employs research staff to investigate relationships across learning, teaching, and space. Lennie Scott-Webber, one of these researchers, produced a seminal publication for the Society for College and University Planners (SCUP) in 2004 that offers a valuable way of understanding the different activities that are central to learning in higher education (Figure 4.13). Since then she and others have produced regular reports examining aspects of workplace, university and college space–organization relationships that both inform product design and underpin consultancy at the company.

Figure 4.12 Steelcase University, Grand Rapids, Michigan, USA
Source: Photos by Jos Boys.

Theme 4.2: Redesigning Processes

4.2.a McGill University, Montreal, Quebec, Canada

Since 2006, McGill University has created an ongoing series of learning spaces projects, through allocating annual core funding and then making a yearly selection of initiatives, based on competitive bidding. Funds are prioritized by a large committee of representatives from across all departments, staff, and student groups, coordinated by the university's educational development unit, the Teaching and Learning Space Working Group (TLSWG). This group "create[s] a vision for classroom development aligned with University directions

ENVIRONMENTS	ARCHETYPAL ATTRIBUTES			
	Icon	Behavioral Premise	Process Steps	Protocol Attributes
Delivering		• Bring information before the public • Instructor led • Knowledge is in one source	• Prepare and generate presentation • Deliver to an audience • Assess understanding	• A formal presentation • Instructor controls presentation • Focus is on presentation • Passive learning
Applying		• Learner-centered • An apprentice model	• Knowledge transferred via demonstration • Practice by recipient • Understanding achieved	• Controlled observation • One-to-one • Master and apprentice alternate control • Informal • Active learning
Creating		• Innovation or knowledge moved from abstract to a product	• Research • Recognize need • Divergnet thinking • Incubate • Interpret into product/innovation	• Multiple disciplines • Leaderless • Egalitarian • Distributed attention • Privacy • Casual • Active learning
Communicating		• Share information • Provide quick exchange	• Organize information • Deliver • Receive and interpret • Confirm	• Knowledge is dispersed • Impromptu delivery • Casual • Active learning
Decision Making		• Make decisions	• Review data • Generate strategy • Plan • Implement one course of action	• Knowledge is dispersed • Information is shared • Leader sets final direction • Situation is protected • Semi-formal to formal • Passive/Active learning

Figure 4.13 Table showing archetypical attributes for knowledge environments
Source: Reprinted from Scott-Webber (2004: 107) with permission.

while promoting sound pedagogical principles, [. . .] establishes teaching and learning space standards, identifies teaching and learning space needs, sets priorities and recommends funding for improvements to classrooms at McGill to enhance these pedagogical environments" (TLSWG, n.d.). The group also works with the university's campus planning and management team during project development and implementation:

> Experience shows that the collaboration between educational developers and building experts has created greater understanding for the need to balance learning-related needs and physical challenges continually in concrete projects. The work has also prepared the ground for closer collaboration between the faculties. The mutual understanding among the university's educational developers and building experts and the collaboration between the faculties strengthen the university when they carry out modernisations and improve their communication and contact with external advisers in modernisation and construction cases [. . .]
>
> This has been an eye-opener to faculty representatives who willingly withdraw their own nominations when they can see a greater and more urgent need at other faculties. One condition for getting a share of the funds allocated to new learning environments is that the rooms must be

included in the university's central booking system. This has increased the efficient use of the rooms.

(Danish Property Agency 2013: 123)

Each year the types of learning spaces developed have evolved as lessons have been learned from past experiences, enabling a incremental improvement in learning spaces overall.

4.2.b Solna Campus, Karolinska Institute, Stockholm, Sweden

The Karolinska Institute, a medical university in Stockholm, Sweden, has also explored how to start from the educational (rather than 'technical') aspects of campus physical and virtual design and how to prioritize improvements during a specific—and major—university development process at its Solna campus. This included research into the existing literature, study visits, and collaborative discussion forums. They also undertook student surveys and, together with consultant architects, produced a design manual (Figure 4.14):

The renovation of the spaces between the lecture halls at Berzelius väg 3 (popularly known as BZ) began at the end of December 2011, and was officially opened for students and staff in February 24th. The once dark and uninviting BZ interior has been radically refreshed with white walls

Figure 4.14 Informal learning spaces, Karolinska Institute, Stockholm, Sweden
Source: Photo by Jos Boys.

and ceilings, new lighting, biowalls, information screens and flexible furnishing upholstered in bright, colourful patterns. Students now have a dedicated meeting place for socialising, group work and self-study.

Architect firm Tengbom won the contract to implement its design concept, which is based on a design manual published by White's. The concept is called Home away from Home and is intended to create a more vibrant, homely environment for students.

(http://ki.se/en/about/renovated-space-
for-students-on-campus)

Projects such as these, of which there are an increasing number, are also part of a shift towards intensifying space usage by adapting 'leftover' spaces in entrance foyers, corridors, and between buildings to support informal learning, thereby improving space utilization and reducing space costs. At the University of Brighton in the UK, for example, the Social and Informal Learning Spaces (SILS) project aims to identify already existing places across the university's campuses that can enable informal learning easily; and can be cheaply and effectively transformed (http://staffcentral.brighton.ac.uk/estateandfacilities/projects/sils-projects.html).

Theme 4.3: Creating Hybrid Spaces

In previous chapters I have already outlined the increasing hybridity and interdisciplinarity of university educational, research, business and civic engagement services. This has of course also had an impact on building types and forms, based on how different kinds of spaces are being unbundled and re-bundled. As Thrift notes, in a study that included a consideration of changing university research spaces, these new building typologies are

> built on a long tradition of trying to design teamwork into buildings, a tradition which had passed through an industrial phase and was becoming interested in buildings which could encompass many modes of social interaction by encouraging both concentration and dispersion simultaneously. So, for example, an office building might contain de-cloistered spaces of semi-public interaction and all kinds of dens in which individuals or smaller groups could make their way (Duffy 1997).

(2007: 44)

He suggests that, with increasing capital funding for the biosciences, this type is not only becoming a norm but also intensifying the 'performative' qualities of space. The architecture itself is now meant to enable the possibility of many encounters between people across time and space, with an infamous example

Figure 4.15 Circulation designed to enhance chance encounters, Stata Center, MIT, Boston, USA
Source: Photo by Jos Boys.

being the Stata Center at Massachusetts Institute of Technology (MIT, Boston, USA; Figure 4.15). Thrift then goes on to outline the key features of such buildings:

> First, they will often include an explicit attempt to represent 'life', whether that be swooping architecture, some forms of public display of science, and similar devices. Second, they are meant to be highly interdisciplinary. As a matter of routine, they usually include not only biologists but also physicists, chemists, computing engineers and so on, all clustered around root technologies like genomics, proteomics, imaging, and the like. Very often, they will place apparently unlike activities (such as computer laboratories and wet laboratories) side by side, or have unorthodox office allocation schedules, all intended to stimulate interdisciplinarity. Third, they are porous. Personnel (for example, scientists arriving and departing on a permanent basis) and information constantly flows through them. [. . .] Fourth, in keeping with an architectural rhetoric about changing ways of working which arose in the mid-1980s and is now an established convention, they are meant to encourage creative sociability arising out of and fuelling further unpredictable interactions. [. . .] Fifth, they are meant to be transparent: there are numerous vantage points from which to spot and track activity, both to add to the general ambience and to point to the values/value of the scientific activity that is going on. In other words, these buildings are meant to encourage a certain kind of notion of interactive knowledge.

(ibid.: 45)

However, as he notes, the mere proximity of different specialists is not enough to 'automatically' create shared dialogue and collaboration (and, in fact, may have the opposite result). The effects of this building type are not often properly evaluated. Such spaces will also need a brokerage strategy, the employment of 'pathfinders' who are explicitly concerned to increase connectivity, and other techniques for preventing silos from forming, or interdisciplinary projects from stagnating.

4.3.a *White Space, University of Abertay, Scotland*

Although smaller, and a relatively cheap conversion rather than a new build, the development of White Space at the University of Abertay offers an innovative alternative way of integrating learning, research and practice by combining staff workplaces, student start-ups, and rentable state-of-the-art facilities to generate a variety of interconnected learning and work-based opportunities. These are specifically focused on providing a space for the new kinds of interdisciplinary interactions happening in computer arts, but also for 'mixing the talents of Computer Arts students, PhD students, lecturers, together with business people, broadcasters and artists' so as to "surround our students with the buzz of a real working environment, allowing them to share real-world knowledge and experience" (www.abertay.ac.uk/about/facilities/whitespace/) (Text Box 4.4; Figure 4.16).

Figure 4.16 Combined MA teaching space and start-up units, White Space, University of Abertay, Scotland

Source: Photo by Jos Boys.

TEXT BOX 4.4 WHITE SPACE, UNIVERSITY OF ABERTAY, SCOTLAND

White Space, University of Abertay, which opened in 2007, is a learning environment and creative incubator for computer arts students, PhD students, and lecturers, together with local businesspeople, broadcasters, and artists from external organizations. The aim of the White Space is to create a work-like environment where students can share real-world knowledge and experience through tutorials, lectures, and group working in informal areas. Additionally, it is expected that students will develop skills in creativity, team working, interdisciplinary working, knowledge, research, enterprise, entrepreneurship, and ethics through working together in the White Space. The University of Abertay intends to adopt White Space thinking in its future estates development.

The key features of White Space are the following:

- In The Institute of Arts, Media and Computer Games, industrial partners are directly involved in delivering part of all of the courses, and undergraduate and postgraduate students share teaching and learning space with lecturers and local businesses.
- Dare to be Digital, developed and organized by Abertay University, is a UK video game development competition for students at universities and colleges of art. An industry judging panel select three games to be nominated for the British Academy of Film and Television Arts (BAFTA) Ones to Watch award, which is awarded to one of the teams at the BAFTA Video Games Awards in London.
- The Hannah Maclure Centre works with contemporary and interdisciplinary artists from the UK and abroad on cultural projects for national and international audiences.
- Other features of White Space are tutorial and seminar spaces for staff and students; a multipurpose space with television, film, digital image, and video facilities; a state-of-the-art digital recording studio with live radio broadcast facilities; a videoconferencing suite; and an informal area with access to refreshments to encourage interaction among staff, students, visitors, and businesses.

For further information see:

Abertay University (2014) *White Space*. Available at: www.abertay.ac.uk/about/facilities/whitespace/ (accessed April 25, 2014).

Abertay University (2014) *White Space Facilities*. Available at: www.abertay.ac.uk/about/facilities/whitespacefacilities/ (accessed April 25, 2014).

4.3.b A More Public Campus?

As already noted, fees for learning, teaching, and academic research are, of course, no longer the only source of funding for universities and colleges. As higher education makes an increasingly hybrid set of relationships with organizations across other educational services, business and the community, its building stock is also changing—suggesting the possibility of acting as a hub for regeneration more widely, and as a source of additional types of income. Academics such as Richard Florida (2002, 2012), from the University of Toronto, have been arguing that universities are part of the rise of a creative class as a key driving force in the development of post-industrial cities and economies. There have been some critiques of both Florida's methods and conclusions (see, e.g., Peck 2005), but the general point remains that universities and colleges can 'make' a place in their wider locality, city, and/or region, both by bringing the wider public onto their campuses and by building out into the community (as already shown with examples in Chapters 1 and 2).

The technical university ETH Zürich is a highly ranked higher education institution, specializing in engineering, science, technology, mathematics, and management. It is also a public university, following the Swiss system, which allows all students who pass the high school 'exit exam' (or an equivalent entrance exam) to go onto university. Although many campus buildings are integrated in the urban area, the university also has a campus on the outskirts of the city, which has now been transformed into a 'science city' with the aim of interconnecting students, academics, and the public and of making a center for sustainability. ETH "sees the demand for dissemination and openness as a possibility of reinforcing professional competences within technology and engineering. The university is literally turning their campus into a multifunctional campus district with an experimental character" (Danish Property Agency 2013: 17).

Because of Swiss law, which gives universities freedom within their own grounds, ETH can use its campus to test new products not yet approved for general use, for example, eco-friendly cars and new types of energy glass. This makes the campus itself a showcase for creative developments. There is a program of demonstrations and tours for the public, and the site aims to act as a platform for dialogue between business and science:

> An innovative urban development strategy aims to develop the Hönggerberg site into a campus that will completely integrate science and society, create a vibrant social scene, and give the public an insight into scientists' lives. [. . .]
> But the aim is for ETH Zürich to become much more than the traditional university campus found in other countries; the goal is to become an intersection between science and society, with its doors open to the

public. 'What is different about Science City is that we have programmes inviting people both in and outside Zürich to come to the campus and meet scientists—to see an MRI scanner in action, or meet a Nobel laureate,' Salzmann explains. 'There's a huge programme to start a dialogue between university people and people outside the university.

(Hager 2008)

EPFL, a sister institution to ETH, situated in a suburban area outside Lausanne, has also used its campus to prototype new kinds of facilities. The Rolex Learning Center (by architects SANAA) has been designed as 'one huge big room' (Moore 2010)—a 10,000-square-meter building to support a campus of 7,000 students and 4,000 research and academic staff. It includes a library, offices, a bookshop, a cafe, a restaurant, laboratories, a 600-seat auditorium, and a branch of Credit Suisse bank. The lettable spaces have been offered to supermarkets, service businesses, and chains of shops, but with the criterion for establishing a shop being that the presentation of a new idea for how the shop is to be run. This is to ensure that the shops feature up-to-date technology and interior design, where new products will be presented and tested. For instance, the bank has a new layout and way of interacting with its clients in a reading lounge–like environment, as well as testing touch-screen technologies that then can be developed at other branches (http://rolexlearningcenter.epfl.ch/page-45197-en.html).

Beyond the Landmark?

In 2008 I wrote an article called "Beyond the Beanbag?' in which I suggested that higher education senior managers were being too easily seduced by the stylistic fads behind many new learning space designs, without undertaking relevant research or evidence-based decision making. We now have many examples of outstanding landmark buildings and individual spaces that are embedding informal and technology-rich learning into higher education campuses, but the underlying issue still remains. How are universities and colleges to act more strategically, across their whole range of services, to develop and manage an appropriate and seamlessly integrated set of virtual and physical spaces, both on and beyond the campus? How can they be sure that those spaces add value, are resource effective and sustainable? And, as well as creating buildings with a strong visual presence that can promote a contemporary identity for a university or college, we also need to have a better understanding of how space and technologies interact with students (and faculty). This is in terms of effective learning, teaching, and research and in relation to well-being, belonging, and engagement—spaces (whether physical or virtual) that help keep students on campus, immersed and supported in their studies. Universities and colleges may have moved on from the 'space norms' of the past, but there is still a long way to go.

5

BEYOND VIRTUAL LEARNING
ENVIRONMENTS

Though eavesdropping today on a meeting of administrators or faculty at most existing universities you might not discern it, whether they know it yet or not, today's education institutions are in the midst of their own conceptual emergency. The knowledge society no longer belongs to the universities but has burst out into virtual Cloud computing spaces that link services, providers and students in multiple ways through the internet.
—O'Hara (n.d.: 4)

Since 2002 the New Media Consortium (NMC) and the Educause Learning Initiative (ELI) have been undertaking longitudinal research into new and emerging technologies and their potential impacts on learning, teaching and critical enquiry across the whole education sector. Each year a report is published, outlining six technology areas that an expert panel thinks will affect higher education over the short, medium, and longer term, supported by examples. The *NMC Horizon Report: 2013 Higher Education Edition* (Johnson et al. 2013) highlighted two technologies—tablet computing and Massive Open Online Courses (MOOCs) as having very immediate effects. Although tablet computers (and smart mobile phones) have been around for a while, the fact that MOOCs did not feature in their 2012 report indicates both the rate of change and the difficulties of making predictions in this area. As they write,

[m]assively open online courses have received their fair share of hype in 2012, and are expected to grow in number and influence within the next year. Big name providers including Coursera, edX, and Udacity count hundreds of thousands of enrolled students, totals that when added together illustrate their popularity. [. . .] MOOCs have enjoyed one of the fastest uptakes ever seen in higher education, with literally hundreds of new entrants in the last year.

(Johnson et al. 2013: 4)

In this chapter, then, I first consider the relative importance of MOOCs to higher education. Are they, as often argued, an example of Christensen's disruptive innovation, or are they unsustainable and likely to peter out? Then, I explore other online and blended learning models and methods, to see the extent to which new communication technologies are already taking learning in universities and colleges well beyond the virtual learning environment (VLE).

The Impact of Massive Open Online Courses

MOOCs grew out of the combination of several factors. The first MOOC started with twenty-five fee-paying students at University of Manitoba, and 2,300 studying the same course, free online:

When Stephen Downes and George Siemens coined the term in 2008, massively open online courses (MOOCs) were conceptualized as the next evolution of networked learning. The essence of the original MOOC concept was a web course that people could take from anywhere across the world, with potentially thousands of participants. The basis of this concept is an expansive and diverse set of content, contributed by a variety of experts, educators, and instructors in a specific field, and aggregated into a central repository, such as a web site. What made this content set especially unique is that it could be "remixed"—the materials were not necessarily designed to go together but became associated with each other through the MOOC.

(Johnson et al. 2013: 12)

Global online networks have thus enabled the (massive) scaling up of learning resources, the ability to generate multiple forms of media-rich content, and the open sharing of those resources. But, as major elite players in higher education such as Massachusetts Institute of Technology (MIT) and Stanford have begun to get involved, the ideas behind MOOCs are shifting. MIT, for example, had already begun accumulating and freely sharing courseware (an issue that will be returned to in the next chapter). It was also developing online infrastructures, with associated research and development, to support the usability and expansion of these resources. Here MOOCs were an obvious next step (Text Box 5.1: MITx), mainly as a form of experimentation:

> MOOCs can expand access to education, for those who are interested and extend institutions' reach and reputation internationally. The 'digital footprint' of learners using the technology is captured in large data sets that can, potentially, provide useful insights into online teaching and learning with very large numbers of students at low or minimal cost. For example, edX institutions such as MIT and Harvard use MOOCs to understand 'how students learn' and 'improve innovations in teaching and learning on campus'.
>
> (Yuan and Powell 2013: 9)

MOOCs, then, have became increasingly promoted by the top-ranking universities as an opportunity to view world-famous professors giving their lectures, making public the reputational USP of these elite institutions, and making their involvement with MOOCs and open courseware (OCW) a loss leader, ultimately aimed at generating applicants for face-to-face courses (Daniel 2012; Cormier 2010, 2013). This in turn has led to a division in definitions between xMOOCs and cMOOCs, the former those offered as a massification of existing eLearning platforms and methods and the latter—developed with the open education movement—that aimed to rethink the whole shape of learning in an internet age (which will be returned to in the next chapter).

TEXT BOX 5.1   MITX

The Massachusetts Innovation and Technology Exchange (MITx) is a non-profit association for the digital marketing and Internet business industry. Started at the end of 2011, MITx produces MOOCs from MIT departments and faculty that appear on the edX platform (co-owned by MIT and Harvard and made available as open-source software in 2013). It supports university-based experiments with scalable learning technologies and research on digital learning and originally included three components: (1) development and offering of massive open online courses, (2) research on the effectiveness of emerging digital learning tools, and (3) the development of an open-source platform for offering massive open online courses.

In September 2013, MITx announced the first of its XSeries Certificate programs, which offer accreditation for the completion of a series of related

MOOC courses (starting with Fundamentals of Computer Science and Supply Chain Management).

MITx has now become part of an institute-wide research initiative on online teaching and learning and acts as a 'knowledge' brokerage across a variety of sectors including digital technology, marketing, online media, professional services and venture capital. It sits under the umbrella of the MIT Office of Digital Learning, which also includes MIT OpenCourse-Ware (OCW), the Office of Educational Innovation and Technology, and Academic Media Production Services.

Source: Adapted from www.mitx.org/ and http://odl.mit.edu/.

As mentioned earlier, the growth of MOOCs has been fueled by the prestigious American universities, in collaboration with private providers. Coursera started at Stanford and is rapidly growing, with more than 200 courses, 30 universities, and 1 million registered learners. EdX was started by MIT and Harvard as a nonprofit business to open their courses globally. Udacity was founded by Sebastian Thrun, an ex-Stanford professor, offering courses mostly in the science and computer programming fields. However, there has been considerable debate about quality and about the problem of dropout rates from MOOCs. As Yuan and Powell write,

> Meyer (2012) reported that the dropout rates of MOOCs offered by Stanford, MIT and UC Berkley were 80–95%. For example, only 7% of the 50,000 students who took the Coursera-UC Berkeley course in Software Engineering completed. There is a similar reported dropout rate in Coursera's Social Network Analysis class where only 2% of participants earned a basic certificate and 0.17% earned the higher level programming with distinction certificate.
>
> (2013: 11).

At the end of 2013, Udacity failed (Siemens 2013a). But by this time, MOOCs had come to be predominantly seen as a scaling up of conventional online learning, based on video lectures, automated tests and self-organized discussion groups, rather than enabling access to, and participation in, open education and debate—that is, as xMOOCs rather than cMOOCs. As some authors have noted, the sudden expansion of MOOCs has actually built on what is already a long history of eLearning and online delivery, particularly in its development of active learning techniques ('learning chunks,' reusable learning objects, problem-based tests and activities, tutor e-moderation, local study groups) but has tended to sell itself as a new innovation, acting as if nothing similar had gone before (Bates 2012). However, although there remains insufficient data, it may be that much learner take up for MOOCs is based on different motives to most online learning; more about simply experiencing studying this way or for intellectual simulation without any expectation of completion (Belanger and Thornton, 2013). It has been suggested that the huge initial take-up will drop off over the next few years, once potential learners are past the novelty factor.

There is also not yet any standard business model for whether or how MOOCs will generate revenue. As the Educause (n.d.) briefing paper notes, venture capital, and philanthropy have funded platform providers such as Coursera and edX. Udacity, for example, aimed to make money through a job board and referral program, rather than from course materials per se. The paper suggests other sources of potential income. This include data mining of student information, charging for associated services such as assignment grading and online discussions, sponsorship advertising, payment for tuition and course credit, a spin-off/licensing model offering the course (or versions of it) to business or othre providers, and licensed institutional use of the MOOC platform itself. None of these has yet been shown to be financially viable. This suggests the need for thoughtful debate:

> As massively open online courses continue their high-speed trajectory in the near-term horizon, there is a great need for reflection that includes frank discussions about what a sustainable, successful model looks like. Some experts believe that the pace at which MOOCs are developing is too rapid for genuine analysis; others maintain that they are not as disruptive of a technology as initially touted. Time will settle those questions, but there is no doubt that MOOCs have already had a significant influence on the future course of online learning, and deserve close attention, study, and continued experimentation.
>
> (Johnson et al. 2013: 12)

However, despite the lack of a workable business model, it has been suggested that the exponential growth of xMOOCs will put the private sector into a stronger competitive position, because many traditional mid-range universities do not have the developmental capacity for this kind of online scaling up:

> If one believes that converging communications technologies could transform higher education in the next five to 10 years, private providers could have an advantage. They may be quicker to capitalise on the opportunities that fast-changing technologies offer to develop new products and services, to create or enter new markets—perhaps through the

opportunities that 'unbundling' of educational processes brings—and to shift into new kinds of businesses. All universities are likely to be challenged by the access to global e-networks and resources that is beyond their capacity but is available to the large private sector conglomerates, both independently and through strategic alliances and joint ventures.

(Fielden et al. 2010: 46)

An underlying question here is about the future development and ownership of MOOC platforms. Virtual learning environments (VLEs), for instance, initially grew through the buying-in of proprietary systems such as Blackboard, but now universities and colleges also have access to an open-source variation in Moodle. How, then, is this situation likely to develop with MOOCs?

Developing a MOOC platform, at least for xMOOCs, would appear to be a much simpler task than creating systems such as those required by the large open universities. When the UK Open University (250,000 students) became the largest user of Moodle in 2007 it made a major investment in order the incorporate the many sub-systems required for the effective operation of this large global institution (Sclater, 2008). An xMOOC platform requires fewer sub-systems but must, of course, be designed to handle very high volumes and inputs from all over the world. However, whereas universities own and operate multiple Moodle installations, the administrative components of MOOCs (especially if they begin to make extensive use of Learning Analytics (Siemens, 2010)) are too complex for a teaching unit in a university to operate without huge resources. For this reason most universities might eventually opt for cloud-hosted MOOC services with control over data releases through contracts with for-profit service providers.

(Daniel 2012: 8–9)

Daniel notes that Google released open source xMOOC software in 2012 as 'an experimental first step' and that has been tested by Google's own MOOC offers. Edx has also recently said that it will make its platform open source, so it remains unclear how this will develop.

Are MOOCs, then, a major disruptive challenge to public universities and to higher education more generally? Daniel argues that they are—most crucially— because they challenge the scarcity model of education, opening up learning resources to a much wider audience. Shirky (2012) also thinks that MOOCs could have a big impact, not so much because more universities and colleges will develop this mode of education (what Daniel [2012] calls the "herd instinct at work as universities observe their peers joining the xMOOCs bandwagon and jump on for fear of being left behind"), but because it represents a "new story rearranging people's sense of the possible, with the incumbents the last to know." The issue, he suggests, is not about comparing the quality and experience of signing up for a MOOC versus attending university, because this is not the reality of actual choices made by learners. It is about what happens to education when it is not only based on selective admission or proprietary control over educational materials and delivery:

> The possibility MOOCs hold out isn't replacement; anything that could replace the traditional college experience would have to work like one, and the institutions best at working like a college are already colleges. The possibility MOOCs hold out is that the educational parts of education can be unbundled. MOOCs expand the audience for education to people ill-served or completely shut out from the current system, in the same way phonographs expanded the audience for symphonies to people who couldn't get to a concert hall [. . .] they try to answer some new questions, questions that the traditional academy—me and my people— often don't even recognize as legitimate, like "How do we spin up 10,000 competent programmers a year, all over the world, at a cost too cheap to meter?"
>
> (Shirky 2012)

Here, I want to suggest that MOOCs exemplify four key aspects of shifts in learning, teaching, and critical enquiry happening more widely across the higher education sector. First, MOOCs are an obvious example of the new kinds of unbundling of traditional educational models (similar to those already outlined in previous chapters) and a rebundling into new forms. These disaggregate learning from its formal accreditation; are less concerned with a strict hierarchy of learning levels and sequences; disconnect subject resources and course design from their supporting tutoring services; and can offer multiple payment modes starting from zero. This kind of unbundling is not new—the UK Open University for instance has always separated out course and materials design from its tutoring, allowed component-by-component study, and through OpenLearn (www.open.edu/openlearn/) is also making part of its course materials freely available. But, following Shirky, the kinds of associated 'stories' are changing. Learning becomes less about achieving an award through an extended period, and more like a series of self-selected, interactive versions of engaging with and discussing, TV-style documentaries, books, or Twitter feeds. Like TV—and increasingly many social media sites—xMOOCs turn their presenters increasingly into 'stars,' public performers whose video lectures can be seen by millions for free, a much greater reach than books or academic articles. Elite universities, use of a "personal faculty brand" (Cormier 2013), then, both perpetuates a conventional ranking system (since Harvard professors are assumed to be better lecturers than those in less-prestigious universities) and makes what was previously privileged knowledge much more accessible. It also allows the audience to participate through self-testing, as a means of accessing how much they have understood. cMOOCs, meanwhile, aim to enable participants to engage with their learning through peer debate facilitated by faculty, to generate debate and reflection.

Second, MOOCs rely on increased collaboration and hybridity in delivery, now embedded into higher education, whether across institutions, between public and private providers, or through outsourcing services. As already noted, MOOC developers need to have the resources to support massive online learning, or be able to form appropriate alliances. Whether development is generated within existing university roles or through a new organization and business proposition, the scaling-up of technological support, educational content, and delivery will mean the forging of new partnerships and relationships.

Third, what MOOCs show clearly is the fast maturing relationships between learning, global online networks and new technologies such as streaming media, web conferencing, interactive forums, intelligent feedback, and micro-payment systems. All these technologies make the experience of online learning increasingly rich, in a dynamic, multimedia environment. MOOCs also challenge a version of online learning that operates only through technology being applied on campus as a complement to the existing classroom experience, such as course web pages, or through a protected and relatively inflexible VLE, or at the level of the development of single courses into 'distance learning' as a basic extension to a wider, geographically spread (but controlled) audience. Working beyond this incremental 'tinkering' requires not only strategic planning and investment but also a critical engagement with the new roles and relationships implied for learners, tutors, academic, and technical support, with the much more hybrid virtual–physical, global–local patterns of provision and with the new of different kinds of services (and service providers) this requires.

Fourth, MOOCs are yet another example of an educational model that is generating tensions and contradictions (as well as gaps and opportunities) around how higher education works, or should work. This concerns the different beliefs and assumptions underpinning this form of delivery, as well as disagreements between supporters of xMOOCs and cMOOCs. For advocates, MOOCs seem to offer the possibility of a valuable mechanism for 'solving' the problem of affordable higher education for the masses. Commercial organizations see MOOCs as a way to enter the higher education market by offering suitable platforms, resources, and support services and by developing partnerships with existing institutions and to explore new delivery models in higher education (Yuan and Powell 2013: 9). Thus, MOOCs are also becoming caught up in dominant discourses about marketization. For Siemens (2013a), one of the (cMOOC) originators, this means that

> MOOCs are already moving into the realm of unloved step-child of education. They are becoming a proxy battle for educational philosophies: what is the role of commercial activity in higher education? How deeply should technology be integrated with teaching and learning? What can software do better than people? MOOCs represent much of the hope of open education advocates (openly accessible education) and the fears of faculty (the take over of public education by for-profits). This dichotomy is being politicized and will only get worse.

What, then, are we to make of the potential massification of education, whether through MOOCs or other online learning services? How can we guarantee quality of student experience and effectiveness of learning in these kinds of environment? How are universities and colleges moving forward in better integrating online and campus-based higher education and in supporting both students and staff in becoming digitally literate? Finally, we need to explore what new kinds of technologies are on the way that, yet again, could have an impact on learning, teaching, and critical inquiry.

Theme 5.1: The Massification of eLearning?

The public hype about MOOCs has been mainly around the potentially dramatic increase in students enrolled for free, as well as the global reach and the reputation-building. Many institutions think they should follow this trend. There are, of course, plenty of other online initiatives that are taking eLearning forward—ones that, like the examples in the first chapter, are also rethinking models for education in varying degrees. In this chapter, the focus aims to be on examples that offer lessons beyond single case-by-case initiatives or simple additive changes within one university or college; exploring how online education can add value, be resource effective, and help us think harder about the implications of the web for advanced learning globally.

5.1.a University of the People

The University of the People (UofPeople) is a nonprofit tuition fee-free online higher education provider (http://uopeople.edu/). Started in 2009, it is based in California and aims to offer undergraduate degrees in computer science and business administration to disadvantaged students across the world. Its services were accredited at the beginning of 2014 by the Distance Education and Training Council in the US, just in time for the completion of its first graduating class. Although students do not pay for tuition, other study elements are charged:

> [. . .] students pay a registration fee determined by the gross domestic product of their country of residence, along with a $100 (£60) administration fee for each exam they sit, those who cannot afford it can apply for a range of scholarships. To complete an undergraduate degree, 40 exams must be passed, bringing the total cost of a degree to around $4,000 (£2,400). The university currently has 700 students from 142 countries, although the first graduating class contains only seven students.
>
> (Parr 2014)

Unlike some of the previous examples in this book, the entrepreneur who set up UoPeople, Shai Reshef, has said that accreditation is important to his potential students, both in attracting them to study with the provider and in validating the standard and type of their studies to employers. By 2016, UoPeople intends to have 5,000 students.

The university uses instructor support combined with student teaching and peer-to-peer learning, through online discussion forums and online communities where students cover readings, share resources, exchange ideas, and discuss assigned questions. Scholars, professors, librarians, master's-level students, and other professionals—many of them volunteers—oversee and participate in both the assessment process and the development of curricula. This volunteer process is central to keeping costs down. The organization has also partnered with a number of other universities and companies.

5.1.b Open Educational Resources University

The Open Educational Resources University (OERu, launched in 2013) also aims to make education accessible to everyone online. It is an independent non-for-profit network, created by the OER Foundation, to offer free online courses for students worldwide. In some cases it also enables them to translate this into (paid-for) academic credit toward qualifications from recognized institutions. All course materials already exist on the internet and are mainly taken by OERu-based learners, although some overlap with existing courses that are taught together with full-time fee-paying students at international partner universities. Unlike many MOOCs, the OERu has a clearly thought through structure, based on what different learners want to achieve from their studies. Courses are offered at three levels of engagement. As the website explains:

1. **Self-directed interest:** Learners in this category select concepts, topics, and activities during the course according to personal interests. You can sip

and dip into sections of the course that you find interesting. Many learners in this category participate actively during all sessions of the course; however, there are no minimum participation requirements for self-interest learners.

2. **Certification for active participation:** Most OERu courses offer certification for participation, based on the achieving the minimum participation requirements for each course. Participation is usually measured by the interactions you post and selected activities you complete during a course. Check the course details to find out more about this certification option for your selected courses.

3. **Learning for credit:** A unique feature of the OERu is that you can submit your work for formal assessment on a 'fee for service basis' from designated OERu partners. Successful students will carry academic credit toward the specified course credits. Our partner institutions normally issue a 'Certificate of Achievement.'

(http://oeru.org/how-it-works/)

OERu also offers what it calls micro-courses or mOOCs—smaller components of units of study that last for two or three weeks but that can still include some accreditation. The overall aim, then, is to provide a 'step-up' mechanism for students who have previously been excluded from higher education by giving them recognized, credit-gaining studies at affordable prices that can then help them apply for degrees.

5.1.c Community College Opening Learning Initiative

As noted in the previous chapter, the US has a strong tradition of charitable foundations sponsoring and supporting large scale and strategic educational change. Carnegie Mellon University has established a consortium of community colleges that aim to improve the effectiveness of their existing course materials, delivery and support methods, and evaluation and improvement. Here, by collaboratively designing and then sharing high-quality and effective learning materials, resources can be saved and college retention and achievement rates can be improved:

> The overarching goal is to demonstrate a 25% higher rate of course completion for students from vulnerable populations, with a focus on gatekeeper courses critical to graduation success. Within three years, the Community College Opening Learning Initiative (CC-OLI) will scale to 40 community college partners and will reach an additional 50–100 classrooms.
>
> (http://oli.cmu.edu/get-to-know-oli/get-involved/
see-our-current-projects/community-college-oli/)

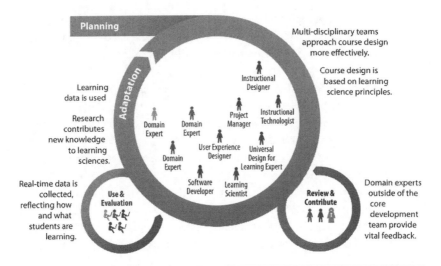

Figure 5.1 Open Learning Initiative Carnegie Mellon University, diagram outlining processes and collaborators

Source: Reprinted from http://oli.cmu.edu/wp-oli/wp-content/uploads/2012/07/OLI_Evaluation_Study_Handout.pdf.

Course development began in 2012, with initial courses in English composition, psychology, precalculus, macroeconomics, biology for majors, and biology for nonmajors. This set of six courses were all created using the Open Learning Initiative (OLI)—a shared content design and delivery platform—and taught across a number of campuses of both community colleges and universities (with partners currently being selected by the organization, and with specific mechanisms in place to buy out staff time and to fund evaluation processes.) The OLI enables free access to online student materials, including labs, assessments, and tutors, as well as faculty tools and analytics providing feedback on students' learning, misconceptions, and progress. Central to the OLI process (Figure 5.1) is that it enables proper instructional design development (rather than being dependent on individual teacher knowhow) and is made resource effective by scaling the use of learning packages across a large number of education providers.

In addition, by using interactive activities and assessments to collect data about how well students are doing (at a detailed level) the development team can see what is working and not working to produce improvements in the next iteration of the courses, to embed 'intelligent' automated tutoring, and to support research about how people learn:

The instructional activities in OLI courses include small amounts of expository material and many activities that capitalize on the computer's capability to display digital images and simulations and promote interaction. Many of the courses include virtual lab environments that encourage flexible and authentic exploration. Perhaps the most salient feature of OLI course design is found in the quasi-intelligent tutors—or "mini-tutors"—embedded within the learning activities throughout the course. [. . .] An intelligent tutor is a computerized learning environment whose design is based on cognitive principles and whose interaction with students is based on that of a human tutor, that is, making comments when the student errs, answering questions about what to do next, and maintaining a low profile when the student is performing well.

(Thille 2012)

The use of automated tutoring through learner analytics is an issue I return to later in this chapter.

Theme 5.2: Seamless Virtual and Physical Integration

If MOOCs provide one kind of development, another is the move toward better integrating university online systems with their physical provision (as already noted in the previous chapter) that is, blending face-to-face and online learning processes. As we wrote in an earlier book (Boys and Ford 2008), this is not just a technological issue, but centrally about the student experience, both as learners and in their myriad other relationships with the university; and has been something where universities and colleges have been uneven in their developments. However, with the ubiquity of web-based systems—and with the ever-increasing availability and ease of use of tablet and mobile computing, with their built-in qualities of touch/movement, photographic, movie, GPS, and networking capabilities—many of the earlier challenges are being eased. Students can now much more easily access everything from timetables to interactive course materials anywhere, anytime. Similarly, difficulties around interoperability, technology costs, and unwieldy databases are now much improved, although it still remains hard to find an example of a public university that has comprehensive—and student-focused—systems in place across all its functions.

In the early days of the Internet, many believed that eLearning would develop quickly to overtake face-to-face contact and would 'inevitably' revolutionize higher education. This has not happened for a variety of reasons, despite the growth of for-profit and nonprofit online educational services. Instead, we have moved toward 'hybrid,' 'enhanced,' and 'blended' learning in universities and colleges, that is, where eLearning systems and materials supplement rather than replace campus-based study and where for the student physical and virtual environments are becoming seamlessly integrated.

5.2.a *Tompkins Cortland Community College, New York*

In September 2011, Tompkins Cortland Community College (TC3) was awarded first place in the Digital Community College's Survey of Small Colleges in the US. TC3 aims to completely integrate the use of mobile technology, modeled on social networking sites such as Facebook. It also, for example, provides free e-textbooks, and integrates streaming digital information into the classroom. TC3 also extends this holistic understanding of technology across all its services, including student record keeping and tracking (Text box 5.2).

TEXT BOX 5.2 TOMPKINS CORTLAND COMMUNITY COLLEGE

Tompkins Cortland Community College (TC3), part of the State University of New York (SUNY) education system, offers thirty-eight associate-degree programs that prepare their 3,000 students for transfer to a four-year college or university. The college's two most important documents are, first, the student folder, which contains registration forms, a certificate of residency, high school transcripts, financial aid information, letters of admission, and grades, and, second, the permanent student record card, which is a document that lists courses, grades, and awarded degrees for each student who attended TC3 prior to 1997.

The student record system employed by TC3 often needed to be accessed by several offices in different locations across the campus, and, together with the fact that the number of student enrollments was also increasing, no longer met the college's requirements. The option of TC3 was to implement a nonproprietary, flexible system to migrate scanned and electronic documents from its previous system and to provide document retrieval over the Internet, and a digitized DocuWare system was introduced to increase accessibility to the student information. The system also enabled the college to deal with a 40 percent increase in student enrolment without increasing staff numbers.

TC3 now has four scanning stations. All the existing student folders were scanned and indexed to the new system, as were the permanent record cards. Now, all incoming information is digitized as it is received. The system has already been expanded to other departments such as Library and Learning Resource Center, and there are further plans to extend it across the campus. The benefits of the system to TC3 have been that retrieval time for information has been reduced and that staff can answer queries with the information they need in front of them. They have found that this has increased job satisfaction and reduced workplace stress for staff.

The registrar's and admission offices now have better workflow processes and can access more up-to-date information than previously. The library can post PDF or TIFF versions of important documents on the website and the Learning Resource Center can create higher-quality images to assist visually impaired students. The benefits at an organizational level are the savings in time spent accessing documents, easier manageability of the document life cycle, and the reduction in the need for physical storage. TC3 has been awarded state and national honors for its use of technology to serve students.

Source: Adapted from Tomkins Cortland Community College (n.d.) *Case Study*. Available at: http://pub.docuware.com/en/tompkins-cortland-community-college#index (accessed April 26, 2014).

5.2.b Central Library, Manchester, UK

The existing library in Manchester, in a historical building (a rotunda), has been revamped to integrate its older—book-based—history with new information and communication technologies. It has a traditional 2,000-square-meter lending library at basement level, as well as a rare-books collection. Visitors enter at ground level into an open-plan atrium containing a café, wall-screen catalogues, interactive displays on local history and interactive tables (Figure 5.2). There are also technology-rich study bays of various types located throughout and a media center providing access to state-of-the-art computing hardware and software. The children's library is themed on local author Frances Hodgson Burnett's book, *The Secret Garden*, with a series of interactive wall and floor play surfaces (Figure 5.3), as well as a gaming area with Xboxes and PlayStations. The library thus very successfully combines older and newer technologies, centered on enabling a coherent and rich set of learning activities.

Theme 5.3: Increasing Digital Literacy

If conventional universities and colleges are often lagging behind in the integration of new information and communication technologies (ICT)—at least compared to private education sector and to business more generally—they are also not yet very effective in facing up to the learning demands of ICT itself. Digital literacy is becoming an essential skill for university managers, academics, and students, and all higher education courses need to include learning resources and delivery methods that support its development. However, definitions of digital literacy remain varied. It can cover access to, and skills in using, appropriate hardware, software, and networks; developing the confidence and motivation to engage with digital resources; and enabling understanding of how to find a way through, make sense of (Siemens 2004), and critically integrate the multitude of digital resources now available on the web. This is in a world where social media (Facebook, Twitter, Instant Messaging) has become ubiquitous; where information-sharing tools such

Figure 5.2 Main foyer, Central Library, Manchester, UK
Source: Photos by Jos Boys.

as blogs, wikis, audio, and photo and video streams abound and are part of an increasing number of online services and apps; and where online forms of exchange—from Amazon to eBay and shopping sites such as ASOS—are becoming part of everyday life. In addition, many educational institutions and other groups are concerned to teach people how to *create* such resources, particularly by developing the requisite programming skills. For example, Stanford's iPhone and iPad application development course can now be freely accessed online through iTunes U. This made iTunes history with 1 million downloads by the seventh week. Another aspect is the increasing interest in

Figure 5.3 Interactive tables and floor surfaces, Central Library, Manchester, UK
Source: Photos by Jos Boys.

maker culture, which is aiming to make programming (across the software and hardware of intelligent devices and robotics) accessible and usable by the public (an issue I will return to later in the next chapter.)

However, if defining digital literacy is complicated and changing, there are already many initiatives examining how it might be better embedded in education. When the European Union explored digital competencies in Europe (Ferrari 2013), it produced a five-point list defining key requirements (Figure 5.4), together with learning outcomes statements at three levels of skills—foundation, intermediate, and advanced.

Dimension 1 Competence areas	Dimension 2 Competences
1. Information	1.1 Browsing, searching and filtering information
	1.2 Evaluating information
	1.3 Storing and retrieving information
2. Communication	2.1 Interacting through technologies
	2.2 Sharing information and content
	2.3 Engaging in online citizenship
	2.4 Collaborating through digital channels
	2.5 Netiquette
	2.6 Managing digital identity
3. Content creation	3.1 Developing content
	3.2 Integrating and re-elaborating
	3.3 Copyright and licences
	3.4 Programming
4. Safety	4.1 Protecting devices
	4.2 Protecting personal data
	4.3 Protecting health
	4.4 Protecting the environment
5. Problem solving	5.1 Solving technical problems
	5.2 Identifying needs and technological responses
	5.3 Innovating and creatively using technology
	5.4 Identifying digital competence gaps

Figure 5.4 Overview of digital literacy competence areas and competences
Source: Reprinted from Ferrari (2013: 12) with permission from European Commission Joint Research Centre Institute for Prospective Technological Studies (© European Union, 2013).

For universities and colleges, effectively teaching digital literacy does have several problems. There is the amount and speed of change, as well as the associated resource and time costs, of keeping up-to-date with the latest trends. There is also the considerable variation in digital skills that both students and academics bring to their work and a lack of clarity of how training (and what kind of training) should be incorporated in either staff development or student programs:

Faculty training still does not acknowledge the fact that digital media literacy continues its rise in importance as a key skill in every discipline and profession. Despite the widespread agreement on the importance of digital media literacy, training in the supporting skills and techniques is rare in teacher education and non-existent in the preparation of faculty. [. . .] we are far from seeing digital media literacy as a norm. This challenge is exacerbated by the fact that digital literacy is less about tools and more about thinking, and thus skills and standards based on tools and platforms have proven to be somewhat ephemeral.

(Johnson et al. 2013: 9)

5.3.a JISC Developing Digital Literacies Programme, UK

The UK Joint Information Systems Committee (JISC) funded a digital literacies program that ran until the end of 2013, with the aim of supporting strategies for UK universities and colleges (www.jisc.ac.uk/whatwedo/programmes/elearning/developingdigitalliteracies). It defined digital literacy as "those capabilities which fit an individual for living, learning and working in a digital society" (Beetham 2013). Interestingly students reported feeling less digitally competent in their learning than in their personal lives and were therefore reliant on faculty to improve both their learning-related and subject-based specialist digital skills. It is also true, however, that many students may be more digitally literate than their tutors, leading to moves in some universities to build on this:

> An emerging trend, being captured by the Developing Digital Literacies Programme is that of students being involved in supporting the digital literacy development of their peers and in the reverse mentoring of staff.
>
> Examples of students working as pioneers and change agents included, digital skills 'clinics' being run by postgraduate and IT support staff, student user groups set up to share tips and tricks in the use of certain digital tools e.g. data analysis software and the involvement of students in the development and testing of new services and applications.
>
> (Payton, n.d.)

As the paper goes on to note, involving students as change agents needs to include clear processes for reward and recognition, and a sustainable program of involvement. It also highlights a worrying gap between engagement with, and knowledge of, the digital world between students and their—supposed—expert advisors. Overall, the JISC initiative supported a number of projects in universities, produced a number of briefing papers and publications, and suggested an overall framework of drivers and emerging themes in higher education (Figure 5.5).

In the next chapter I look at other recent ideas about digital literacy, as expounded by George Siemens (2003, 2004), who sees this less as a list of skills and more as an ability to make and evaluate *content*, that is, its meanings, patterns, and context.

5.3.b Ball State University, Indiana, US

I have already outlined how the CC-OLI recognizes and explicitly supports the skills and amount of work involved in designing good learning resources. This is

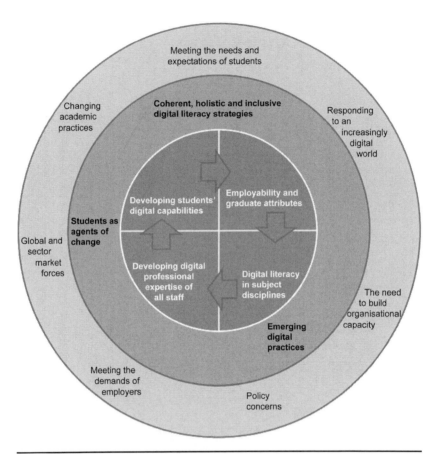

Figure 5.5 The JISC Developing Literacies Programme: drivers and emerging themes

Source: Adapted from JISC *Developing Digital Literacies* briefing paper (n.d.: 4) www.jisc.ac.uk/media/documents/publications/briefingpaper/2012/Developing_Digital_Literacies.pdf.

because the shift to more active, blended or problem-based learning requires more 'up front' and integrated course design and development than traditional lecture–seminar–lab programs (or, rather, makes the need for course learning *design* more obvious). This issue will be returned to in the next chapter. Here what is important is how universities and colleges are building in processes to help academics develop effective online or blended learning, for example through training or by providing instructional design expertise. At Ball State, for example, the Interactive Learning Space (ILS) Faculty Development Program aims to improve the type and quality of pedagogy used in its various learning spaces. This was both to challenge the tendencies in higher education to compartmentalize learning development across several different specialists—teachers, information technologists making decisions about technology, and facilities managers procuring and designing learning environments (Bickford and Wright, 2006: 4.1); and to face the challenges of faculty having varying knowledge and skills as in both education and technology. As Pavlechko and Jacobi explain,

> Our university's effort to provide innovative space and technology led to addressing faculty development necessary for a successful transition to learning spaces designed specifically for active learning. Since our campus faculty development programme is divided into two support units—one for face-to-face instruction and the other for online instruction—the Office of Educational Excellence, responsible for the former, was charged with overseeing the redesign of the classrooms and creation of a faculty development programme to support instruction in the newly designed learning spaces.
>
> (Forthcoming)

Academics must apply to join the progam and then take part in a six semester skill development process, which enables them to design courses that effectively engage with the university's interactive learning spaces, as well as reflect on their teaching practice, collaborate with peers, improve on their scholarship of teaching and learning, and strengthen their professional networks for mentoring throughout the year. The program concludes with the dissemination of research findings regarding faculty members' ILS Initiative experiences.

Theme 5.4: Using Big Data

I have already outlined the increasing amount of information, in a multitude of formats, now available publically through the web. As well as social media, this includes governmental, business, and other organizational data. As Greller and Drachsler (2012) write, data-driven companies such as Google, Yahoo!, Facebook, and Amazon, among others, are growing exponentially by commercially exploiting such data for marketing or in the creation of new personalized services:

> The new "data economy" empowers companies to offer an increasing amount of data products at little or no cost to their users (e.g., Google Flu Trends, bit.ly customised URLs, Yahoo Pipes, Gapminder.com). This growth in data also renewed the interest in information retrieval technologies. Such technologies are used to analyse data and offer personalised data products customised to the needs and the context of individual users.
>
> (2012: 42)

The 'massification' of data in easily accessible forms offers huge research potential to universities. For example, Essex University UK recently completed a Data Research Centre for Smart Analytics that "will make data, routinely collected by business and local government organizations, accessible for academics as a national resource in order to undertake outstanding research in the social sciences in ways that safeguard individuals' identities" (www.data-archive.ac.uk/news-events/news.aspx?id=3725; Text Box 5.3).

Box 5.3 ESSEX UNIVERSITY DATA RESEARCH CENTER

In the UK, new university-based data research centers are being funded to coordinate research into data routinely collected by business and local government organizations. These are overseen by the Administrative Data Network (AND) and mark the first phase of the Economic and Social Research Council's (ESRC) £64 million investment in a Big Data Network. Two further phases will establish new centers for business and local government data and third sector for social media data.

The centers will make large data sets accessible to academics to develop social sciences studies in ways that safeguard individuals' identities, providing an evidence-base to inform policy development, implementation, and evaluation. Almost £5 million went to the University of Essex for the Administrative Data Service (ADS) element of the new Big Data network, providing a one-stop shop for finding, learning about, and requesting access to administrative data for research:

> Its core responsibilities will be: to provide a first point of contact for administrative data users and owners; be the central point for managing research access requests; ensure there is consistency in standards and practice across the network; engage with data owners, users and the public to develop a culture of effective and secure data sharing to enable better research for the public benefit; and to develop capacity and skills in using administrative data for research.

The UK Data Service is delivered by the UK Data Archive, based at the University of Essex, in partnership with Mimas and the Cathie Marsh Centre for Census and Survey Research (University of Manchester), School of Geography (University of Leeds), Geography and Environment (University of Southampton), and EDINA (University of Edinburgh).

Source: Adapted from www.essex.ac.uk/depts/ukda.aspx and http://ukdataservice.ac.uk/ (accessed 14 August 2014).

As Greller and Drachsler continue, this exponential growth in online data will affect research processes:

> The new data economy has made data collection very much an afford-able activity. It is based on the highly economic electronic data mining of people's digital footprints and the automated analysis of behaviours of the entire constituency rather than sampling. Because data mining is not a separate act to normal user behaviour, the information retrieved is also highly authentic in terms of reflecting real and uninterrupted user behaviour. As such, data mining is more comparable to observational data gathering than to intrusive collection via direct methods.
>
> (2012: 42)

However, universities and colleges have been relatively slow at mining their own electronic data to support their understanding of a whole range of educational processes. Initially, as Kennedy et al. note, this has tended to be about how databases could support institutional reporting and decision making, with an increasing interest in using big data to highlight students at risk (as outlined in Chapter 2 on enhancing student performance):

> For example, in their paper on academic analytics, Campbell, DeBlois and Oblinger (2007) provide a number of examples where institutions in the United States have made use of data such as GPA, SAT scores, visits to campus, and students' use of the learning management system to predict outcomes such as students who are at risk and student retention. Similarly, Arnold (2010) reports on a system at Purdue University called "Signals", which takes data from the University's central systems and, using algorithms, "generates a risk level with supporting information for each student, represented by a green, yellow or red indicator."
>
> (2013: 172)

The scaling-up represented by MOOCs, through global online networks, exponentially increasing web-based resources, and personal mobile devices, is also having an impact on how universities can track their students, offering richer feedback because of the amount and type of data that can be collected. This is because, as online learning became more common, researchers have been exploring how to use the web's tracking potential to understand what tasks students engaged with and how different students moved through the materials. This emerging field is known as Learning Analytics (Siemens and Gasevic 2012; Long and Siemens 2011; Kennedy et al. 2013) and focuses on learning (rather than administration and management), with the aim of developing detailed information and feedback that is useful to students as well as educators. This, in turn, is linked to personalized learning, to the potential of students being able to customize their learning to their own needs and preferences:

> The proliferation of interactive learning environments, learning management systems (LMS), intelligent tutoring systems, e-portfolio systems, and personal learning environments (PLE) in all sectors of education produces vast amounts of tracking data. But, although these e-learning environments store user data automatically, exploitation of the data for learning and teaching is still very limited. These educational datasets offer unused opportunities for the evaluation of learning theories, learner feedback and support, early warning systems, learning technology, and the development of future learning applications.
>
> (Greller and Drachsler 2012: 43)

Learning analytics is still in early stages of implementation and adoption within higher education (Johnson et al. 2013: 10), and its definitions remain contested (http://en.wikipedia.org/wiki/Learning_analytics). The big issues here, then, are about how learning analytics can develop as a pedagogically strong tool for learners and tutors alike. As with the VLE proprietary systems such as Blackboard, the problem of a one-size-fits-all solution (especially with the associated tendency towards creating a monopoly) is that it can embed particular assumptions into its frameworks as to what is tracked and why. These then become the norm and effect, in turn, how learning can be 'shaped.' Private providers, such as Pearson Education, have already developed CourseSmart Analytics, a tool for tracking students' activity as they interact with online texts and for interpreting that data for educators, providing them with an engagement score for a particular text. Pearson Education is also in partnership with Knewton, which offers a personalized learning platform (www.knewton.com), where adaptive learning technology tracks each student's particular strengths and weaknesses and can make detailed automated recommendations for improvement.

Many developers and educators are arguing that the educational grounds on which data from these platforms are collected also needs to be made explicit and transparent, and not lost within programming, scalability and cost demands. As Siemens and Gasevic write,

> Learning analytics currently sits at a crossroads between technical and social learning theory fields. On the one hand, the algorithms that form recommender systems, personalization models, and network analysis require deep technical expertise. The impact of these algorithms, however,

is felt in the social system of learning. As a consequence, researchers in learning analytics have devoted significant attention to bridging these gaps and bringing these communities in contact with each other through conversations and conferences.

(2012: 1)

The technical complexities of learning analytics (as with other online learning systems development), together with the continuing lack of, and lack of support for, instructional design expertise in universities, means that not-for-profit higher education's lagging behind in these areas is likely to continue. Whilst there have been several good briefing papers for educators (ELI 2011; Brown 2012; Buckingham Shum 2012; Cooper 2012; Ferguson 2012; Powell and MacNeil 2012) we still urgently need research and development that can bridge the gap. A number of research networks and groups are already responding to this concern, such as the Society for Learning Analytics Research (www.solaresearch.org), the Lytics Lab at Stanford University (http://lytics.stanford.edu/), and a Learning Analytics Google Group (https://groups.google.com/forum/#!forum/learninganalytics).

5.4.a Learning Analytics Research Group, University of Melbourne, Australia
Another example is the research group at the University of Melbourne, as part of its eLearning Incubator—a space for bringing together diverse expertise in the university across academic departments, Information Technology Services (ITS), the library, and the Centre for the Study of Higher Education, as well as faculty-based teaching and learning groups:

> The eLearning Incubator provides a University focal point for research and development activity in a range of areas including:
> - The design and development of leading edge eLearning, online learning and mobile learning resources, applications and programs.
> - The design, development and implementation of the University's open learning agenda, through the provision of Massive Open Online Courses (MOOCs) offered in partnership with Coursera.
> - The development, use and refinement of learning analytic techniques using data repositories from enterprise University systems and the University's Coursera courses (MOOCs).
>
> (http://le.unimelb.edu.au/elearning/larg.html)

The group is concerned to explore large data sets of staff and students' interactions in electronic learning environments, to better understand student motivation and autonomous learning in MOOCS and the effects of gamification and game based learning environments on learning (a subject that will be returned to in the next chapter). They also want to model how student interactions occur in open curriculum structures. Finally, they are examining how data mining, machine learning, and predictive analytics, together with social network analysis and network modeling, can help in creating adaptive learning environments that can provide personalized feedback on progress to students and tutors.

5.4.b Exploratory Learning Analytics Toolkit, RWTH Aachen University, Germany

Dyckhoff et al. (2012) outline another initiative aimed at educators, where learning analytics tools can be used to visualize and then reflect on learning and teaching, through an online dashboard. eLAT (exploratory learning analytics toolkit) was designed to enable faculty to easily review how students engaged with their learning resources:

> A pre-eminent barrier is the additional workload, originating from tasks of collecting, integrating, and analyzing raw data from log files of their VLE [. . .] The main aim of eLAT is to support reflection on and improvement of online teaching methods based on personal interests and observations. To help teachers reflect on their teaching according to their own interests, the desired Learning Analytics tool is required to provide a clear, simple, easily interpretable and usable interface while, at the same time, being powerful and flexible enough for data and information exploration purposes. Therefore, eLAT was designed to enable teachers to explore and correlate content usage, user properties, user behavior, as well as assessment results based on individually selected graphical indicators.
>
> (Dyckhoff et al. 2012: 59)

Theme 5.5: Open Badging

The exponential expansion of web information and resources has both created problems in accessing and selecting appropriate data from the huge amount available, and offers the means for agglomerating and filtering that information. Various gateways, portals, repositories, wikis, utilities, and apps compete to become *the* place to go for particular types of information, as Google has for online searches and Wikipedia has for sourcing basic information. The proliferation of web-based courses, learning materials, and more general resources such as TED Talks makes these difficult to search for effectively and comprehensively, making such services (as I noted in Chapter 2) a growing and competing area for dominance. At the same time, and as was also mentioned earlier, accreditation of learning is moving beyond simply formal certificates from universities, colleges, and other higher education providers:

Learning has evolved from simple "seat time" within schools to extend across multiple contexts, experiences, and interactions. It is no longer just an isolated or individual concept, but is instead inclusive, social, informal, participatory, creative, and lifelong.

(Knight and Casilli 2012: 279)

Services such as LinkedIn now offer an online network for individuals to display their achievements across formal, informal, and work-based learning, as well as their interests and expertise. Additionally, LinkedIn provides a function where peers can endorse skills and projects and give references. Another competitor in this area is Degreed (degreed.com)—punch line 'Jailbreak the Degree'—that tracks achievement of MOOC courses (both those it and others deliver) as well as other educational projects and activities. It also offers learning resources. Barber et al. (2012) suggest that "these developments could offer more accurate and up-to-date assessments of an individual's qualifications and real skills than a stamp of approval from a prestigious institution" (p.36).

Most recently, open badging, a development from gaming, is being explored as a way of describing and accumulating different kinds of recognition that can be publically accessed. This requires an infrastructure through which different kinds of badges can be allocated and validated, independent of any educational institution. The badges can be 'carried' with the learner and can be combined to form an ongoing history of skills and competencies:

Advocates of open badging systems point to the egalitarian quality of a system where the rules are clear and the platform's ability to explain much more in the way of accomplishments and goals than a college transcript. Purdue University has developed two mobile apps, Passport and Passport Profile that integrate the Mozilla Open Infrastructure software. The badging system was adopted by Purdue in order to identify skills that are not represented by a student's degree, and to provide educators with another outlet to recognize student accomplishment and concept mastery.

(Johnson et al. 2012: 21–22)

5.4.a Mozilla Open Badge Initiative
Mozilla has been in the forefront of these developments. Its argument is that in gaming environments and elsewhere, the concept of badges acts as a motivator, a recognition of achievement, and a means of sharing that achievement:

From the Boy and girl Scouts to PADI diving instruction, to the more recently popular geo-location game Foursquare, badges have been

successfully used to set goals, motivate behaviors, represent achievements, and communicate success in many contexts. [. . .] And yet in
the current formal education and accreditation systems, much of this
learning goes undetected and unrecognized. Institutions still decide
what narrow types of learning "count," as well as who has access to that
learning.

(Knight and Casilli 2012: 279–80)

The project was first developed through a partnership between Mozilla and
Peer 2 Peer University (P2PU) that was offering free online web-developer
training. The pilot was built around fourteen badges,

including hard-skill badges such as JavaScript, value badges such as
Accessibility, social or peer badges such as Good Collaborator, and participation badges such as Active Responder and Peer Editor.2 The goal
was to use badges to capture hard and soft skills that are important for
web developers, as well as to guide community-beneficial behavior.

(ibid.: 281)

Mozilla differentiates between digital badging and open badging; with the
latter, the badge has embedded metadata that guarantees its validity and is
transferable across different online environments:

Open Badges take that concept [of digital badges] one step further, and
allows you to verify your skills, interests and achievements through cred-
ible organizations and attaches that information to the badge image file,
hard-coding the metadata for future access and review. Because the system is based on an open standard, earners can combine multiple badges
from different issuers to tell the complete story of their achievements—
both online and off. Badges can be displayed wherever earners want
them on the web, and share them for employment, education or lifelong
learning.

(https://wiki.mozilla.org/Badges)

To move to open badging, then, a personalized, comprehensive, and cross-
platform process will need to be underpinned by a common infrastructure that
can 'hold' badges from many different sources, that has comparability based on
agreed metadata standards that 'sit behind' each badge, that has a method for
individuals to collect and sort their badges, that has appropriate display sites
(that can also check authenticity), and that has the possibility of additional
endorsements (Figure 5.6).

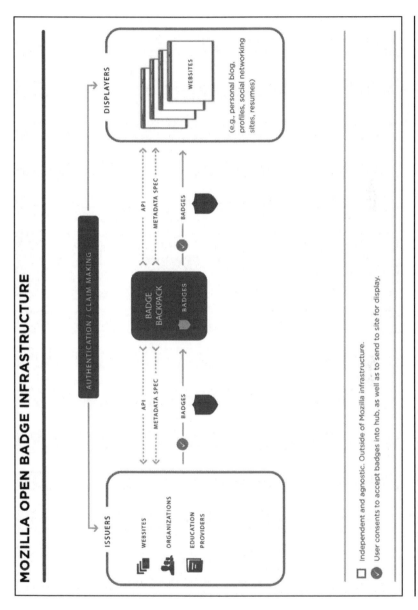

Figure 5.6 Mozilla Open Badge Infrastructure

Source: Adapted from Knight and Casilli (2012: 281); http://net.educause.edu/ir/library/pdf/pub7203cs6.pdf. Reprinted with permission from EDUCAUSE.

When Knowledge No Longer Belongs to Universities

How are universities and colleges to respond to endlessly changing information and communication technologies, or to assess their potential and implications for higher education? Although some of the highest-ranking universities such as Harvard, MIT, and Stanford have invested heavily in experimenting with the latest developments, much of the sector lags behind, often relying ultimately on ICT department expertise without effective integration across all activities and with ICT planning not always explicitly strategically or educationally driven. But as Sheets et al. write, and as the examples here suggest, it is not just a matter of using new technology while still hanging onto existing assumptions and structures:

> In Christensen's framework the most important drivers of disruptive innovation are not the technological innovations themselves, though they usually receive the most attention. Instead they are the innovative business models that can harness the power of these new technologies and the value networks that support them in the context of the standards and regulatory environment.
>
> (2012: 5)

This, in turn, cannot just be resolved by 'adding' online learning to existing provision:

> What we face in higher education is a far more daunting task than "let's all run MOOCs" or "online learning is the future". We face challenges around access, digitization of education, move to granular learning (courses to competencies), growth of startup/maker culture [covered in Chapter 6], for-profit presence, global learner base, reduced public funds, autonomous and informed learners, participatory learning, privacy, digital identity, power shifts from institution to individual, new roles for educators in creating content and methods of teaching, and so on. The last thing we need is a light treatment of MOOCs or change in general. We need an analysis that moves away from simple answers toward complex questions. [. . .] We need to raise the quality of discourse around higher education so that we can suitably respond to the dramatic and historic changes impacting the university.
>
> (Siemens 2013a)

In a previous book (Boys and Ford 2008) we argued that the universities could learn from the best of e-business, not so much by directly following their business models as by understanding how the growth of the web was changing the shape of their operations in every way. In that text, we focused on ways that new technologies were enabling individuals from different departments, organizations, and countries to work effectively together sharing knowledge and information across both functional and physical boundaries: and how it could make it much easier for students, staff, and other stakeholders to access relevant information and communicate their requirements quickly, accurately, and from any location. We proposed that higher education also needed to start from the key issues of customer focus (however, this needed to be defined in relation to students and other stakeholders), organizational integration, and common systems. What is critical about recent developments is not only that they make this holistic approach to new technologies even more relevant, but also that we are now amid a large-scale change—the massification of learning—that will require web-based and interoperable infrastructural systems that can operate seamlessly and effectively well beyond the boundaries of any single university or college.

For these infrastructural systems to enhance the quality of higher education in all its myriad forms, they need to make the learner experience and the effectiveness of learning central to design development; be fully integrated across organizational, physical, educational, and virtual spaces; and be based on common standards that enable interoperability and 'massive' sharing. If the mainstream of universities and colleges do not engage fully with these underlying issues, then it is very likely that the central players in this emerging market will be, on one hand, for-profit online educational providers and, on the other, creative web-based players working outside of universities who are already creatively exploiting the many interesting gaps and opportunities that are now opening up. In the next chapter, then, I explore some of these developments in more detail.

6

THE IMPLICATIONS OF NEW
TECHNOLOGIES FOR LEARNING

[O]ur world is very different than the one in which the current education system was developed and standardized. With the advent of the web and its core principles of openness, universality, and transparency, the ways that knowledge is made, shared, and valued have been transformed, and the opportunities for deeper and richer learning have been vastly expanded.
—*Knight and Casilli (2012: 280)*

As discussed in the previous chapter, we are now in a world of integrated, easily accessible digital networks and resources, accessed via multiple mobile devices and supported by cloud-based storage capabilities. The amount of information and resources online is continually increasing, and interactive web content has become much simpler to create. Higher education is already exploring how developments such as social media connect with its traditional services. But this has also produced problems, because education-specific virtual learning environments (VLEs) can lack the immediacy of Facebook, Flickr, and Twitter for students, yet at the same time, merely using preexisting web apps and templates may not be the most effective forms for learning and teaching activities or can appear forced. In addition, image and streaming media sites such as YouTube, infotainment sources like Buzzfeed, apps such as iBook Author, blogging and wiki software such as Wordpress, educational repositories such as iTunesU, RSS feeds and bookmarking services to organize content (such as

HOLA, grsshopper, DiGG), and antiplagiarism software to check for validity all offer educators a massive array of possibilities but nevertheless may need 'translation' to be properly embedded into courses.

So there is now a much wider range of learning opportunities available to universities and colleges beyond the lecture hall and seminar or laboratory, including online learning, hybrid learning and collaborative models, and learning is seen as much more than the simple transmission of knowledge to passive subjects. But there are not yet clear pathways through the increasing mix and variety of information and media, of ways to access that media, and in having methods for framing it for effective learning. And the complexity will continue, with new technologies such as 3D printing and an increasing move toward the 'Internet of Things' (where objects and material spaces can have computer-based properties), again shifting relationships between the virtual and the physical.

Meanwhile, as concluded in the last chapter, students already spend much of their free time on the Internet searching sources and exchanging information, often via their social networks, so that what counts as knowledge and expertise and where it can be found is blurring far beyond the boundaries of the traditional higher education. Knowledge really does no longer belong to the university. The overabundance of 'stuff' available to students and faculty, and the numerous modes of analyzing, reflecting on, and communicating what has been distilled from that 'stuff,' creates very different conditions from the days of the scholarly academic publication and the peer-reviewed research journal. Besides keeping up with all these new technologies, and predicting which are likely to last, the biggest challenge is to understand the implications for higher education of these new tools and systems. How can we use them productively and creatively for learning, not just as add-ons to conventional methods (or problematic innovations to be avoided) but as part of a rethinking of the whole shape of learning and teaching? How can we embed these new tools effectively, and what are the implications for how and when we learn?

Change is already happening. The Khan Academy (www.khanacademy.org) has famously challenged conventional models of education based on face-to-face lectures and seminars supported by self-directed study, through its 'flipping the classroom' model (Text Box 6.1). By reversing these arrangements and using an online video to provide knowledge content, learners can absorb the material at their own pace, and review several times if required; this means that contact time (whether online or face-to-face) can instead focus on mentored practice and development. In what other ways, then, are these alternative ways of delivering content affecting learning, teaching, and critical inquiry in higher education?

TEXT BOX 6.1   KHAN ACADEMY

The Khan Academy, a not-for-profit organization, was set up in 2006 by Salman Khan to provide free education worldwide. It receives funding from a number of organizations such as the Bill & Melinda Gates Foundation, Google, and the Carlos Slim Foundation, among others, and actively encourages people to donate to the organization through a number of different options, which are identified on the website. There is an extensive library of resources, including math, science, economics and finance, humanities, computing, and test preparation. There are also sections on content provided by partners, videos of talks and interviews and materials for use in coaching and in the classroom. Khan Academy employs content specialists and interns and encourages volunteers to translate content into different languages. It serves 10 million people a month with 5,000 videos.

Students can choose the subjects and the level at which they want to study. Each topic has a short, approximately ten-minute video, and after watching this students are encouraged to share their knowledge about the topic with others, as well as make comments, ask questions, give feedback on comments posted by other students, and highlight any errors in the videos.

There are a series of interactive challenges and assessments that students can undertake. These tests are randomly generated to ensure students have plenty of examples on which to work and enable them to practice at their own pace. Through a series of different color codes, students can immediately identify which courses have been successfully completed and which need further work. If a student finds a particular test difficult he or she has access to a video on the topic. Each student has access to personalized learning through a 'Learning Dashboard,' which uses state-of-the-art, adaptive software to identify gaps and show progress. To encourage students to learn, badges are awarded badges for achievement at different levels of learning. Some of these are awarded for relatively easy tasks, while others may require years of work to obtain. Teachers, coaches, and parents can access instant data to track students' progress in real time and can identify any topics that are problematic for students.

For more information see:

Khan Academy (2014) Available at: https://www.khanacademy.org/about (accessed April 27, 2014).

Selingo, J. (2014) "To Reach the New Market for Education, Colleges Have Some Learning to Do," *The Chronicle of Higher Education*, March 24. Available at: http://chronicle.com/article/To-Reach-the-New-Market-for/145499/ (accessed April 27, 2014).

Talbers, R. (2013) "Khan Academy Using Contractors for Accuracy Checking—Some Thoughts," *The Chronicle of Higher Education*, October 23. Available at: http://chronicle.com/blognetwork/castingoutnines/2013/10/23/khan-academy-using-contractors-for-accuracy-checking-some-thoughts/ (accessed April 27, 2014).

Open Learning Anywhere?

When the expert advisory panel for the New Media Consortium (NMC) Horizon 2013 report (Johnson et al. 2013) was asked what were the key trends affecting higher education realities they put openness at number one. By this they meant that concepts such as open education resources (OER) and open sourcing are having a big impact on how education is both being 'thought' and being delivered. This is in several ways—in potentially undermining traditional expertise and authoritative sources, in the increasing overabundance of easily available information, and in the increased ease of access to content creation for non-experts. They also note the differences between 'open' and 'free'. For open education supporters 'open' means more than just without cost; it also implies freedom to copy and remix, lack of barriers to access or interaction, and sharing and collaboration (ibid.: 7). The report goes on to suggest that the skills developed through this kind of learning are as valuable for employability as more formal, accredited skills.

However, like the divisions between xMOOCs and cMOOCs, open education approaches, based on accessibility and free sharing, such as open courseware (OCW) projects and OER, also have their tensions:

> The first decade of OCW focused primarily on content creation by encouraging faculty and universities to share their educational materials with the world. A sufficient breadth and depth of materials were needed as building blocks for the improvements in teaching and learning that this sharing was expected to bring. Content creation was largely up to each contributor, with no master plan in place for soliciting contributions in particular areas. Intentional creation of OCW and OER to fill in the gaps is needed, which requires a thorough inventory of existing available resources.
>
> (Forward 2012: 297)

The open education movement, then, has tended to reproduce academic autonomy, as individual educators, course teams or groups of collaborators have developed transferable learning materials, based on what they already do.

So, overall, resources remain fragmented and uncoordinated, accumulated out of various projects and interests, rather than from local, regional, national, or international educational strategies. This, together with issues of searching and selection; of quality, relevance and transferability; and in academic resistance to resources reuse have all affected the take-up—and therefore economies of scale—made possible by open sharing.

Designing open educational resources can involve either (re)using materials that are already especially purposed for educational use or 'curating' web-based information into shareable educational packages. Such repurposing, contextualising, sharing, and questioning already existing materials also has an impact on how we think about course design. The tutor's role becomes that of selecting, adding to, and building learning materials around, existing online sources. Although in many ways this is also what the conventional lecture–textbook–seminar format does (provides a block of content and then orchestrates discussion/writing about it), the sheer abundance of cross-media web-based sources—as well as its gaps—suggests that we need to explicitly use learning and teaching methods that enable students to negotiate, analyze, and develop a position in relation to that material. Open education in a connected world also needs to have a clear learning and teaching process for peer participation, for crowdsourcing and crowd-sharing, and for mentoring and moderating online groups (Salmon 2004), as well as for offering responsive and personalized feedback, some of it based on effective learning analytics (as outlined in the previous chapter). Cormier, discussing his experience of studying through a MOOC, notes this shift to reuse:

> Every bit of the content that I saw in the course [. . .] was open access. Due to the crazy international laws around copyright, try to get a contract with a publisher for access to a journal for 300,000 people. At least, not under any current model. So we have maybe 100 items of open content being curated by the instructors and then seen by potentially thousands of other teachers.

> (2013)

We are thus in a position where academics have 'an embarrassment of riches' requiring different skills and use of time in searching, filtering and 'translating.' But there are also gaps in what is available, affected by both copyright issues or other formal protections (whether by academic protocols, publishers costing models or commercial confidence.) and by who predominantly puts content online (e.g., as in the areas that get marginalized or ignored by Wikipedia).

Once so much knowledge and information comes from outside the boundaries of the university (and without the gatekeeping processes that the academic publishing industry has historically provided), issues of ownership, quality, permissions, and costs become more complex and problematic. Plagiarism becomes easier for students, and awareness of assessing the validity of multiple sources becomes much more important. Primary resources of varying quality (books, journals, articles, lectures) are increasingly available for easy public access on the web. This may be legally—both free and paid-for—as e-books or articles uploaded by academics (e.g., through academia.edu) or other media (videos, websites, blogs, wikis, etc.); and less legally through, for instance, complete academic books scanned in as PDFs. This is leading to problems, around Intellectual Property Rights (IPR) and other legal concerns with reuse (especially on a MOOC-sized massive scale). This is an issue both for learning and for research, because several licensing mechanisms now operate from creative commons through to full copyright, and online academic journals have an increasing range of business and pricing models for making research papers available. In addition, new modes of scholarship, beyond the conventional journal article or book, are presenting significant challenges for university libraries in how scholarship is documented and what business models can support these activities:

> The emergence of new scholarly forms of authoring, publishing, and researching outpace sufficient and scalable modes of assessment. Traditional approaches to scholarly evaluation such as citation-based metrics, for example, are often hard to apply to research that is disseminated or conducted via social media. New forms of peer review and approval, such as reader ratings, inclusion in and mention by influential blogs, tagging, incoming links, and re- tweeting, are arising from the natural actions of the global community of educators with increasingly relevant and interesting results.
>
> (Johnson et al. 2013: 9)

These changing patterns of scholarly engagement, which reach out beyond the circles of academia, are being unevenly developed and recognized (Weller 2011). This is both in the extent to which mainstream faculty are comfortable operating in these new spaces and in how much support comes from academic decision makers and from the regulatory systems for research across different subjects, institutions, and countries.

Theme 6.1: Changing Learning and Teaching Methods?

In the previous chapter I outlined how MOOCs grew out of two different models of education, one from the open education movement (cMOOCs) and the other from the scaling-up and potential monetization of conventional eLearning (xMOOCs) through videos, quizzes, and testing—what has been called 'drill and grill' (Daniel 2012: 8). Many of the educators designing and writing about cMOOCs argue that these challenge both traditional and more recent understandings of learning. Diana Laurillard (1993) famously framed learning as a dialogue between tutor and student (underpinned by experiential practice), where learning happens through students 'talking back' what they have learned. This work, though, assumes the academic as authoritative expert, supported by a 'controlled' access to knowledge and information, even as Laurillard centrally engaged with the potential of new information and communication technologies. George Siemens, by contrast, starts from the world already described earlier, where learners have access to huge amounts of information; where expertise is not only more available but also dispersed and unchecked; where lines between the knowledgeable expert and others is blurring, making experts less trusted and peer learning more central; where learning occurs all the time and not just in formal settings; and where there is a positive emphasis on learners as creators and coproducers rather than passive receivers of knowledge.

Siemens proposes that learning is best understood as what he calls connectivism (2004). This is based on developing abilities for navigating around the overabundance of information and knowledge available—'wayfinding'—and then developing skills in 'sensemaking' (2013a). These activities are also based on continuous dialogue and feedback, through both expert tutorial and peer-group conversation, and where students take control of routes they want to follow, engaging with some discussions and not others and reaching their own conclusions:

> Learning is a process that occurs within nebulous environments of shifting core elements—not entirely under the control of the individual. Learning (defined as actionable knowledge) can reside outside of ourselves (within an organization or a database), is focused on connecting specialized information sets, and the connections that enable us to learn more are more important than our current state of knowing.
>
> Connectivism is driven by the understanding that decisions are based on rapidly altering foundations. New information is continually being acquired. The ability to draw distinctions between important and unimportant information is vital. The ability to recognize when new information alters the landscape based on decisions made yesterday is also critical.
>
> (Siemens 2004)

Various mechanisms (blog posts, diagrams, videos) become not just source materials but also the means through which learners generate and share their own 'artifacts,' as a means both of making sense of something and of communicating it to and with others (Text Box 6.2).

TEXT BOX 6.2   SOME PRINCIPLES OF CONNECTIVISM

- The integration of cognition and emotions in meaning-making is important. Thinking and emotions influence each other. A theory of learning that only considers one dimension excludes a large part of how learning happens.
- Learning has an end goal—namely the increased ability to "do something". This increased competence might be in a practical sense (i.e. developing the ability to use a new software tool or learning how to skate) or in the ability to function more effectively in a knowledge era (self-awareness, personal information management, etc.). The "whole of learning" is not only gaining skill and understanding—actuation is a needed element. Principles of motivation and rapid decision making often determine whether or not a learner will actuate known principles.
- Learning is a process of connecting specialized nodes or information sources. A learner can exponentially improve their own learning by plugging into an existing network.
- Learning may reside in non-human appliances. Learning (in the sense that something is known, but not necessarily actuated) can rest in a community, a network, or a database.
- The capacity to know more is more critical that what is currently known. Knowing where to find information is more important than knowing information.
- Nurturing and maintaining connections is needed to facilitate learning. Connection making provides far greater returns on effort than simply seeking to understand a single concept.
- Learning and knowledge rest in diversity of opinions.
- Learning happens in many different ways. Courses, email, communities, conversations, web search, email lists, reading blogs, etc. Courses are not the primary conduit for learning.
- Different approaches and personal skills are needed to learn effectively in today's society. For example, the ability to see connections between fields, ideas, and concepts is a core skill.
- Organizational and personal learning are integrated tasks. Personal knowledge is comprised of a network, which feeds into organizations and institutions, which in turn feed back into the network and continue to provide learning for the individual. Connectivism attempts to provide an understanding of how both learners and organizations learn.
- Currency (accurate, up-to-date knowledge) is the intent of all connectivist learning.

- Decision-making is itself a learning process. Choosing what to learn and the meaning of incoming information is seen through the lens of shifting reality. While there is a right answer now, it may be wrong tomorrow due to alterations in the information climate impacting the decision.
- Learning is a knowledge creation process . . . not only knowledge consumption. Learning tools and design methodologies should seek to capitalize on this trait of learning.

Source: Adapted from www.connectivism.ca/about.html.

This connectivist model also understands peer participation in a particular way, as exemplified by the cMOOC framework, where large numbers interact (at least initially), giving choices in grouping. Here students are envisaged as taking responsibility for their educational decisions and as wanting to be engaged through critical inquiry:

> Higher education generally homogenizes learners through pre-requisites or subject streams (programs). Most learners in a course will be at a roughly similar stage—or so the program structure suggests. In reality, learners are a diverse group, even in reasonably small classes. They come to a course with different beliefs, live experiences, knowledge, aspirations, and learning habits. The uniformity of university program tracks masks the differences of learners.
>
> In an open course, participants aren't filtered in the same way. Participants range from "absolutely new to the topic" to "have written many books on the topic". As a result, filtering (or forming sub-networks/ groups/discussion clusters) happens once the course is underway. The first few weeks are a bit tumultuous—it's really a sociological and psychological process of identifying yourself to others and positioning yourself meaningfully in the conversation.
>
> [. . .] This fluidity of interaction across novice-intermediate-expert networks is one of the main points of value in open courses. And one of the main differentiators from traditional courses.
>
> (Siemens 2011)

To knowledge construction as wayfinding and sensemaking through shared artifacts, Stephen Downes—Siemen's partner in what is considered the original 2008 MOOC—adds the concept of pattern recognition:

> We have through the industrial age depended on a model of knowledge as a set of theses that are hypothesized and tested against experience. In this model, articulation and measurement are essential skills. But our

understanding of what it means to know, to infer, and to give reasons evolves in an environment where knowing consists of pattern recognition. [. . .]

[This means] some of our long-standing ideas about community and collaboration need to be reconsidered. The most important function of a person in a community is no longer conformity, but rather, creativity and expression. It is through the cooperation of autonomous and diverse individuals that communities function most effectively, not through collaboration or cohesion.

(2012: 10)

Interestingly—in its 'ideal' form at least—the kind of scaling-up embedded in cMOOCs does not necessarily rely on mass-replication of content and delivery, supported by automated testing (i.e., with everyone studying the same resources). Rather, it based on a changing and responsive agglomeration of relevant online resources that are then explored through an underlying structured framework of relevant skills development and tutor and peer discussion. In many ways this can be seen as much more in line with a traditional academic role.

6.1.a Alternative MOOCs

FemTechNet is a network of scholars, artists, and students working across technology, science, and feminism in a variety of fields. They

collaborate on the design and creation of projects of feminist technological innovation for the purposes of engaging the interests of colleagues and students on advanced topics in feminist science-technology studies. This project seeks to engender a set of digital practices among women and girls, to teach and encourage their participation in writing the technocultural histories of the future by becoming active participants in the creation of global digital archives.

(http://femtechnet.newschool.edu/the-network/)

As part of this, the group developed an alternative experiment to MOOCS, which they called Distributive Open Collaborative Courses (DOCCs), with the first run in 2013 titled "Dialogues on Feminism and Technology":

A MOOC (massive open online course) is pedagogically centralized and branded by a single institution. The fundamental difference is that a DOCC recognizes and is built on the understanding that expertise is distributed throughout a network, among participants situated in diverse institutional contexts, within diverse material, geographic, and national settings, and who embody and perform diverse identities (as teachers, as students, as media-makers, as activists, as trainers, as members of various publics, for example).

(http://femtechnet.newschool.edu/docc2013/)

The DOCC framework is smaller, more distributive, and locally specific than either xMOOCs or cMOOCs are. Rather than relying on 'talking-head' lectures of famous experts, the core video resources are centered on dialogue, bringing together prominent and innovative thinkers and artists in debate. These learning materials are developed across universities and colleges by collaborating tutors (from a variety of subject areas) and then configured to a particular educational setting, with credit offered through already existing mechanisms within each institution. The first FemTechNet DOCC involved fifteen universities and colleges over a ten-week period. The idea is also that course content grows through the exchange among participants. One outcome was a project called Wikistorming (http://femtechnet.newschool.edu/wikistorming/), where students participated in adding entries to Wikipedia that covered currently ignored areas around feminism and technology. On the first iteration the numbers were small (200 credited, with 25 'drop-in learners), but as Balsamo and her colleagues note, the start-up costs were small compared to MOOCs, and the retention rate was 99 percent (Balsamo et al. 2014).

Another MOOC generating project explicitly explores how it might work across the arts and design subjects. Arts Massive Open Online Course (artsmooc) is an experimental social enterprise approach to integrating online open courses into practical face-to-face based arts subjects for those in creative industries (www.artsmooc.org). The aim is to address problems for the arts (some of which have already been outlined in Chapter 1), including the reduction of arts-based courses in schools, university education becoming less affordable for some social groups, colleges and universities requiring support to provide MOOCs, and the lack of Internet and digital literacies in online learning communities. With artsmooc, arts-sector stakeholders—such as artist run groups, clubs, studios, colleges, schools, universities, and galleries—work in partnership with online resource networks, art support networks, arts OERs and MOOCs. The artsmooc community creates, contributes to, and codevelops freely available arts resources, events, workshops, and communities of practice to support specialist groups, subjects, and disciplines. Each artsmooc is developed alongside other artsmooc communities of practice within the wider ecosystem in a collaborative and supportive environment, in either online or face-to-face learning.

6.1.b Games and Gamification

If connectivism draws from an analysis of changing conditions produced by the web—an overabundance of resources and global networks—then other methods for learning have also grown out of web-based developments. These include Web 2.0 and social media as well as immersive environments such as Second Life, Sim City, Multi-User Dungeons (MUDs), and Massively Multi-player Online Role-Playing Games (MMORPGs). There has been a growing interest in how games and 'gamification' can be translated into teaching and learning, built on the considerable success of online gaming, now often called serious gaming. This transfer to education centers on three aspects. First, online games work by immersing the participant in the action, so that they literally navigate their way around contexts and situations, often with the cooperation (or competition) of other participants. Games most commonly involve scenarios or simulations, which involve the playing-out and experimenting in a virtual version of the material world, thus going beyond a reliance on texts and discussion into experiential learning (and allowing practice and crucially failure that could not be undertaken in real-life situations). Second, games tend to be built on a system of levels (or quests or other structures) with explicitly increasing types of difficulty, in which participants can have some degree of choice over what challenge they want to take next, but can also feel real achievement as they move from one level to the next. Third, a system of badges (as noted in the last chapter), through the accumulation of points or other rewards, offer recognition of achievements; and the ranking of relative success transparently shows progress, and motivates interest through competition (with oneself and/ or with others). Gamers, then, can become deeply engaged in personal challenges. As the NMC Horizon 2013 report (Johnson et al. 2013) notes, major corporations and organizations, including the World Bank and IBM, already use game experts to develop their online training, because it develops these characteristics.

The translation of gaming strategies into mainstream university and college education has however, been slow and uneven (despite it being on the NMC list of innovations for many years). This is probably mainly because of the still relatively untested impact for learners, the levels of institutional support required (JISC 2007) and the considerable up-front development time and expertise required for materials development. At the most simplistic level the emphasis on individual competition and ranking (rather than connectivism's sensemaking and sharing) equates much more directly to a neo-liberal viewpoint based on self-interest and incentives. In many cases in education, the emphasis has tended more toward simulations and scenario building and to different kinds of puzzles as a form of both collaboration and competition. One example from the NMC Horizon 2013 report is from the IE Business School in Madrid:

> [S]tudents are learning the complexities of global economic policy through a game called "10 Downing Street". In this simulation, students

take on the role of the British prime minister and work with key figures including Paul Krugman, Margaret Thatcher, and Milton Friedman
to come to an agreement that will affect the well being of the national
economy. In teams of six, students engage in debates to determine the
most viable policy option, which is then put into practice after a general election. Scenarios like this one demonstrate the power of games to
mimic pressing issues, requiring students to do higher-level thinking and
exercise skills pertinent to their area of study.

(Johnson et al. 2013: 21)

Online serious games like these are mainly just extending existing methods in higher education (particularly in the vocational and professional areas)
where real-time role-playing and real-world simulations are common. The bigger challenge to universities and colleges is in the effects of game-type activities
on motivation. As Shantanu Sinha, president of the Khan Academy, writes,

One of our biggest problems is that our education system has a very
poorly designed motivation and incentive system. It just doesn't work for
the majority of people. Currently, our pitch to young students goes something like this: "You should study and work hard because otherwise you
will get bad grades. If you get bad grades, you won't get into college or get
a good job. You don't want to struggle in 10 years, so go study now." [. . .]
    So what better ways are there to motivate people? This is where we
can truly learn from the game industry. They have turned motivation
and incentive systems into a science. Being in Silicon Valley, I've had
the privilege of meeting some senior leaders in the game industry. I have
always been astounded by how well they understand human behavior.
One CEO of a game company recently told me, "If we build a game in
which someone is demotivated or disengaged for 45 seconds, we know we
need to improve." Forty-five seconds! Imagine if we thought this way in
education. I think I went *years* demotivated at school when I was growing
up. And, that's likely the norm, not the exception.

(2012)

He suggests that universities and colleges can learn from a critical engagement with the games industry and its knowledge in structuring activities.
    Serious games are also increasingly bridging physical and virtual worlds;
potentially adding the motivation and engagement that embodied tasks can
offer (research shows positive correlations between physical activity and learning), as well as linking into creativity and the positive state of concentration and
absorption in a task that has been called 'flow' (Csikszentmihalyi 1990). New

kinds of web-based community games are being invented, of which geo-caching (www.geocaching.com) is probably the most famous, where participants can interact both online and through undertaking activities in the physical world. SF Zero or SF0 (http://sf0.org) is another such game, originating from San Francisco. Players earn points by completing a wide variety of different tasks, often with a focus on creativity, exploration, community, or performance. Although the game was originally intended for San Francisco residents, its player base has expanded to include many other localities both in and outside of America. It was created and is managed by a nonprofit organization dedicated to producing free immersive art games that use new technologies in significant ways.

Theme 6.2: Open Sourcing and Sharing

Although academics have traditionally shared research and scholarly activity through publications, networks, and conferences, they have generally resisted sharing learning materials beyond individual course teams or units of study. This is despite a long history of government and other funding for the development of publicly available and transferable learning materials, and an increasing number of development consortia and expert groups, such as the OCW Consortium formed in 2005 (www.ocwconsortium.org). As already mentioned, there have been accumulating initiatives aimed at improving access to, and quality control over, relevant online sources. These have included different subject-based gateways, portals, and repositories; the development of Reusable Learning Objects (RLO), aiming to supply courses with generic 'learning chunks' that can be built into bigger components; OER, as already discussed; various OCW projects; the increasing availability of free digital textbooks (from producers such as Flatworld and BookBoon); and open licensing mechanisms such as Creative Commons. In addition, and as mentioned in the previous chapter, there are new open source infrastructural systems being developed, of which Moodle is only one:

> As the value of OER and OCW for both formal and non-formal learning became more apparent, developing support for learners was a logical next step. Several interesting models have emerged. Some, such as NIXTY (http:// www.nixty.com), are built around a learning management system that functions similarly to platforms students use at many higher education institutions. Others, such as OpenStudy (http://openstudy.com), use a virtual-peer study- group model, organizing study groups around broad content areas or specific OCW courses. Learners can ask questions on the topic, either based on their own studies or on OCW materials, to which peers and volunteer mentors provide responses. Peer 2 Peer University (www.p2pu.org) has a learning platform based on peer support

for learning, offering some courses that incorporate challenges and peer reviews as a means to build knowledge and skills.

(Forward 2012: 296)

In addition, crowdsourcing and crowd-sharing initiatives are having an enormous impact on the web, of which Wikipedia is only the most well known. Now many 'lifelong learning' websites are based both on open sharing of knowledge and information and on peer support and knowledge or skills exchange. Like some of the alternative universities outlined in Chapter 1 and the social enterprise examples given in Chapter 2, these initiatives understand learning widely and as something that happens through social media, peer support and knowledge exchange. Here the web acts to connect various individuals and groups. Horsesmouth (www.horsesmouth.co.uk) is an online peer-mentoring and coaching site that is built on volunteer exchanges of expertise. Similarly, the School of Everything (http://schoolofeverything. com) enables learners to search for teachers in their area, and vice versa. There is no registration fee, and the site caters to educational organizations and individual teachers who charge for their lessons as well as those who offer lessons for free or as part of a skill swap.

Some of these crowd-sharing sites have a hybrid cost model, combining skills swaps with paid-for classes. Livemocha, now owned by Rosetta Stone, is an online language learning site that not only has free beginners materials and offers a network of global language speakers who mentor each other for free but also provides more advanced online learning resources, supported by instructor-led classes:

> The Livemocha community is made up of language enthusiasts: teachers, language experts, other language learners, and native speakers proud of their language and heritage. Community members help each other learn in a myriad of ways: they leave comments in response to practice exercises, build mini-lessons within exercise feedback, have practice conversations via text, video or audio chat, provide language practice and culture tips, and give much-needed encouragement.

(http://livemocha.com/)

Others are using the framework of crowdsourcing and sharing to challenge conventional academic repositories and portals. DHThis is a crowd-sourced site for Digital Humanities (DH) News. It challenges the framework of most digital portals and repositories, which, while aggregating content, also tend to act a selection filter (through editorial control) to offer guarantees of relevance, accuracy, and quality in a particular subject area to users:

DHThis flips that model, shifting control of new developments in DH to wider publics. Using a Slashdot-style system of user engagement, [where people posting comments themselves become moderators] DHThis gives registered users the opportunity to upvote and downvote articles and gives karma points that reward active (and useful) participation in the community. DHThis is built on an ethos of open access and open engagement and provides an ongoing forum for defining DH in the moment. [. . .]

Registration is free and open to anyone. A submission needs 5 votes to appear on the front page. Registered users may give votes using the thumbs up/thumbs down feature on the post. Votes are also accorded by 5-star ratings and karma, and users need a minimum 100 karma value before a post they submit will appear on the front page. Users accrue karma through actions including submission, upvoting, and comments.

(www.dhthis.org/page.php?page=www-dhthis-orgaboutus)

DHThis thus takes the crowd-sourcing model from parts of social media and applies it back into an educational and academic context.

6.2.a Open Educational Resources

There is no standard definition of OER, but OER Commons (www.oercommons.org), a digital content hub, offers the following (see also http://loumcgill.co.uk/oer-terminology for more on terminology):

Open Educational Resources (OER) are teaching and learning materials that are freely available online for everyone to use, whether you are an instructor, student or self-learner. Examples of OER include: full courses, course modules, syllabi, lectures, homework assignments, quizzes, lab and classroom activities, pedagogical materials, games, simulations, and many more resources contained in digital media collections from around the world.

As outlined at the beginning of this chapter, OER operate at a variety of levels. As the JISC explains,

it is helpful to consider learning resources by their levels of granularity and to focus on the degree to which information content is embedded within a learning activity:

- Digital assets—normally a single file (e.g. an image, video or audio clip), sometimes called a 'raw media asset';
- Information objects—a structured aggregation of digital assets, designed purely to present information;

- Learning objects—an aggregation of one or more digital assets which represents an educationally meaningful stand-alone unit;
- Learning activities—tasks involving interactions with information to attain a specific learning outcome;
- Learning design—structured sequences of information and activities to promote learning.
     (https://openeducationalresources.pbworks.com/w/page/24836860/
          What%20are%20Open%20Educational%20Resources)

The type and the size of learning resource, then, are likely to have an impact on reusability. A larger, pedagogically designed 'chunk' is not only likely to be more resource effective (in reducing the amount of learning materials designed on a case-by-case basis) but also potentially more in need of adaptation, less generally relevant to a particular group of students, and less attractive to academics. But the rolling out of shared OER cannot just a matter of individual faculty preference, used only by individual enthusiasts. For universities and colleges to develop OER effectively requires—most crucially—an underpinning strategy, particularly in partnership with wider networks and partners. It requires the finding and creating of appropriate and reliable sources (e.g., through specialized search engines such as Jorum and DiscoverEd), investment in providing and supporting suitable hosting, metadata and management infrastructure, decisions on development processes (open source, in-house, outsourced, through partnerships, etc.), and the embedding of processes across learning, teaching, and critical inquiry. To be successful—to add value and resource effectiveness—OER need to be fully integrated into strategic planning and implementation, including the development of practical support for both faculty and students by engaging with issues around academic culture and autonomy, development time, instructional design skills, and technical and legal issues.

As well as effective learning and cost savings, OER is also about widening educational participation by making learning available beyond conventional and Western academic institutions. The William and Flora Hewlett Foundation is currently funding a global initiative to increase the use of OER across all educational levels. It offers

a roadmap for transforming teaching and learning by shifting OER from a small-scale movement to standard education practice. The early adopters of OER believed that education is a public good and that openness, embedded as an essential element of the teaching and learning process, can have a strong, positive effect in education. The goal is not to further OER as a movement itself, but to contribute to the equalization of access to knowledge for all and demonstration that the teaching and learning experience can be improved even as fiscal resources decline. Bringing this aspiration to fruition in mainstream education will require focus, collaboration, and a community of supporters from multiple sectors.

(William and Flora Hewlett Foundation 2013: 3)

The foundation has set the goal that by 2017, OER will be becoming standard education practice, and that OER producers will supply high-quality, personalized instructional materials for a wide range of courses—from the most basic, primary school–level subjects to the most popular credit-bearing courses in colleges in the United States. Those materials will be organized in a way that enables in-classroom adoption that is simple enough to encourage widespread use. At the same time, "key OER providers around the globe will be on a path to sustainability, receiving funding from governments, other philanthropies, institutions, revenues and other private sources" (ibid.: 4). The project has a detailed logic model of activities, and learning outcomes (Figure 6.1) as well as initial metrics and targets (ibid.: 31).

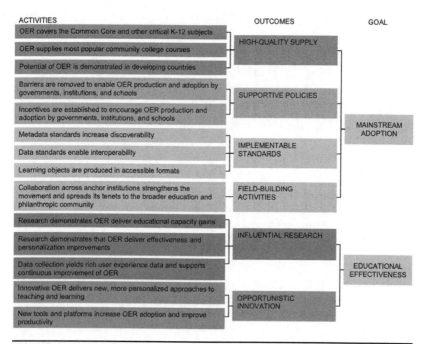

Figure 6.1 Detailed Logic Model: showing intended OER activities, outcomes and goals

Source: Reprinted from William and Flora Hewlett Foundation (2013: 21), www.hewlett.org/sites/default/files/OER%20White%20Paper%20Nov%2022%202013%20Final_0.pdf.

6.2.b Project Kaleidoscope

Project Kaleidoscope (PKAL) focuses more precisely on using OER to improve student success, through a partnership of fourteen colleges across the US. The group aims to use OER in all courses and to support with well-structured course design and coworking. It has three basic aims:

1. Eliminate textbook cost as a barrier. Faculty members across institutions collaboratively create open course frameworks that use the best existing OER, and reduce required textbook costs to $0.
2. Drive assessment-driven enhancement of open course frameworks. Project resources analyze assessment, activity and success data to guide faculty members in continually improving the effectiveness of the open resources.
3. Create a collaborative community to share learning and investment. The project emphasizes institutional engagement, allowing institutional leaders and faculty members to benefit from sharing and collaboration within and across institutions.

(www.project-kaleidoscope.org/)

Kaleidoscope has been developing what it calls "Open Course Frameworks" for ten high-enrollment courses in colleges. Current learning resources include algebra, reading, writing, English composition, and college success, with introductory materials in business, geography, biology, chemistry, psychology, and other subjects in development. These courses are used and then improved through an iterative process of seeing how well students have performed. The development team says it has enabled "an improvement in student success (completing with a grade of C or better) that was greater than 10%, with strong gains by low-income students" (www.project-kaleidoscope.org/courses/).

6.2.c ALTO Project, University of the Arts, London, UK

As well as generating OER, universities and colleges must decide about where these sit within university systems and on what platform. The ALTO (Arts Teaching and Learning online) project (http://alto.arts.ac.uk/) at the University of the Arts in London (UAL) is a developmental project to enable all staff and students across the institutions to create, collaborate, and publicly share learning resources. It also acts as a portal for existing OER, provides a personalized repository for individuals to collect their content in one place and allows control over degrees of access (Figure 6.2):

> We have been developing a rich model for publishing OERs in practice-based arts subjects, which we hope to take forwards in further research and development projects. The working title for this is the 'ALTO

Figure 6.2 ALTO website, University of the Arts, London, UK
Source: Reprinted with permissions from University of the Arts London.

Ecosystem'—this has the ambitious goal of creating a reusable and adaptable model for providing appropriate IT, cultural and policy support for OER and collaboration in the Art and Design sector.

(http://process.arts.ac.uk/content/alto-ecosystem)

Rather than using the existing OER portals, or any of the existing open-source platforms (such as MIT OCW, Open Learn, or MERLOT, a database-driven central website with distributed web 'feeder' sites), ALTO was developed as a customized infrastructure and interface. The university already had a project exploring similar issues through an existing UAL social media initiative called process.arts (Text Box 6.3), funded through a staff teaching fellowship. This has therefore offered opportunities for experimentation and prototype development.

TEXT BOX 6.3   PROCESS.ARTS UNIVERSITY OF THE ARTS, LONDON UK

Process.arts is an open online community that aims to share art, design, and media practice, not just within one university but also beyond it, encouraging communities of practice to develop and bringing together individuals, groups and organizations worldwide. The site is deliberately designed to offer a rich media experience, which is important to the subjects it covers. Although process.arts developments were a central and valuable starting point for the university's own ALTO project, its structure

> does not map onto courses; meta data links user-generated pieces of openly licensed text, image, video and audio content together through individual profiles and subject specific interest groups. Like many web2.0 environments used for education, process.arts can neither really be described as a repository nor as a VLE. Because of this it provides a novel and alternative VLE environment that encourages and supports rich media experimentation and informal learning, a welcome alternative for many to commercial alternatives.
> (http://process.arts.ac.uk/content/about-processarts)

6.2.d PATINA

As digital repositories become more commonplace, there is also the issue of how these might move beyond a text-based online database and storage service. For example, the Personal Architectonics of Interactions with Artefacts (PATINA) project is exploring how different ways of conceptualizing, visualizing, and communicating research data could affect the way in which material is stored and engaged with. Funding via the Research Councils UK (RCUK) Digital Economy Programme, was for three years from October 2010. Led by the University of Bristol, with Brighton, Greenwich, Newcastle, Southampton, and Swansea, it also involved Microsoft Research, Nokia Research, and the Victoria and Albert Museum. This project aimed to explore repositories as 'architectonic'—by both developing web-based spaces linked to metaphors of physicality (e.g., around how we navigate) and integrating virtual space with material devices, as tangible user interfaces. It also wanted individual researchers to be able to design their own private, institutional, and public research spaces. As the project reports,

> PATINA will provide researchers with new opportunities to create research spaces that emphasise the primacy of research material, and support the sharing of research activities as well as results. Through recording of research practice the project will also enable you to 'walk in the footsteps' of other researchers, and explore how the provenance of your developing ideas links with theirs through shared objects that exist both online and in the real world.

The consortium will build wearable prototypes that can enhance research objects by projecting related information back into their research space. These technologies will also provide the means to capture, record, and replay the researcher's activities to support intuitive archiving, sharing and publication of interactions with research objects. The design of the technologies will draw on theoretical frameworks of space developed from studies of research spaces as diverse as libraries, museums, homes and archaeological fieldwork sites.

(www.patina.ac.uk/)

One example of the kinds of 'spaces' being developed here is the chronotape, "a tangible timeline for family history research" (www.chronotape.com/) designed by Peter Bennett at the University of Bristol.

Theme 6.3: Embodied Learning

Just as universities and colleges have begun to understand more about how Web 2.0 applications can or might interact with learning and teaching methods and modes of delivery, new developments in robotics and nano- and biotechnologies are again shifting the possibilities of online and face-to-face education. Whilst there is a long tradition in higher education of experiential learning (Dewey 1938; Kolb 1984) and, to a lesser extent, object-based learning (Chatterjee 2009; Boddington and Boys 2011), the potential of objects to support nonverbal, tacit and creative learning remains under developed in universities and colleges. Now, with the increasing embedding of information and communication technologies into objects and spaces, the potential of a more 'physical' learning is opening up again, together with new kinds of possible interactions between humans and the material world.

The Internet of Things (IoT)—the networked connection of objects— enables objects and spaces to have built-in information and intelligent properties that can be responsive to the user, to other artifacts, and to computer data, producing, analyzing and reacting to flows of information. Google Glass (www.google.com/glass/start/what-it-does/) is probably the most well known of these kinds of developments in wearable computing, but there are now many other interactive resources in which the virtual and physical are incorporated, through bodily augmentation and smart clothing and through augmented and virtual reality environments. These developments are not new. MIT Media Lab, for example, has been exploring wearable computing for many years. But nano- and biotechnologies are becoming more available and inexpensive. For example, we have already become used to touch-screen computing and GPS-enabled operations, and gesture-based computing is close. These changes will be hard to keep up with:

We've seen with our own eyes a violin, with perfect pitch, that was 3D printed at Exeter University; a wallet at the MIT Media Lab that knows how much money you have in your bank account and gets progressively harder to open the more you spend. Wearable computing, such as Google Glasses and pulse monitoring watches, is already here. Three states in the US—California, Nevada and Florida, if you want to avoid them—have already made driverless cars legal. [. . .] We haven't even mentioned the biotech revolution that is happening in parallel.

(Barber et al. 2012: 9)

At the same time, research groups such as the Centre for Speckled Computing at the University of Edinburgh continue to push the boundaries of what is technically possible:

Specks will be minute (around 1 mm^3) semiconductor grains that can sense and compute locally and communicate wirelessly. Each speck will be autonomous, with its own captive, renewable energy source. Thousands of specks, scattered or sprayed on the person or surfaces, will collaborate as programmable computational networks called Specknets.

Speckled Computing is the culmination of a greater trend. As the once-separate worlds of computing and wireless communications collide, a new class of information appliances will emerge. Where once they stood proud—the PDA bulging in the pocket, or the mobile phone nestling in one's palm, the post-modern equivalent might not be explicit after all. Rather, data sensing and information processing capabilities will fragment and disappear into everyday objects and the living environment.

(www.specknet.org/)

Higher education has already been investing in laser-cutting, computer numerical control (CNC) machines and 3D printing, especially for science research, in lab settings and in arts and design, enabling staff and students to create 3D models for visualizing concepts or enabling the handling of exact copies of precious objects. The museum community in particular has built on this service, creating and sharing replicas of artwork, sculptures, and fossils. Other innovations are being developed commercially. The Augmented Reality Development Laboratory (ARDL), for instance, has designed a tool that enables the portrayal and manipulation of virtual 3D objects using simple 2D cards, which is already being developed for a variety of educational uses (Text Box 6.4). This trend will continue. The University of Nevada, Reno's DeLaMare Science and Engineering Library, for example, is just one of the first academic libraries in the US to allow students, faculty, and the public to use 3D printing and scanning tools, as this technology becomes affordable (Johnson et al. 2013: 29). But perhaps the more crucial aspects of these new technologies are in how they make learning 'embodied,' both in how we engage with information and communication technologies and in how we can cocreate through them.

TEXT BOX 6.4   AUGMENTED REALITY DEVELOPMENT LAB

Digital Tech Frontier (DTF) creates, manufactures, and markets interactive educational programs using experiential technology and has played a fundamental part in the development of the Augmented Reality Development Lab (ARDL). This is a revolutionary concept that makes virtual, 3D objects appear as though they were real. Virtual objects are very useful to convey spatial, temporal, or contextual concepts. Users looking through either a Virtual Reality POV Viewing Device or a screen can see virtual objects that can be attached to cards, book pages, interactive whiteboards, the floor, or the wall to provide a 3D animated replica that fills the room. It is particularly useful for viewing objects such as dinosaurs, the human heart, volcanoes, or planets in ways that would not be possible in the real world or when real objects would be too expensive, dangerous, or fragile to work with. With Augmented Reality, users have the opportunity to collaborate and interact with virtual objects and other users, and different objects can be viewed in proximity to each other.

New content can be created professionally, or users can create their own content by using programs such as Google SketchUp, Lightwave, 3D Max, Ogre, or Maya to create models that are then imported into the ARDL Model Creation Tool and converted into an Augmented Reality platform ready to be placed into an interaction paddle, which allows objects to be manipulated and examined in a number of different ways.

Source: Adapted from http://augmentedrealitydevelopmentlab.com/ (accessed April 29, 2014).

6.3.a Wearable Technologies and Tangible User Interfaces

Wearable technologies are an expanding area that is likely to have a longer-term impact on learning and research, particularly because they enable real-time data sensing. A MIT Media Lab project, for example, allows users to turn any surface into an interface. SixthSense (www.pranavmistry.com/projects/sixthsense) is based on a pocket projector, a mirror, and a camera. The hardware components inside this pendant-like, wearable device project information onto any surface, while the camera recognizes and tracks a user's hand gestures. Another example is from the Pedagogic Research and Support groups at the Ecole Polytechnique Fédérale de Lausanne (EPFL) which develop new technologies for learning. The unit's researchers have developed an interactive table that registers how speaking time is distributed around the table, helping students to measure how balanced their collaborative talk is (Danish Property Agency 2013: 37). In a similar project, from the Institute of Aesthetics and Communication at Aarhus University in Denmark, researchers are exploring how a table might support students' wider reflection:

> ReflecTable is a project aiming to design a setting that students can use to train their design and innovation skills. The theoretic underpinnings of the ReflecTable is the work of Donald A. Schön, who originated the idea of the reflective practicum. [. . .] The reflective practicum is based on the view, that design—and other practices—can't be taught using the traditional university means, but must be learned-by-doing. The reflective practicum is a setting that mirrors key elements of practice and enables the students to try—and reflect on—practice.
>
> The main feature of the project was, initially, an interactive table—hence the name "ReflecTable"—but hardware alone makes no reflective practicum. The main challenge of the project is figuring out what activity the table should facilitate and which rules should govern this activity.
>
> (http://reflectable.dk/about/)

Although many of these tools with an explicit learning dimension are being developed and experimented with, it is still too soon to see how embedded they will become into mainstream higher education.

6.3.b Maker Spaces

What has seen considerable growth, as part of the open education movement, has been what is usually called maker culture, which is concerned to make emerging digital technologies easily available to everyone, together with the associated knowledge and skills required, across programming and physical construction:

> Those involved in the many Maker communities around the world emphasize invention and prototyping. The MakerBot is a 3D desktop printer that allows users to build everything from toys to robots, to household furniture and accessories, to models of dinosaur skeletons. In 2012, MakerBot Industries released the Replicator 2, with a higher resolution compatibility and build volume. Relatively affordable at under $2,500, the MakerBot has

brought 3D printing to the masses; the technology had previously only been found in specialized labs.

(Johnson et al. 2013: 28)

Websites such as Thingiverse (www.thingiverse.com) offer source files that anyone can use to print objects without original designs. The do-it-yourself aspect is also supported by open-source programming applications, and there is a strong element of using and learning practical skills, not just across electronics and robotics but also metalworking, woodworking, and other, more traditional craft skills. Maker culture is thus centrally concerned with creative learning, personal achievement, and collaborative engagement, through what it calls 'tinkering.' Through hacker spaces, 'Fab Labs,' and other collaborative workshop spaces, people can come together to share facilities and ideas (Figure 6.3).

Many universities and colleges now have Fab Labs and maker spaces in some form. There are also projects that have looked at how this kind of learning can be up-scaled and offered at a distance. The UK Open University's My Digital Life course tested the cost-effective production and distribution of SenseBoard kits to all its learners on a unit of study introducing basic computer science and programming (Kortuem et al. 2013). The aim was to make the IoT central, because the interrelations between computing and objects are becoming

Figure 6.3 Maker Space, Newcastle upon Tyne, UK
Source: Photo by Jos Boys.

increasingly important. The course had almost 2,000 students participating, and involved a range of activities including collaborative and collective programming of real-world applications. Course design and development therefore had to both engage with key pedagogic issues and solve the practicalities of providing hardware kits to such large numbers.

6.4.c Creative Collaborations and Co-creation

In parallel to, and often overlapping with, maker culture is an interest in developing smart machines and interfaces that allow a creative, public engagement with the world through technologies. As already outlined, some of these are simple web-based interactive collaborations such as Geo-Caching or iSpot (www.ispotnature.org/), where physical artifacts and events are exchanged and commented on, through objects, activities, photographs, videos, audio files, etc. Some enable the crowdsourcing of and the sharing of data. Others are concerned to use robotic machines to enhance people's engagement with an activity (such as Rusty Squid, a Bristol-based collective of roboticists, puppeteers, and model makers who design and build 'corporeal' creatures that can interact with people and their environment (http://rustysquid.org.uk/)) or to empower people to understand more about their environment. As Juliet Sprake and Peter Rogers write of their various projects,

> [p]articipatory sensing is an emerging field in which citizens are empowered by technologies to monitor their own environments. Harvesting and analysing data gathered in response to personal or local enquiries can be seen as an antidote to information provided by official sources. Democratising sensing means that ordinary people can learn about and understand the world around them better and can be a part of the decision-making in improving environments for all.
>
> (Sprake and Rogers 2011: 753)

They give examples of three projects:

> In the first of these projects, Located Lexicon, we wanted to find out whether a lexicon of terms derived from user-generated content could enable the formation of Twitter like groups that allow users to engage in finding out more about their location. In the second project, Where's Fenton? we made a publicly available app that involves users in counting the abundance and logging the location of deer in a park. This project focused specifically on anonymity of the user in collecting data for a specific enquiry.
>
> In the last project, Tall Buildings, we experimented with using dimensions of altitude, distance and speed to encourage users to physically

explore a city from its rooftops. In all of these projects, we experiment with the pedestrian as a human sensor and the methods and roles they may engage in to make new discoveries.

(Sprake and Rogers 2014)

Other groups use a mixture of low-tech and high-tech creative technologies to enable public participation in local politics. The Institute of Infinitely Small Things is an informal network that "conducts creative, participatory research that aims to temporarily transform public spaces and instigate dialogue about democracy, spatial justice and everyday life. The Institute's projects use performance, conversation and unexpected interventions to investigate social and political 'tiny things'" (www.ikatun.org/institute/infinitelysmallthings/). The group Proboscis also centers on social engagement through creative research, what it calls "co-discovery for uncommon insight" (http://proboscis.org.uk/). It mainly develops activities that help people create, communicate, and share things through collaboration and co-discovery. They use a range of creative technologies, listed on their website as "pervasive urban play, mobile spatial mapping, sensors and citizen science, public data mash ups, experimental robotics, hybrid digital/physical outputs from digital experience" (http://proboscis.org.uk/projects/ongoing/public-goods/; Figure 6.4). The Public Goods project, for example, focuses on

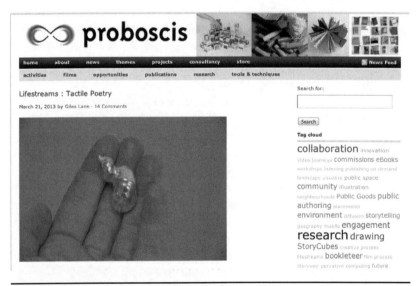

Figure 6.4 Proboscis, Tangible Souvenirs project, London, UK
Source: http://proboscis.org.uk/tag/tangible-souvenirs/.

making and sharing tangible representations of the *intangible* things we feel are *most precious* about the places and communities we belong to, such as stories, skills, games, songs, techniques, memories, local lore and experiential knowledge of local environment and ecology.

(ibid.)

In this there is a shift from their previous aim to make public data more accessible and understandable to people who do not or cannot access them at present. Rather,

We believe that creating new kinds of interfaces and feedback mechanisms that make such data and its visualisations tangible and tactile will offer enormous benefits to people who suffer from blindness, low or no reading ability or simply do not use the typical devices (smartphone, tablets and computers) that are ordinarily used interact with such data. We will be examining how to create *tangible souvenirs* from public data: creating physical, material outputs of public data visualisations or even sonifications.

(ibid.)

Proboscis are therefore aiming to make a series of prototypes that create physical outputs from 'mash-ups' of online public data, as a means of making this information more tactile, engaging, and understandable. They also suggest that such 'tangible souvenirs' could, in turn, act as a feedback loop, through which information can then flow from physical back to the digital.

Such initiatives have been happening both within universities and beyond them—through maker, academic, artist, and community groupings. They deserve a critical engagement from educators more generally, to help understand how learning is changing and to explore how to take advantage of such creative pedagogies, and the associated material devices in higher education.

Toward Open Educational Practices

As Kortuem et al. write,

[t]he Internet of Things is seen as the next revolution in IT. Emerging originally out of an industrial context, in the public view the Internet of Things is still primarily associated with the interests of large industrial players. However, unless we willfully expand the discussion and assign the needs, desires and fears of ordinary citizens as much importance as the requirements of industrial players, there is a danger that the Internet of Things falls short of its potential.

(2013: 60)

As with the web more generally, some of this is about data protection and legal issues. Who has a right to gather data, whose data is being collected and what is being done with it? With the increasing use of location data (RFID and GPS) as well as other source sensing devices such as CCTV, this issue can only expand (www.opensourcesensing.org). But for universities and colleges it is also about user-led innovation, about students as citizen producers, about generating social enterprise and social engagement, and about exploring and implementing both online resources and more physical interfaces. As many authors have noted, this is not merely to ask individual higher education institutions to design more online resources and to improve digital access to those resources but about what is being called open educational *practices* (Conole and Ethlers 2010; Luckin et al. 2012; McGill et al. 2013). These argue for a more strategic and mainstream move toward practice change, through institutional and wider cultural change, as well as better evaluation and improvement processes. Organizations such as the Open Education Quality Initiative (OPAL; see Text Box 6.5) have been set up to map, support, and extend such open educational practices.

TEXT BOX 6.5   OPEN EDUCATION QUALITY INITIATIVE

The Open Educational Quality (OPAL) Initiative was a two-year Europe-wide project running from 2010 through 2011 that was concerned to move OERs beyond small initiatives and the issue of access to innovation and quality, using the concept of Open Education Practices (OEP). The first stage was to map barriers to OER take up. They found that concerns over quality, the absence of trust on the part of learners and educators, a lacking of sense of ownership of the materials, and only modest levels of support from institutions all hindered wider acceptance of OER. The initiative offered 5 principles in its final report for enabling better take-up:

A. A policy environment for supporting the usage of OER is important
B. Institutional support strategies are fostering open educational practices
C. Networks of Innovation play an important role for shaping OER developments and open educational practices
D. Specific quality assurance processes for OER are viewed necessary
E. Open educational practices are supported through cultures of innovation and in turn provide innovation in organisations

(Andrade et al. 2011: 8–10)

The project also set up an OPAL Award to recognize outstanding achievements in the field of OEP; undertook a process of dissemination through conferences, papers and presentations, and workshops and seminars; and set up consultative groups and linked into existing networks and organizations.

Reference:

Andrade, A., Ehlers, U. D., Caine, A., Carneiro. R., Conole. G., Kairamo, A-K., Koskinen, T., Kretschmer, T., Moe-Pryce. N., Mundin, P., Nozes, J., Reinhardt, R., Richter, T., Silva, G., and Holmberg, C. (2011). *Beyond OER: Shifting Focus from Resources to Practices the OPAL Report* Available at: https://oerknowledge-cloud.org/?q=content/beyond-oer-shifting-focus-open-educational-practices.

Further information from:

"Open Education Quality Initiative—OPAL" Available at: www.icde.org/ICDE+to+play+key+role+in+Open+Educational+Quality+Initiative.9UFRzW5W.ips (accessed May 15, 2014).

And, as Luckin et al. write (and as was emphasized in the last chapter), this is not about the technology but about the interrelationships between learning and the possibilities offered by that technology:

> Our starting point is that digital technologies do offer opportunities for innovation that can transform teaching and learning, and that our challenge is to identify the shape that these innovations take. To aid us in this task, we have rejected the lure of categorising innovations by the type of technology employed. The only answer to questions such as "do games help learning?" is to say, "it depends." instead we argue that more progress comes from thinking about the types of learning activities that we know to be effective, such as practising key skills, and exploring the ways that technology can support and develop these effective learning activities in innovative ways [. . .].
>
> (2012: 8–9)

Like Scott-Webber's work, outlined in the previous chapter, Luckin et al. (2012) go on to offer a useful categorization of different kinds of learning practices that help us see how and where various technologies can support learning. Their report, entitled "Decoding Learning" (http://www.nesta.org.uk/sites/default/files/decoding_learning_report.pdf) is framed around learning from experts, with others, through making, through exploring, though inquiry, though practicing, from assessment, and finally by learning in and across settings. Here what is most important is to understand is first, why so many existing universities and colleges still seem unable to challenge the worst aspects of the 'cultural baggage' of higher education, with its limited assumptions that learning design should be undertaken on a case-by-case basis; second to really invest effectively and strategically in instructional design and development; or thirdly to properly engage with the potential impacts of new technologies on learning. Although this book has shown how much universities and colleges have moved on in responding to both internal and external pressures, I suggest that in these areas much still needs to change, a point that is returned to in the last chapter.

CONCLUSION

LEARNING IN A POST-UNIVERSITY WORLD?

In 1997, Peter Drucker had been confident that: "Thirty years from now the big university campuses will be relics. Universities won't survive. It's as large a change as when we first got the printed book."
—*Harrison and Hutton (2013)*

I started this book by suggesting that today's universities and colleges are facing many tensions—even contradictions—as ever-increasing and various demands are made on what higher education can and should achieve. I also proposed that debates about, and opportunities arising from, this complexification are being distorted in many ways; through the framing of dominant education discourses, because of the heavy weight of academic tradition and practice, through a continuing tendency to emulate elite universities, and because university and colleges are still failing to learn enough about themselves through appropriate kinds of evidence-based educational research.

Building Better Universities has therefore summarized a few of the new approaches and projects in contemporary higher education worldwide. It has not aimed to suggest solutions but to open up the questions we need to ask. Through a review of how current universities and college are responding 'on the ground' we can now reengage with the bigger questions of the *idea* of the university (Newman [1852] 2014; Oakeshott 1950; Barnett 2010, 2011) and what universities are *for* (Collini 2012). Most crucially, this means addressing how we can better conceptualize twenty-first-century higher education, the range and types of institutions that should be delivering it; what their teaching, learning, and research models should be; and how they can guarantee both resource effectiveness and added value to their learners.

There are, of course, already many proposals about what the university of the future might be like. Some suggest a shift in focus, for example, toward the 'ecological' as an institution "that takes seriously its relationships with the total environment and [. . .] does what it can to further the wellbeing of that total environment" (Barnett 2011: 5) or socially committed to "provide the structures for public debate between expert and lay cultures" (Delanty 2004: 252). Others suggest that it needs renaming, for instance, as a multiversity (Kerr [1963] 2001) or that we employ a term reflecting a 'subversive' strategy for working in and around the current swing toward corporatism and managerialism, by calling it a paraversity (Rolfe 2013). What happens, then, to the question of what a university is for and what it should be like in the future, when viewed through some of the actual strategies, spaces, and technologies currently being applied in real situations and contexts, as reviewed in this book? I suggest that this focuses us on some concrete questions such as

- What are the key contemporary issues for universities and colleges?
- What kinds of developments in response to these issues are required at the individual institutional level, across partnerships, and in terms of influencing debate and policy?
- What kinds of research and data do universities and colleges need to be gathering that can inform strategic decision making across educational and other goals, resource effectiveness, and impact?
- What will be the effects of contemporary issues on the range and type of institution offering higher education into the future?

Although some universities and colleges are already engaging with these questions through their educational and business models, I have been suggesting that many still tend to jump on the existing multitude of 'bandwagons'— adding online learning courses, or building an international campus or two, signing up to business partnerships, promising their students employability skills but ignoring or avoiding major underlying shifts. They are neither strategically rethinking their educational and business models, nor shifting their traditional approaches to, and methods for, learning, teaching, and critical inquiry. In the rest of this chapter I draw out what are, for me, the most important current considerations for universities and colleges in responding creatively and effectively to the increasing complexification of their aims and objectives. These are not the only conclusions that can be drawn from the preceding review—and different institutions and individuals may have other interpretations and focus on different concerns—but the eleven points outlined below aim to capture some key issues about where we are, across the contemporary higher education sector.

1. Beyond the Scarcity Model of Learning?

One of the central emerging themes of *Building Better Universities* has been the continuing social and economic divide between who is likely to study quality liberal arts or science education and who undertakes mass vocational training, now often online. Universities have historically developed an elite and scarcity model of higher education based on restricting entry to 'the brightest and the best.' This is being reinforced through the prevalence of both national and global ranking systems and by a continuing tendency among many higher education institutions to emulate the 'top' universities. But this approach, as Daniel notes, is both self-perpetuating and means that quality and reputation are decided at admissions –based on what learners bring with them- rather than on completion (with what has been added through their studies):

> Elite institutions, of course, usually define their quality by the numbers of applicants that they exclude, not by the teaching that happens on campus after admission. My late Athabasca University colleague Dan Coldeway called this the principle of 'good little piggies in, make good bacon out'. It is a venerable academic tradition but hardly seems fit for the 21st century, not least for institutions that have suddenly discovered a mission to open up to the world.
>
> (2012: 12–13)

xMOOCs, for example, have been developed within this tradition, by signaling quality through 'star performers' and the status and reputation of the institution, rather than through any evidence of effectiveness of teaching and learning on the courses themselves. But the scarcity model is being challenged from many places. This is because it fails to educate the whole population effectively (to support both the economy and wider societal and cultural aims) and because it tacitly accepts and reproduces social inequality. Much online education from for-profit providers is exploiting this 'gap' in the higher education market, whereas the open education movement and other public participatory organizations beyond the higher education sector are challenging its assumptions by aiming to open up learning to a much wider audience.

Daniel cites the UK Open University as a successful example that has long ignored the scarcity model of higher education. It has no academic admission requirements but "has awarded over a million highly regarded degrees to its students. Entry to the Open University is easy; exit with a degree is difficult" (2012: 12). Many case studies here have been about colleges and other organizations finding ways to improve their performance for the least advantaged in society. Examples such as Western Governors University that are centered on learning outcomes, enable students from all sorts of background to achieve mastery of a specific set of knowledge and skills by taking the time that it needs; and the University of the People is based on enabling a more open access to learning, by making higher education available free or at an affordable price for low income students across the world.

As Casey et al. write, there are now interesting contemporary tensions happening with the scarcity model everywhere, because elite universities such as Harvard and Massachusetts Institute of Technology (MIT) are now making their courses publicly available and other institutions are engaging with the open education agenda:

> The potential of open public spaces (both physical and online) to act as a conduit for social change are considerable [. . .]. Linking universities to such spaces [. . .] can be seen as both extending the reach of the traditional academy and at the same time subverting it and, potentially, reforming it. In the process, institutions that are so place-based as universities run the risk of exposing practices and values that make little sense to the outside world.
>
> (2011: 197–198)

But even though the scarcity model is being challenged, it remains powerful, particularly in the conventional public university and college sector. I already noted in the introduction that concepts of 'excellence,' of particular forms of data collection about 'success' and of assessing and ranking universities as total institutions—rather than say by subject—is part of the perpetuation of an elitist scarcity model of higher education at a time when many contemporary changes are pushing in a different direction. Particular ways of measuring performance can also reproduce this model—both by shaping what is framed as relevant in particular ways, and by making that shape become 'natural' and 'obvious':

> The rise of the measurement culture in education has had a profound impact on educational practice, from the highest levels of educational policy at national and supra-national level down to the practices of local schools and teachers. To some extent this impact has been beneficial as it has allowed for discussions to be based on factual data rather than just assumptions or opinions about what might be the case. The problem is, however, that the abundance of information about educational outcomes

has given the impression that decisions about the direction of educational policy and the shape and form of educational practice can be based solely upon factual information.

(Biesta 2007: 2)

As I have argued throughout this book, higher education has become so framed by international rankings, league tables and performance metrics that we can easily fail to see beyond this or to critique it. Yet producing factual data is not a substitute for decision making and—more crucially—does not help with essential *value* judgments about what higher education ought to be like or how to improve it. In fact, concepts such as 'excellence' (as discussed in the Introduction) or 'quality' have become ubiquitous precisely because they *appear* to express values. This means that explicit debate about what ought to be valued in higher education is overlooked or avoided, and that universities and colleges find themselves locked into a specific set of implied and constraining values. Biesta shows how this works:

> An example of this can be found in discussions about educational effectiveness. Apart from the fact that it is difficult to make a case for education that is not effective—which gives the idea of educational effectiveness a prima facie plausibility—'effectiveness' is actually a value. This seems to suggest that an argument for effective schooling or teacher effectiveness is exactly doing what I am suggesting we should do. The problem is, however, that effectiveness is an instrumental value, a value which says something about the quality of processes and, more specifically, about their ability to bring about certain outcomes in a secure way. But whether the outcomes themselves are desirable is an entirely different matter—a matter for which we need value-based judgments that are not informed by instrumental values but by what we might best call ultimate values: values about the aims and purposes of education.

(Biesta 2007: 35)

Concepts such as effective education, then, cannot be criticized—you could not possibly want the opposite—but do not actually tell us what makes for *good* education nor help us agree its purpose. As Biesta goes on, concepts such as this only make sense if we ask, "Effective for what?" and "Effective for whom?" Yet there remains a "remarkable absence in many contemporary discussions about education of explicit attention for what is educationally desirable. There is much discussion about educational processes and their improvement but very little about what such processes are supposed to bring about" (Biesta 2007: 3).

What then, are these assumed values that have become hidden behind a particular type of measurement culture? How can we open up for more explicit debate questions of what constitutes academic knowledge; about the relative importance of science, technology, engineering, and mathematics or traditional liberal arts; about educational quality and ranking being only about 'brightest and the best'? To what extent are these versions, explicitly argued for, and defended against, of higher education, rather than just oft-repeated clichés? How are such assumptions, and the language in which education is now couched, framing one way of thinking, doing, and reasoning rather than others? These are the sorts of questions university managers and academics ought to be asking if we are to break free from both the scarcity model of education.

However, this is not about doing away with measurement. It is about what and how we measure. What, would higher education look like for example, if it judged academic, vocational, and professional success more explicitly as enabling achievement (e.g., in relation to defined graduate attributes or of what constitutes university-level critical inquiry) rather than through simply getting a degree from a 'good' university? Barber et al. suggest that universities themselves could choose to develop a different system of rankings, which puts greater weight on outputs and outcomes and less on inputs (2012: 62). The work done through the ESRC-funded project Pedagogic Quality and Inequality in University First Degrees (Ashwin et al. 2012), summarized in the Introduction, offers one example of how universities could go about this.

Challenging the dominance within universities and colleges of an elite model of provision and a seriously flawed measurement culture is about more than merely wanting to widen access to existing definitions of 'good' education. It is about more than seeing online learning as a solution to the serious gap between the high quality assumed in elite institutions and the 'inevitably' reduced quality of massification of higher learning (whether online or on campus). Rather, it is about the *purpose* of universities and colleges, in both improving individual employment and career prospects across society, and in supporting wider societal, cultural, and economic goals.

Newman et al. (2004) for example, have suggested that universities should meet (and be audited against) the following individual *and* societal needs:

- academic success for an ever expanding share of the population;
- university responsibility for efficient use of resources;
- university recognition that teaching and learning matter;
- preserving scholarship integrity;
- preparing students for tomorrow's democracy;
- deepening outreach and service.

(quoted in Brown, n.d.: 1–2)

It is a very real question for today's publicly oriented universities and colleges as to whether these kinds of goals are getting lost in complexification, in the scramble to meet external pressures, and because of an inability to resolve internal dilemmas. Throughout this book I have suggested that social responsiveness and concern for the public good is, or should be, a key goal of universities and colleges, particularly in clarifying their differences from some for-profit providers, who explicitly do not engage in these wider aims. But this kind of commitment remains uncertain:

> Although there appears to be a normative consensus around the importance of the social responsiveness of higher education and for the idea that HEIs should engage with their publics, there are different understandings and approaches to what this means by way of concrete interventions, strategies and indicators of achievement, and the nature of the social partnerships and networks which reflect this focus.
>
> (Singh and Little 2011: 42)

For individual public institutions, this means a more explicit priority setting across its noneconomic and profitable forms of public engagement, including broadening educational opportunities both within and beyond the campus walls. To reiterate—the problem is not in fact the differences between for-profit 'low quality' providers and 'high-quality' nonprofit providers but between better and worse education across the whole sector (see also Siemens 2013a). As online private providers develop and as technologies become increasingly supportive (e.g., for tutoring via streaming media, with interactive hardware), *all* educational institutions will have to address how to provide valuable and relevant learning to large numbers of people effectively. In this context, I am suggesting that public universities and colleges in particular need to be explicitly arguing for the added value of social engagement. They need to build it into their activities across all levels (such as the University of Northampton, UK, has with social enterprise); to find ways to cost/co-fund/cross-subsidize where necessary; to develop metrics that can properly measure educational and social impact; and to raise the level of public and political debate around these issues.

2. Alternatives to Increased Segmentation and Differentiation

If the three main roles of the university can be outlined as learning and credentialing, research and development, and general business services that support learning and research (Sheets et al. 2012) then how can the increasing complexification—and associated tensions and potential contradictions—be dealt with? Rubin (2013) outlines the value propositions contained within these three roles for the traditional, nonprofit university (Figure 7.1). This

Core Business	Existing Value Proposition
Learning and teaching	Support transition into adulthood
	Improve individual employability and career prospects
	Develop specialist subject knowledge and skills
	Develop individual ability as learner and scholar
	Develop citizenship
Research	Create new knowledge that benefits society
	Create new disciplinary knowledge
	Produce new scholars
	Support individual business development and economic growth
Service	Enable community engagement
	Support community-based activities
	Widen access to learning and scholarship

Figure 7.1 Value propositions of traditional nonprofit universities
Source: Adapted from Rubin (2013).

shows that they have far more value propositions than do most business organizations. Despite this, Rubin is clear that, although priorities differ across different universities and colleges, there remains, in general, a commitment to all these areas of operation.

In addition, although with some variations depending on the affect of the new managerialism on particular institutions, decision making in the public universities and colleges remains relatively flat, consensus based, and with day-to-day practices not formally documented. The response from the market to this unwieldy and resource-ineffective complexity is clear: focus on core business, with a one or two value propositions, then outsource or cut non-core activities. Again, Rubin (2013) gives a precise summary of how for-profit education providers work:

> For-profit universities and colleges focus on providing the first two value propositions: developing skills efficiently and obtaining a degree for career mobility. This is particularly true for those using online learning,

and the narrow focus allows very tight standardization of procedures and a mass-production design, which increases efficiency. The business model is value-added (Christensen et al., 2011), and the organization is highly specialized, with work broken up into discrete units that can be done consistently and routinely. Decision-making is centralized at the top and decisions are implemented through middle-management.

As I have shown in earlier chapters of this book, the for-profits aim to increase profit margins by limiting their value propositions and are happy to compete against universities and colleges still attempting a more comprehensive model. They do this through scaling-up, by reducing noncore costs through not undertaking supporting research or other nonlearning activities, and by standardizing procedures, both for faculty and for students. Although this enables consistency of experience (often an ignored problem inherent in traditional universities 'cottage industry' tradition, which is discussed later in this chapter) it does not value learning as an expansive or questioning process, or research as important for societal knowledge, entrepreneurship, and culture. It is an approach that also tends not to meet Rubin's third and fourth teaching value propositions: the development of independence in young adults and the development of cognitive skills that are difficult to master such as critical thinking, writing and ethical decision making. It puts little emphasis on the whole student experience, that is, the social, cultural, and citizenship activities embedded in most traditional universities, or the potential value in integrating learning into a research-based knowledge creation environment.

Still, the advice from the market is to focus the value proposition, for example, by unbundling learning from research, or by limiting the amount of research and/or other activities; to standardize educational and management systems; and to scale up teaching and learning delivery through repetition and replication. However, many of the examples in this book instead offer alternative ways of incorporating a range of value propositions, or parts of them. These, I would argue, challenge current assumptions of a developing bifurcation between high-ranking and 'mediocre' institutions, between research and teaching, or between liberal arts and vocational training, that is, a predicted higher education future in which universities and colleges are *either* elite, academic, and research-intensive institutions *or* mass, training, and teaching-intensive institutions. For me, it is especially the integration of research and learning that is central to the university as a key site of knowledge creation and critical inquiry. Part of the problem lies in how higher education itself continues to be unclear about the relationships of research to teaching and learning processes. I have written elsewhere that what is centrally distinctive about higher education is that it simultaneously needs to 'reproduce' itself (as a center of learning, teaching, and research) and to educate its students for life outside the academy:

> This, of course, is part of the inherent tensions in higher education which separate it from education at primary and secondary levels; it brings learning as a means to develop expertise in a subject discipline which will be used outside the academy together with learning as a means to enable the growth and change of the academy-as-a-centre-of-knowledge itself. Teachers, tutor-practitioners, researchers, research students, teaching assistants, educational development workers and students are all engaged to varying degrees not only in their subject area, but also in the post-compulsory educational community of practice which has historically had knowledge creation and development at its core.
>
> (Boys 2010: 70)

The neoliberal emphasis on externally facing and applied research continues to marginalize knowledge production and development more generally, and to underplay the sense of universities and colleges as a community of practice (Lave and Wenger 1991; Wenger 1998) where students are not just learning their subject, or enhancing their employability, but also co-engaging in knowledge sharing, contestation and improvement. The example of the Student as Producer from the University of Lincoln (Chapter 1) is just one way that universities and colleges can refuse to separate out learning from research, and highlight the value and importance of the academy.

3. Leveraging Learning

It should be clear in reading this book, that the model of a single form of university and college learning, linearly developing through a structured three- or four-year undergraduate, one- to two-year postgraduate, and then PhD process (and where access to this learning is bounded to a particular place and by a set of entry requirements) does not meet the myriad needs of many learners across the different stages of their lives. Competence-based learning models already start from a critique of achievement as the 'clocking up' of a certain number of credit hours at different levels, rather than a flexible student-centered pattern. In theory, universities could develop learning and teaching resources and delivery methods that enabled a multitude of entry points, reasons for study, length and type of study and differential exit points. Continuing Professional Development (CPD) units of study could be one unit of study in a master's courses, or adult education learners (e.g., who do not want accreditation) could do elements of a degree together with its undergraduate students. Some of the examples here (such as OERu) both acknowledge that learners want different levels of engagement with their studies and offer differential fees to match, based on the same learning resources. This could increase resource effectiveness, offer a diversity of types of participation, and enrich the student experience. What would a university look like that integrated a 'School of Life' (Chapter 1) or a expanded version of the Danish university extension system (Chapter 2) within its conventional degree structures, offering a variety of levels of engagement (attendance, tutoring, and/ or course-work assessment) and accreditation? Online micro-payment systems make it simple to offer differential pricing for various levels of service. Could universities build in peer exchange, skills swapping, volunteering, and so on as embedded elements in a program? Baltic 39 at Northumbria University, UK, already does this, albeit on a very small scale (Chapter 2), as do many educational institutions that support community-based volunteering as credit-bearing activities. What might happen if this was also connected to differential pricing and variations in badging, which would enable students to make real choices about payment—through labor, time, and/or money; about what constitutes added value; and about how much it does or does not link to formal accreditation for their own career and personal development?

What is preventing these kinds of development? At a practical level existing university structures—in the UK at least—separate out research, educational, and 'third-stream' revenues and cost, pricing, and accounting processes, and therefore struggle to operate seamlessly across hybrid initiatives. This self-perpetuating division prevents learning being leveraged for greater effect across a multitude of possible services. In addition, the lack of standardization and explicit course design that can differentiate across levels of study (access, beginners, intermediate, advanced, professional) or that recognizes and integrates learner diversity (international student, placement, retired, specialist) into teaching methods mean that most courses are currently not well framed for multiple access learning. This is also true across many open education offerings as well as MOOCs; because entry is based on student choice alone, the suitability of the learning materials to individual level and interest is poorly articulated and so does not help potential students make informed choices.

It should also be noted that these kinds of hybridized learning opportunities go in a different direction too much of the current literature based on improving marketization, by potentially adding complexity rather than simplification. It is likely that more the effective leveraging of learning as a core business would require that a university or college simplify, reduce, or forego other aspects of contemporary higher education 'mission statement' lists.

4. Rethinking Credentialing

The issue of a range of forms of accreditation, beyond the university degree certificate, and of how different types of achievement might be recognized and validated, has been a recurrent theme in this book. Universities and colleges often provide intermediate credentialing for students who complete part of a course, but—in my experience—this is seen by students and staff alike as a failure rather than as an achievement. Historically, universities and colleges have used their accreditation powers as a unique selling point (USP), enabling collaborations with international higher education providers, by providing the status and reputation of a specific university 'brand.' But institutions could also learn from some of the educational providers, outlined in Chapter 1, who are focused much more on the learning experience and achievement than on it's credentialing. On one hand, this is by emphasizing the status and reputation of the provider (i.e., building on traditional ranking methods but not bothering with formal certification); on the other hand, it is by enabling a community of learners to engage with affordable and effective studies that suit their needs, so that a formal award becomes unimportant. This can be seen both in the alternative arts schools outlined in Chapter 1 and in some MOOCs. Although there are examples here, particularly those offering online learning internationally, that have made accreditation an important part of their offer, the massively expanding variety of learning opportunities—online, face-to-face, and blended—suggests that degree credentialing alone will no longer have such a hold. This, in turn, means that the moves toward open badging systems (that can be properly checked and communicated), such as that being developed by Mozilla, are likely to have a much bigger impact in the future.

5. Unbundling the Academic Role

Perhaps the biggest potential shift implied by both for-profit educational models and MOOCs is in finally and decisively unbundling what an academic does. A typical academic in a university or college combines, in some variation, the roles of knowledge producer, course designer, tutor, mentor, and assessor, as well as a responsibility for maintaining accreditation standards. Each of these roles is subject to personal capabilities and preferences, tradition and practice, institutional dynamics, and external pressures. The production and dissemination of knowledge through scholarly inquiry has in the UK, for example, had demands made on it to be relevant to the economy and employability, to generate income for the university, and to have recognizable impact on society. Increased external auditing of educational standards has demanded more bureaucracy and explicit paper trails. Meanwhile, pedagogic theory has been arguing for a shift away from the dissemination of knowledge to interactive learning and from subject expert to facilitator, and new technologies are increasing the range and type of media through which learning can take place.

It is in this context that faculty are often seen as 'resisting change' by not adapting flexibly to these new framings. It is certainly true that both the history of university faculty as subject specialists (rather than, say, trained teachers or researchers) and an associated tradition of academic freedom has led to what Johnstone (2002) calls a 'cottage industry' of course design and tutoring and a tendency for silos between subjects and between academics and student support services. Rubin (2013) usefully summarizes this typical academic culture of universities:

> In strongly decentralized universities, programs and courses are added based on faculty preference, whether individually or by committees; student demand may or may not be considered. [. . .] each course is designed independently and generally idiosyncratically, with few standards or rules, although in some cases core required courses are standardized in terms of textbooks and syllabi, and occasionally use a common final examination. All aspects of the courses are the intellectual property of the faculty member. In order to support this, graduate teaching assistants and adjunct faculty are used to reduce expenses and provide faculty time to conduct research and engage in collegial decision-making about all academic aspects of the institution.

In fact, it is exactly this blurring of both the complexities of what academics do across their different roles and the amorphousness of their 'autonomy' that makes such resistance more understandable. This is particularly in a context for many faculty worldwide, where research is taking precedence over teaching, making the *educational* aspect of many higher educational institutions increasingly marginalized. Thus, thinking about a positive unbundling of the academic role has two components—what might be separated out and undertaken by different kinds of specialists, and what additional 'space' needs to be opened up for a rebundled academic role to be undertaken more effectively.

In *Building Better Universities* I have shown that the kind of scaling-up models that private online universities and MOOCs offer (as well as projects like the Open Learning Initiative) are challenging higher education's conventional mode of case-by-case course creation as never before. Massification of learning, in whatever form, necessarily means an explicit consideration of how (and by whom) resources are developed, and how these are delivered and supported. The business model of the for-profit educational sector has long separated out learning materials development and its delivery:

> [For-profit higher education] entrants generate course material in three primary ways. First, they can hire their own staffs to develop new materials. Second, they can license existing courses from colleges and universities. Third, they can contract directly with individual faculty or other

experts for material and courses, similar to a traditional book publishing arrangement. [. . .]

The data suggest that entrants are keeping their sourcing options open. Indeed, several major players appear to be pursuing all three options. While deals at the university level are attractive, thus far they have been quite expensive; the long-term trend will probably be for entrants to source material directly from faculty.

(Collis 2002: 13)

Pearson Education, for example, invite educators to put proposals forward for eLearning development and products, in much the same way they would previously have written a book proposal (http://catalogue.pearsoned.co.uk/educator/beawriter/index.page).

Interestingly, it is perhaps the very invisibility of their role as course designers that has made the current generation of university and college faculty less entrepreneurial in selling their expertise (and its associated IPR) to the private sector. Or it may be that most academics currently do not yet have either the appropriate technical skills or the pedagogic design skills:

Most academics are not using new technologies for learning and teaching, nor for organizing their own research. Many researchers have not had training in basic digitally supported teaching techniques, and most do not participate in the sorts of professional development opportunities that would provide them. This is due to several factors, including a lack of time and a lack of expectations that they should. Many think a cultural shift will be required before we see widespread use of more innovative organizational technology.

(Johnson et al 2012: 10)

This is also linked to institutional inertia with its continuing lack of strategic integration of online and blended learning, little understanding of the amount and type of specialist instructional design skills required, or the up-front effort and costs of course content development when it does not rely on a case-by-case and 'just-in-time' approach. Learning materials development using new technologies is still not always part of universities' recognition and rewards systems (such as in promotion and tenure reviews); and experimentation or innovative applications of technologies tend to be marginalized in many higher education institutions and are thus mainly undertaken on a voluntary basis by individual enthusiasts:

If you are just doing what we usually do in higher education, running the technology project like a cottage industry with a single faculty member serving a group of students, it doesn't work too well in terms of ultimate cost. You also tend to burn out the faculty member. [. . .]

How do we sort through institutional models that can support the roles of individuals to make the use of these technologies feasible? The structure we have now really just doesn't work. We need to shift traditional faculty roles. We need to create additional definitions for professionals working within higher education on the teaching and learning process. We also need to balance what that means in terms of status and costs to the institution that is supporting them.

(Johnson 2002: 17–20)

Worryingly, although these concerns for higher educational institutional commitment to online and blending learning have been voiced for many years, developments remains uneven. Digital resources such as online lectures, guides and website references may now be standard practice (White and Manton 2011), but effective seamless integration between virtual and physical learning remains elusive. Even with the advent of MOOCs we do not yet have anything like a post-cottage-industry form of educational design and delivery or resource-effective scaling-up, large-scale sharing, and the reuse of materials.

How, then, can this be changed? This is, first, about the kinds of roles outlined earlier (trained teachers, student advisors, course design developers, educational researchers, instructional designers, and researcher-teachers) all of which need to be better articulated. Second, it is about improving learning and teaching methods and modes of delivery more generally. If we are to properly embed the kinds of open educational practices (OEP) outlined in Chapter 6, and an academic culture of sharing and reusing resources, then we need to build this into continuing professional development for academics. This would also include explicit debate about the changing forms of pedagogy being offered, both in better understanding different types of educational activities (as outlined in this book in the work of Scott-Webber [2004] and Luckin et al. [2012]) and by exploring contemporary ideas about teaching, such as those suggested by Siemens, Downes, and others, around curation and 'connectivism' (Chapter 6).

Here the key point is that a new structure of recognition, rewards, and career paths available to academics needs to be formalized and properly supported in ways that do not just take into account parallel but differential roles but also the widening array of forms of digital scholarship and of teaching and learning opportunities through which those roles are undertaken.

6. Biting the Scaling-Up Bullet

The biggest strategic challenge for most English-speaking universities is probably in moving beyond the craft and 'cottage industry' approach to learning and teaching—not just unbundling the academic role but also integrating it within more strategic educational development. This is not because the conventional lecture–seminar–course work model is wrong (although many educationalists would argue that it is not the best or only way for teaching and learning) but that it does not scale up effectively. Existing course design practices also result in an unevenness of educational experience for students:

> There are advantages and disadvantages to this [cottage industry] approach. The outcomes are highly variable; some courses are brilliantly designed and taught, and others not. Some faculty will prepare their courses carefully, while others will still be designing—or redesigning—them throughout the course, causing confusion. [. . .]
>
> Courses can be customized to meet different learning goals, with a range of activities from debates to case analyses, negotiations to building and taking intelligence tests. Variety in pedagogy and design can heighten students' interest. However, such an approach requires intensive training in course design as well as technology; support from an instructional designer; and a high degree of commitment on the part of the faculty. And, of course, the individualized approach is extremely expensive.
>
> (Rubin 2013)

As Rubin says, to improve course design and delivery demands the investment of time, resources and relevant expertise—a process that this book has already shown is happening in community colleges, but much less so in the traditional, nonprofit universities. This is because it challenges the autonomous and individualized pattern of much program design and teaching. Once learning materials are no longer developed on a case-by-case basis, their creation requires collaboration, research and development, and planning. And, for this to be cost effective, it also demands a scaling-up, whether within an institution by increasing entry figures; by extending the number of learners studying a particular unit beyond the institution (e.g., through online learning or international franchising), or by collaboration across subject specialists, and/or institutions teaching core courses based on the same resources (as the FemTechNet DOOC does). This scaling-up, however, is about much more than resource effectiveness and profit margins. The Carnegie Mellon Open Learning Initiative (OLI) and the William and Flora Hewlett Foundation OER projects, outlined here, are just two examples which show how the professional and collaborative design of learning materials (whether face-to-face, online, or blended) can improve effectiveness of learning, patterns of retention and achievement, and can widen educational participation across the world.

Although I have suggested that public universities need to examine how to have an integrated research–teaching–learning process as a core value proposition, I also believe—from the evidence gathered in *Building Better Universities*—that we need to *separate* out course design from its delivery, and develop effective and relevant scaling-up mechanisms. As already mentioned, these kinds of divisions are not new, as with various open universities across the world and with many of the online private providers also working in this way. The OLI proposes a mapping of the different roles and processes (Chapter 6) and in another version of such a model Rubin (2013) argues for four separate roles—or specialisms—for educators: instructors (who are trained in teaching and learning), student advisors (who support students across all needs), academic course designers, and instructional designers (who enable the creation and management of learning resources). There are already specialist instructional designers and learning technologists in universities, but this usually remains an often-marginalized and under-resourced activity. Such a model would also require a fuller integration of student support staff into course teams.

Materials and course development is then planned over time, rather than as a 'just-in-time' process, and is orchestrated through university guidelines, auditing, and process improvement processes. The look and feel of resources becomes standardized and repeatable, as are course delivery methods. Courses can now be delivered on a rolling cycle, with frequent starts, and in a variety of modes. Scaling-up does demand more standardization, of a kind that many academics continue to resist; but this in turn can support better, more-thought-through course design and delivery that has consistency, robustness, and sustainability (and where effectiveness can be tracked through learning analytics so as to inform an ongoing process of improvement).

A final point: scaling-up does not need to mean that all higher education degree courses somehow become the same. By forcing a clarity as to what are the foundational and essential attributes for any graduate of a particular discipline or area of study, and what is distinctive and special about what specific programs offer (and the university or college that is supplying the service) scaling-up can communicate much more precisely the different kinds of added value embedded in learning between educational institutions.

7. Improving Resource Transparency and Effectiveness

The dominance of neoliberal values across the English-speaking world has focused debate, policies, strategies, and initiatives on higher education as a personal good, undertaken primarily through self-interest and that should be bought and sold in a competitive free market, to enable both individual employability and societal economies. As many authors have noted, much of higher education in the Western world is actually a quasi-market (Collini 2013; McGettigan 2013; Marginson 2013) where tensions between the desires of governments to control and regulate universities and colleges for a variety of reasons is at odds with a attempts to construct a free market, for example through the removal of any kind of public subsidy. In the UK context, for instance, if governments reduce their funding to higher education institutions, then they may no longer have real leverage if those providers choose to ignore advice. Similarly, as private universities are increasingly accessing the public purse (through taxpayer-underwritten student loans), then their relative lack of current regulation needs reviewing.

There has also been much debate about whether learning in its widest sense can be properly expressed through free market mechanisms (Robinson 2011; Sandel 2012). Many of the examples here have suggested other forms of exchange beyond the market, both through some kind of central planning (as in the very different regulatory frameworks of China, Singapore, and Denmark) or through variations of reciprocity, as in open education, crowd-sharing, skill-swapping, and co-creation. There are already well-tested social enterprise models that offer more hybrid goals across both individual and social gains, and that mix for-profit activities with free exchange mechanisms.

To reiterate what I outlined at the beginning of this book, for universities and colleges in the twenty-first century, the divide is not—as it often appears in debate—between being driven by the profit motive and the market versus insisting on academic freedom and learning 'for its own sake.' Rather, it concerns the development and proper implementation of explicit, transparent, and sophisticated costing models that can simultaneously deal with the conventional cost–benefits analysis of strategies and initiatives and with appropriate metrics for non-financial relationships. Importantly, these kind of models need to be discursive—with figures that help clarify the implications of particular actions, not as a 'answer' but as a means to inform debate over priority setting (Shapiro and Schroeder 2008):

> Simply allowing market demands to determine who gets what, however, will not work [. . .]. There clearly needs to be a greater reliance upon market-related factors, but these factors need to be filtered and structured through a governing set of educational principles and goals, which in turn need to be subject to constant review.
>
> (Smith 2004: 75)

The continuing lack of effective pricing and costing models to inform decision making for higher education has been covered elsewhere (Johnstone and Marcucci 2010; McGettigan 2013), suggesting a need for more research into barriers and drivers, as well as into alternatives that avoid both the oversimplifications of cost–benefit analysis (Ackerman 2008) and can critically analyze the current quasi-markets that many universities and colleges find themselves in. This, in turn, needs to inform policy and public debates about pricing and affordability for potential students and about who pays for higher education and through what mechanisms. Worryingly, many universities and colleges are a long way off from more-sophisticated resource planning:

> Current financial systems are designed to ensure that funds provided to a university for a specific purpose are used for that purpose, not to provide accountability for performance. As a result, there are few useful ways to acquire information about the cost effectiveness of various activities. This separation of performance-related information from financial data prevents a clear understanding of the relationship between the income, expenses, and results associated with the production of teaching, research, or other university undertakings. [. . .]
>
> The academic side expends the vast majority of the money in higher education institutions (on average 70 percent in research universities, according to IPEDS). Without dividing the academic side into its units (colleges and departments), its functions (teaching, research, service), and its sources of revenues (state appropriations, tuition, contracts and grants, and gifts), no one can properly manage an institution or understand its true productivity.
>
> (Capaldi and Abbey 2011)

Without transparency or the ability to assess the relative costs and benefits of different strategies—preferably in ways that can engage all staff including academics in resource-effective decision making—universities and colleges will continue to be at a disadvantage compared to for-profit operators.

8. Investing in Learning Literacy

As student numbers increase (often combined with a decreasing level of resource) we can no longer assume that students come already with the learning literacy appropriate for higher education. The traditional university may have relied on selection and entry restriction to bring in students who already had the knowledge and skills required for study at an advanced level; but these skills now need to be explicitly taught, along with a clearer introduction to the 'rules of the game' of what being a university or college student involves. Pre-access, access, and foundation programs already recognize this, as do the English language and academic skills development for international students, now frequently outsourced by universities to for-profit providers.

Without a doubt, most incoming students would benefit from a more explicit introduction to what being an undergraduate (or postgraduate or PhD) student means, particularly as a higher proportion of their work is self- and

Figure 7.2 Vitae, services for researchers
Source: www.vitae.ac.uk/doing-research.

peer-directed rather than formally taught. The increasing number and quality of informal learning spaces that cater for these activities (as discussed in Chapter 4) illustrates the associated importance of helping students to use these spaces effectively (as well as evaluating and improving the number and types of such spaces provided). As noted in Chapter 2, the organization Vitae already offer this kind of support to research students. This is provided as an outsourced service available to universities, in this case through an international program led and managed by the Careers Research and Advisory Centre (CRAC), a not-for-profit registered UK charity dedicated to active career learning and development and funded by the UK Research Councils (Figure 7.2). Yet how we learn to 'be a student' mainly remains left up to individual faculty or a course team. Building in relevant learning skills–related OER would be an effective way of filling this gap (or, rather, supplying a more consistent whole-university approach) and is likely to improve retention and achievement rates (as evidenced by the Higher Education Academy's "What Works" project outlined in Chapter 2).

However, some of the cases cited here suggest that this is not enough. Educators such as George Siemens and groups such as the Singularity University and the University of the Third Horizon argue that higher education should no longer be so much about understanding a specialist subject as about developing the underlying capacities to engage effectively and creatively with a complex and uncertain world across multiple subjects. This understanding concerns the core activities of higher education, what it is that students should be learning and how they can do that most effectively. Discussions about curation and connectivism as pedagogic approaches and varying views on what might constitute graduate attributes are not just for educational 'specialists' but need to inform curriculum development at the highest levels. We need to ask explicitly just what are the key competencies that all students need to have developed during their university education, and how are these similar or different across disciplines? This should be a matter of positive contestation, not a reliance on current fads.

The other crucial aspect of competencies highlighted in this book is digital literacy for both students and faculty. This is central, not because the internet has become ubiquitous, but because it brings to the table a massive over-abundance of knowledge and information and—increasingly—informal learning resources and supporting infrastructures. As I have shown, this incredibly creative explosion has been happening mainly *outside* the conventional university, which can be seen to be lagging painfully behind in terms of technological understanding. Whether through online learning and skills-swapping spaces, such as Horsesmouth or LiveMocha (Chapter 5), or privately developed online learning support, such as the Khan Academy (Chapter 2), much of this web-based innovation only highlights the digital and creative gulf between such developments and the knowledge and interest of many academics, university managers, and higher education institutions. This is exacerbated by the fast-moving take-up of new *educational* technologies across the commercial world, not just as an 'addition' to business as usual but as completely embedded within a value proposition as well. A company such as CISCO not only undertakes its own educational development and delivery, but incorporates a digital knowledge repository into everyday business life, both giving its employees access to the latest intelligence and expecting that they engage with, and add resources, as part of an ongoing on-the-job learning process. The Muse (www.themuse.com) seamlessly brings together job searching with careers advice and online training courses. Qstream is a mobile apps for sales forces (which was developed at Harvard) that combines reporting and analytics into real-time intelligence for employees, and training and testing—using "simple, scenario-based questions challenge users and keep their knowledge sharp. Built-in game mechanics drive user engagement and keep them coming back for more" (http://qstream.com/how-it-works/). By the time this book is published, all of these will have been superseded by other creative, educational, online innovations. Meanwhile, many mid-range universities will still be arguing over how to persuade faculty to teach in other ways beyond the lecture and seminar and will be trying to increase use of their firewall-protected virtual learning systems.

This is because in higher education generally there are few procedures for ongoing CPD updating about the educational implications as web technologies improve and change; nor enough analysis of the kinds of competitors being enabled by the web. What is more, there remains little understanding—particularly at senior management level—of how new information and communication technologies have the potential to both revitalize and shift traditional educational models and academic roles. Whether by accessing a richer range of resources (in a multitude of formats), by exploiting the values of blended learning, or by flipping the classroom, a hybrid pedagogic understanding across material and virtual spaces is becoming increasingly essential to all levels of academic work.

However, this is not about a simplistic (and false) divide between digital natives and their predecessors (Jones and Shao 2011). Many students also come with relatively limited digital skills, and, as shown in Chapter 5, digital literacy is about much more than just having the technical understanding of basic hardware, software, and networks. It is now a central educational requirement of universities that they enable competencies in engaging effectively with the digital world. This demands an improvement both in their own digital literacy as organizations and in its more explicit and effective teaching and learning. As with moving toward a scaling-up and leveraging of learning, there remains a serious lack of investment of either time or resources across the nonprofit educational sector in this issue.

9. Learning as Coproduction

This book has deliberately emphasized examples from open education, crowdsourcing and sharing, skills exchange, and maker culture, both because these areas are growing so rapidly in the current period, and as a means of exploring educational models that work beyond the market, particularly by building on reciprocity rather than financial and contractual exchange. This also raises wider issues about relationships between students and educators. As already mentioned, at the University of Lincoln for instance, higher education can be framed around an idea of the student as producer, as a colleague in knowledge development and a member of a learning community of practice (Lave and Wenger 1991; Wenger 1998). This notion is also central to much open education and to the co-design processes increasingly used in public participation. It deliberately aims to challenge the assumption that students have become merely consumers of higher education, instrumentally focused on their career and earnings prospects. Other universities bring students together beyond their specific courses as part of developing creative and engaged citizens (Chapter 1). Envisaging learners as coproducers of knowledge at a series of levels (where responsibility is increasingly passed to the student) has in fact been inherent in a traditional model of university and college life in which learning and research are integrated. The articulation of an explicit educational model here by the public universities and colleges would (as noted earlier) be an important step forward in engaging with the best of open education movement's approaches.

10. Enabling Global Citizenship

As outlined in Chapter 3, almost all Western universities have been expanding their global dimension, both through taking on international students and by opening campuses in other countries. More recently, non-Western countries and educational sectors have been examining how they too might expand their offer globally and attract foreign students. For many this is a mainly economic decision; as already noted, in UK universities, international students have been subsidizing home students for years. But I have also suggested that internationalization has not included enough of a critical review of educational and cultural differences, nor has it made sure that international students have equivalent learning experiences and opportunities to their local peers (in many UK universities, for example, international students tend to get lower degree awards overall). The case study outlines in this book offer some directions. Some see educational internationalization as a central means to make improvements to aspects of the world's problems. Others find opportunities for enabling students to improve their critical thinking abilities as they find out about different perspectives from across the world and negotiate complex and difficult relationships and situations. There have also been projects to investigate how an idea of global citizenship should affect the higher education curriculum and much other research and publication in this area (Shiel and McKenzie 2008; Caruana 2010; Kennedy et al. 2014). Again, the concern is the extent to which this work is deeply informing institutional strategies and developments, beyond just adding 'global citizenship' as yet another clichéd concept in higher education's mission statements.

11. Embedding Educational Research

Finally, we need to ask what kinds of research and data universities and colleges need to be doing to inform their own activities. There have been two main types of research highlighted in this book. First, we need more evidence-based research that can properly underpin university strategy development and decision making. Second, we need to support and enhance research into learning and teaching, the impacts of new technologies and different kinds of learning spaces on pedagogy. Although this latter exists, it continues to be undervalued compared to subject-based research and is rarely embedded into higher education institutions as a means of finding out more about themselves.

Redesigning the Plane While Flying It

> Whom is higher education meant to serve—individual students, poten-
> tial employers, the state, humanity, or some other entity? Is education
> meant to be primarily a personal experience, an economic apprenticeship,
> civic training or moral enlightenment? To what extent is higher education
> meant to preserve and sustain the received wisdom and knowledge of the
> past, and to what extent is it responsible for generating new knowledge?
>
> —Smith (2004: 70)

In 2010 Graham Leicester of the International Futures Forum (IFF) gave a
conference talk entitled "Redesigning the Plane whilst Flying It":

> [T]he talk was surprising [because of] the severe doubts Leicester
> expressed about the capacity of today's educational institutions to meet
> the needs of tomorrow on its current path and without a new round of
> game changing innovations so radical as to substantially alter the educa-
> tional institutions we work in today. [. . .]
>
> The task ahead is not only to redesign the plane but to steer it in a
> new direction that we cannot—and may never—clearly see. Instead of a
> strategy of clearly identifying desired goals, measuring the gap between
> the ideal state and the present reality and defining the success path to
> close the gap—a logic that has been at the core of Western industrial
> thought for centuries—an uncertain future requires a different more cre-
> ative stance.
>
> (O'Hara, n.d.: 2)

Ultimately in *Building Better Universities*, I am suggesting that universities
and colleges can find ways to challenge a neo-liberalist agenda that seems to
want to perpetuate and even increase the bifurcation of higher education into
elite, well-funded, research-intensive institutions, on one hand, and mass-pro-
duction-style, cost-cutting teaching 'mills' on the other. To do this, however—'to
redesign the plane'—the middle ground of HEIs in particular needs to shift
its aims away from emulating the elite (e.g., through increasing entry standards, or 'promoting' themselves—meaninglessly—as 'academically excellent')
or relying on simplistic clichés around globalization or the knowledge economy.
Instead, universities and colleges that are concerned with defending the public
purpose of higher education need to go back to first principles, to critically
address what they currently do and to envisage what a socially responsive, publicly engaged university should look like. This would involve thinking creatively,
cost-effectively, and transparently about what to provide and how; and then
implementing the necessary unbundling and rebundling of existing services. It

would include developing and promoting alternative metrics to existing ranking and student satisfaction league tables, that can explicitly argue (and support with evidence) other ways to describe the effectiveness of teaching and learning in higher education. And this would need to happen at individual institutional level, across partnerships, and more widely to influence debate and policy.

The big questions are whether contemporary public universities can change enough, whether they can cut through accumulated tradition and practice and clarify their aims beyond all-purpose, overly complex, and mainly vague mission statements (Pinheiro et al. 2012); implementing instead more explicit, focused, value-adding, and resource-effective educational models. These questions also imply further questions—what would such a higher education landscape look like more generally, and what does it mean about future changes to our traditional ideas of the university? This book has argued that we can go beyond the current dominant binary discourse in higher education and develop other possible—creative and socially purposeful—variations on what a university can be like, of which many of the examples here have give some sense of possible directions. But it is also true that many universities and colleges may well be stuck in what has been called the second horizon (Figure 7.3). In the three-horizon model, the first level is business as usual (leading to stagnation and decline), the second involves some positive initiatives and innovations, and the third is reached through the development of a new paradigm. Being in

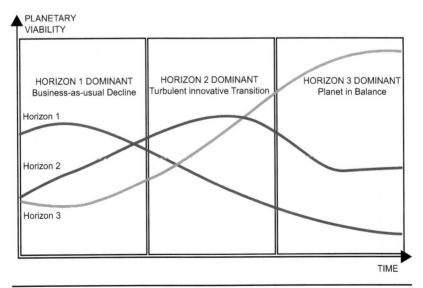

Figure 7.3 University of the Third Horizon (H3Uni) Three Horizons Model

Source: http://h3uni.net/h3uni/context/. Reprinted with permission from University of the Third Horizon (H3Uni).

the second horizon generates both crises and opportunities; for higher educa-tion, moving up is dependent on whether institutions rethink or adapt their practices beyond emulation, ranking, and conventional bandwagon responses to the major contemporary challenges outlined here—marketization, globaliza-tion, and the impact of new technologies.

As I said at the beginning of *Building Better Universities*, higher education is in a world of shifting boundaries, whether it wants it or not. Ultimately, this is not just about taking a position on profit versus nonprofit provision, or elitist versus egalitarian models of learning, or campus versus online education, or on local versus global services. It is about some dramatic underlying changes, the effects of which we still cannot predict. I suggest that almost all of these relate most crucially to the impact of the web on learning.

First, what happens when universities lose—as in fact they already have—the 'right to title,' given by unspoken tradition and practice and reinforced historically by their literal presence in the material landscape? Now we have many organizations calling themselves universities or colleges without either external validation or regulation, or any formal 'internal' credentialing powers. Educational content and the importance of learning are taking on a value that is not only recognized through the status and reputation of a particular edu-cational institution. Whatever these different incomers call themselves, their locus is predominantly outside the traditional academy. We already live in a post-university world.

Higher education may have came historically in 'standard' packages of undergraduate, postgraduate and doctoral degrees, and stood at the center of 'official' knowledge, as both generator and judge of that knowledge. But such a role is now much more blurred and insecure:

> Today anyone with a smart phone can access a universe of information about anything instantly and can download entire degree programs for free [. . .]. The implications of these possibilities are beginning to register on investors, philanthropists, content developers and potential employers and signal the start of another era in higher education, with different games and different rules.
>
> (O'Hara, n.d.: 4–5)

Second, what happens to universities when education—learning in all its myriad forms—takes place across a much broader landscape, particularly as the web shifts the locus of activity predominantly online? Universities and colleges may be looking most anxiously at their own position in the ranking systems, and at competing with private providers for part of the market. However, the competition is not only from for-profits but also from the open education movement, from the wave of open-source and crowd-sharing models developed out of web-based activities and increasingly being returned to the physical world. This has a radical, progressive and resonant view of learning (however hard to achieve) based on coproduction and creation, and is not going to be going away anytime soon.

Finally, and as part of the global interconnectivity made possible by the web, an alternative to the liberal arts or science education versus vocational training divide is revealing itself. This has a focus beyond specialist subject knowledge and departmental silos and towards developing the generic knowledge and skills necessary for dealing with complexity and uncertainty. It makes contemporary and world problems *the* central issue (while enabling local actions). In their various ways—through very different educational and business models—Singularity University, the University of the People, the School Of The Damned, and the University of the Third Horizon all refuse existing university assumptions about what higher education is and how to deliver it.

These are big issues for universities and colleges, but many seem to be failing to notice. By illustrating some of the ways that universities and colleges are innovating, the hope is that *Building Better Universities* can move these kinds of concerns to center stage. This is not about agreeing with, or merely following, what is written here, but to enable more explicit and constructive arguments. It is to help support and improve the quality of debate about where higher education is going and to inform—even influence—decision making about how to build better universities into the future.

BIBLIOGRAPHY

Ackerman, F. (2008) *Critique of Cost-Benefit Analysis, and Alternative Approaches to Decision-Making*. Available at: www.ase.tufts.edu/gdae/Pubs/rp/Ack_UK_CBAcritique.pdf.

Alexi Marmot Associates (AMA) (2006) *Spaces for Learning: A Review of Learning Spaces in Further and Higher Education*, Scottish Funding Council.

Altbach, P. G. (2010) "The State of the Rankings," *Inside Higher Ed*, November 11. www.insidehighered.com/views/2010/11/11/altbach.

Apple, M. (2004) *Ideology and Curriculum*, Routledge.

Araya, D., and Peter, M., A. (2010) *Education in the Creative Economy: Knowledge and Learning in the Age of Innovation*, Peter Lang.

Arnold, K. (2010) "Signals: Applying Academic Analytics," *Educause Review Online*, March 3. Available at: www.educause.edu/ero/article/signals-applying-academic-analytics (accessed May 23, 2014).

Ashwin, P., McLean, M. and Abbas, A. (2012) *Quality and Inequality in Undergraduate Courses: A Guide for National and Institutional Policy Makers*, University of Nottingham. Available at: www.pedagogicequality.ac.uk/index.php.

Bailey, M. (2011) *The Assault on Universities: A Manifesto for Resistance*, Pluto Press.

Ball, S. J. (2012) *Global Education Inc.: New Policy Networks and the Neoliberal Imaginary*, Routledge.

Balsamo, A. (2011) *Designing Culture; the Technological Imagination at Work*, Duke University Press.

Balsamo, A., Juhasz, A., and Galijia, R. (2014) *A Feminist Cyber-Learning Experiment: Hybridizing Online and Residential Learning*, March 8. Available at: https://ols.berkeley.edu/sites/default/files/presentations/OLS2014_AnnBalsamo.pdf.

Barber, M., Donnelly, K., and Rizvi, S. (2012) *Oceans of Innovation: The Atlantic, the Pacific, Global Leadership and the Future of Education*, IPPR. Available at: www.ippr.org/publication/55/9543/oceans-of-innovation-the-atlantic-the-pacific-global-leadership-and-the-future-of-education.

Barnett, R. (2000) *Realising the University in an Age of Supercomplexity*, Open University Press.

Barnett, R. (Ed.) (2005) *Re-Shaping the University: New Relationships between Research, Scholarship and Teaching*, Open University Press.

Barnett, R. (2007) *A Will to Learn: Being a Student in an Age of Uncertainty*, McGraw-Hill/Open University Press.

Barnett, R. (2010) *Being a University*, Routledge.

Barnett, R. (Ed) (2011) *The Future University: Ideas and Possibilities*, Routledge.

Barnett, R. and Temple, P. (2006) *Impact on Space of Future Changes in Higher Education (UK Higher Education Space Management Project, 2006/10)*, Higher Education Funding Council for England (HEFCE).

Bates, T. (2012) "What's Right and What's Wrong about Coursera-Style," MOOCs, August 5. Available at: www.tonybates.ca/2012/08/05/whats-right-and-whats-wrong-about-coursera-style-moocs/ (accessed February 2, 2104).

Batty, D. (2013) "Alternative Art Schools: A Threat to Universities?" *The Guardian*, October 21. Available at: www.theguardian.com/education/2013/oct/21/alternative-art-schools-threaten-universities (accessed April 20, 2014).

Beetham, H. (2007) *Rethinking Pedagogy for a Digital Age: Designing for 21st Century Learning*. Routledge.

Beetham, H. (2011) *Developing Digital Literacies*, Briefing Paper Joint Information Steering Committee (JISC). Available at: www.jisc.ac.uk/media/documents/funding/2011/04/Briefingpaper.pdf

Beetham, H. (2013) *Digital Literacy*, Joint Information Steering Committee (JISC).

Beetham, H.K., and Sharpe, R. (2007) *Rethinking Pedagogy for a Digital Age: Designing and Delivering E-learning*, Routledge.

Beichner, R.J. (2008). *The SCALE-UP Project: A Student-Centered Active Learning Environment for Undergraduate Programs*, BOSE Commissioned Paper, National Academy of Sciences Board on Science Education. Available at: http://www7.nationalacademies.org/bose/Beichner_CommissionedPaper.pdf.

Belanger, V., and Thornton, J. (2013) "Bioelectricity: A Quantitative Approach—Duke University's First MOOC." Available at: http://dukespace.lib.duke.edu/dspace/bitstream/handle/10161/6216/Duke_Bioelectricity_MOOC_Fall2012.pdf.

Bell, L., Stevenson, H., and Neary, M. (Eds.) (2009) *The Future of Higher Education: Policy, Pedagogy and the Student Experience*, Continuum.

Benneworth, P. (Ed.) (2013) *University Engagement with Socially Excluded Communities*, Springer.

Benneworth, P. (2014) "Decoding University Ideals by Reading Campuses: Exploring beyond the Democratic Mass University," in P. Temple (Ed.) *The Physical University: Contours of Space and Place in Higher Education*, Routledge, 217–242.

Berglund, E. (Ed.) (2009) *Growing by Degrees: Universities in the Future of Urban Development*, Building Futures RIBA. Available at: www.buildingfutures.org.uk/projects/building-futures/universities.

Bickford, D. J., and D. J. Wright. (2006) "Community: The Hidden Context for Learning," in D.G. Oblinger (Ed.) *Learning Spaces*, Educause, 4.1–4.22.

Biesta, G. (2007) "Why 'What Works' Won't Work: Evidence-Based Practice and the Democratic Deficit in Educational Research," *Educational Theory* 57 (1): 1–22.

Biggs, J., and Tang, C. (Eds.) (2007) *Teaching for Quality Learning at University*, McGraw-Hill/Society for Research into Higher Education & Open University Press.

Bligh, B., and Pearshouse, I. (2011) "Doing Learning Space Evaluations," in A. Boddington and J. Boys (Eds.) *Re-Shaping Learning: A Critical Reader*, Sense Publishers, 3–18.

Boddington, A., and Boys, J. (Eds.) (2011) *Re-Shaping Learning: A Critical Reader*, Sense Publishers.

Boddington, A., Boys, J., and Speight, C. (Eds) (2014) *Museums and Higher Education University Working Together: Challenges and Opportunities*, Ashgate.

Bok, D. (2013) *Higher Education in America*, Princeton University Press.

Bourn, D., McKenzie, A., and Shiel, C. (2006) (Eds.) *The Global University: The Role of the Curriculum*, DEA. Available at: http://clients.squareeye.net/uploads/dea/documents/dea_global_university_curriculum.pdf.

Boyer Commission (1998) *Reinventing Undergraduate Education: A Blueprint for America's Research Universities*, Carnegie Foundation for the Advancement of Teaching.

Boys, J. (2009a) "Beyond the Beanbag? Towards New Ways of Thinking about Learning Spaces," *Networks Magazine*, no. 08 (Autumn). Available at: www.adm.heacademy.ac.uk/resources/features/beyond-the-beanbag-towards-new-ways-of-thinking-about-learning-spaces (accessed March 28, 2013).

Boys, J. (2009b) "Creative Differences: Deconstructing the Conceptual Learning Spaces of Higher Education and Museums," in B. Cook, R. Reynolds, and C. Speight (Eds.) *Museums and Design Education: Looking to Learn, Learning to See*, Ashgate, 43-60.

Boys, J. (2010) *Towards Creative Learning Spaces: Re-Thinking the Architecture of Post-Compulsory Education*, Routledge.

Boys, J., and Ford, P. (Eds.) (2008) *The e-Revolution and Post-Compulsory Education: Using e-Business Models to Deliver Quality Education*. Routledge and JISC Online. Available as free e-book from: www.jisc.ac.uk/publications/generalpublications/2008/erevolutionebook.aspx

Boys, J., and Hazlett, D. (Forthcoming) "The Spaces of Relational Learning and their Impact on Student Engagement," in C. Nygaard, J. Barthlomew, P. Branch, and L. Scott-Webber (Eds.) *Learning Space Design in Higher Education*, Libri Publishing.

Boys, J., Melhuish, C., and Wilson, A. (2014) *Developing Research Methods for Analyzing Learning Spaces that can Inform Institutional Missions of Learning and Engagement*, SCUP Publications.

Boys, J., and Smith, H. (2011) "What Do We Know about What Is Being Built? New Typologies of Learning Spaces," in A. Boddington and J. Boys (Eds.) *Re-Shaping Learning: A Critical Reader*, Sense Publishers, 33–48.

Brennan, J. (2011) "Higher Education and Social Change: Researching the 'End of Times,'" in *Higher Education and Society in Changing Times: Looking Back and Looking Forward*, Centre for Higher Education Research and Information (CHERI) Open University, 6–12.

Brennan, J., King, R., and Lebeau, Y. (2004) *The Role of Universities in the Transformation of Societies—An International Research Project: Synthesis Report*, Association of Commonwealth Universities/Centre for Higher Education Research and Information. Available at: www.open.ac.uk/cheri/documents/transf-final-report.pdf.

Brennan, J., and Shah, T. (Eds.) (2011) *Higher Education and Society in Changing Times: Looking Back and Looking Forward*, Centre for Higher Education Research and Information (CHERI) Open University. Available at: www.open.ac.uk/cheri/documents/Lookingbackandlookingforward.pdf.

Brennan, J., and Singh, M. (2011) "Playing the Quality Game: Whose Quality and Whose Higher Education?," in D. Rothen and C. Calhoun (Eds.) *Knowledge Matters: The Public Mission of the Research University*, Columbia University Press, 401–426.

Brint, S. (Ed.) (2002) *The Future of the City of Intellect: The Changing American University*, Stanford University Press.

Britner, P., A. (2012) "Bringing Public Engagement into an Academic Plan and Its Assessment Metrics," *Journal of Higher Education Outreach and Engagement* 16 (4): 61–77.

Brooks, R., Fuller, A., and Waters, J. (Eds.) (2012) *Changing Spaces of Education. New Perspectives on the Nature of Learning*, Routledge.

Brown, M. (2012) *Learning Analytics: Moving from Concept to Practice*, Educause Learning Initiative Briefing. Available at: www.educause.edu/library/resources/learning-analytics-moving-concept-practice.

Brown, R. (n.d.) *Higher Education and the Market: Further Thoughts and Reflections*, OxCHEPS Occasional Paper No. 20, Oxford Centre for Higher Education Policy Studies. Available at: http://oxcheps.new.ox.ac.uk/MainSite%20pages/Resources/OxCHEPS_OP24.pdf.

Brown, R. (Ed.) (2010) *Higher Education and the Market*, Routledge.

Brown, R. (2011) "Looking Back, Looking Forward: The Changing Structure of UK Higher Education, 1980–2012," in J. Brennan, and T. Shah (Eds.) *Higher Education and Society in Changing Times: Looking Back and Looking Forward*,Centre for Higher Education Research and Information (CHERI) Open University. Available at: www.open.ac.uk/cheri/documents/Lookingbackandlookingforward.pdf.

Brown, R., with Carasso, H. (2013) *Everything for Sale? The Marketisation of UK Higher Education*, Routledge.

Browne (2010) *Securing a Sustainable Future for Higher Education. Independent Review of Higher Education Funding and Student Finance in England*, chaired by Lord Browne of Madingley, England, 9 November. Available at: www.gov.uk/government/uploads/ system/uploads/attachment_data/file/31999/10–1208-securing-sustainable-higher-education-browne-report.pdf.

Buckingham Shum, S. (2012) *Learning Analytics Policy Brief*, UNESCO. Available at: http:// iite.unesco.org/files/policy_briefs/pdf/en/learning_analytics.pdf.

Busch, G. (2013) "The People Want to Learn," May 17. Available at: www.dandc.eu/en/ article/why-many-brazilian-students-choose-go-night-school-after-work (accessed February 14, 2014).

Calhoun, C. (2006) "The University and the Public Good," *Thesis Eleven* 84 (February): 7–43.

Campbell, J.P., DeBlois, P. B., and Oblinger, D. G. (2007) "Academic Analytics: A New Tool for a New Era," *Educause Review* (July/August): 41–57. Available at: http://net. educause.edu/ir/library/pdf/erm0742.pdf.

Capaldi, E.D. (2009) "Intellectual Transformation and Budgetary Savings through Academic Organization," *Change: The Magazine of Higher Learning* (July–August). Available at: http://newamericanuniversity.asu.edu/docs/Change_Magazine_Intellectual_Transfomation.pdf.

Capaldi, E. D., and Abbey, C. W. (2011) "Performance and Costs in Higher Education: A Proposal for Better Data," *Change: The Magazine of Higher Learning* (March–April). Available at: www.changemag.org/Archives/Back%20Issues/2011/March-April%20 2011/better-data-full.html (accessed March 14, 2014).

Carey, K. (2011) "Disrupting College," *The Chronicle of Higher Education*, February 10. Available at: http://chronicle.com/blogs/brainstorm/disrupting-college/32019 (accessed October 8, 2014).

Carnegie Foundation for the Advancement of Teaching (n.d.) *First-Time Classification Framework*. Available at: http://classifications.carnegiefoundation.org/downloads/community_eng/first-time_framework.pdf.

Caruana, V. (2010) "Global Citizenship for All: Putting the 'Higher' Back into UK Higher Education," in F. Maringe and N. Foskett (Eds.) *Globalization and Internationalisation in Higher Education, Theoretical, Strategic and Management Perspectives*, Continuum, 51–64.

Carvalho, L., and Goodyear, P. (Eds.) (2014) *The Architecture of Productive Learning Networks*, Routledge

Casey, J., Greller, W., Davies, H., Follows, C., Turner, N., and Webb-Ingall, E. (2011) *Open Spaces for Arts Education—The ALTO Ecosystem Model*. Available from: http://process. arts.ac.uk/sites/default/files/deol_2011_alto_paper_25–10–11.pdf.

Chatterjee, H.J. (2009) *Object-Based Learning in Higher Education: The Pedagogical Power of Museums*. Available at: http://edoc.hu-berlin.de/umacj/2010/chatterjee-179/PDF/ chatterjee.pdf.

Chatterton, P. (2000) "The Cultural Role of Universities in the Community: Revisiting the University-Community Debate," *Environment and Planning A* 32: 165–181.

Christensen, C. M., and Eyring, H. J. (2011) *The Innovative University: Changing the DNA of Higher Education from the Inside Out*, John Wiley.

Christensen, C. M., Horn, M.B., Caldera, L., and Soares, L. (2011) *Disrupting College: How Disruptive Innovation Can Deliver Quality and Affordability to Postsecondary Education*, Center for American Progress and Innosight Institute. Available at: www. americanprogress.org/issues/2011/02/pdf/disrupting_college.pdf.

Clark, B. R. (2004) *Sustaining Change in Universities: Continuities in Case Studies and Concepts*, Open University Press.

Coiffait, L. (Ed.) (2012) *Blue Skies: New Thinking about the Future of Higher Education*, Pearson. Available at: http://pearsonblueskies.com/wp-content/uploads/2012/09/Blue-Skies-UK-2012-FINAL.pdf.

Colby, A., Beaumont, E., Ehrlich, T., and Corngold, J. (2007) *Educating for Democracy: Preparing Under-Graduates for Responsible Political Eengagement*, Jossey Bass-Carnegie Foundation for the Advancement of Teaching.

Collini, S. (2012) *What Are Universities For?*, Penguin.

Collini, S. (2013) "Sold Out," *London Review of Books* 35 (20): 3–12. Available at: www.lrb.co.uk/v35/n20/stefan-collini/sold-out (accessed October 30, 2013).

Collis, D.J. (2002) "New Business Models for Higher Education," in S. Brint (Ed.) *The Future of the City of Intellect: The Changing American University*, Stanford University Press, 181–202.

Conole, G.C., and Ehlers, U.D. (2010) "Open Educational Practices: Unleashing the power of OER," paper presented to UNESCO Workshop on OER, Windhoek, Namibia. Available at: http://cdn.efquel.org/wp-content/uploads/2012/03/OEP_Unleashing-the-power-of-OER.pdf.

Cooper, A. (2012) *A Brief History of Analytics A Briefing Paper*, JISC CETIS, November. Available at: http://publications.cetis.ac.uk/wp-content/uploads/2012/12/Analytics-Brief-History-Vol-1-No9.pdf.

Cormier, D. (2010) MOOCs, Knowledge and the Digital Economy—a Research Project," December 20. Available at: http://davecormier.com/edblog/2010/12/20/moocs-knowledge-and-the-digitial-economy-a-research-project (accessed August 16, 2014).

Cormier, D. (2013) "Some Things MOOCs Are Good For," October 29. Available at: http://davecomier.com/edblog/2013/10/29/some-things-oocs-are-good-for (accessed August 16, 2014).

Cote, J. E. and Allahar, A, L. (2007) *Ivory Towers Blues: A University System in Crisis.* Toronto: University of Toronto Press.

Cote, J.E., and Allahar, A, L. (2011) *Lowering Higher Education: The Rise of Corporate Universities and the Fall of Liberal Education*, University of Toronto Press.

Crow, M. (2011) *A New American University Reader: Selected Writings on University Design and Related Topics*, July, Arizona State University. Available at: http://president.asu.edu/sites/default/files/New%20American%20University%20Reader%20072611%20%282%29.pdf.

Csikszentmihalyi, M. (1990) *Flow: The Psychology of Optimal Experience*, HarperCollins.

Currie, J (2004) "The Neo-Liberal Paradigm and Higher Education: A Critique," in J. K. Odin and P. T. Manicas (Eds.) *Globalization and Higher Education*, University of Hawaii Press, 42–62.

Daniel, J. (2012) *Making Sense of MOOCs: Musings in a Maze of Myth, Paradox and Possibility*, Academic Partnerships.

Danish Property Agency (2013) *Campus Planning: Method and Process (Campusudvikling Metode og process)*, Bygningsstyrelsen. Available at: www.bygst.dk/media/142181/campusudvikling.pdf.

de Freitas, S. (2006) *Learning in Immersive Worlds. A Review of Game-Based Learning*, JISC Publications. Available at: www.jisc.ac.uk/whatwedo/programmes/elearning_innovation/eli_outcomes.

de Freitas, S., Savill-Smith, C., and Attewell, J. (2006) *Educational Games and Simulations: Case Studies from Adult Learning Practice*, Learning and Skills Research Centre. Available at: www.lsneducation.org.uk/research/centres/RCFTechEnhanceLearn/computergames.

Deiaco, E., and McKelvey, M. (2012) "Universities as Strategic Actors in the Knowledge Economy," *Cambridge Journal of Economics* 36 (3): 525–541.

Delanty, G. (2001) *Challenging Knowledge: The University in the Knowledge Society*, Society for Research into Higher Education and Open University Press.

Delanty, G. (2004) "Does the University Have a Future?," in J. K. Odin and P. T. Manicas (Eds.) *Globalization and Higher Education*, University of Hawaii Press, 241–254.

DeMillo, R., A. (2011) *Abelard to Apple: The Fate of American Colleges and Universities*, The MIT Press.

Dewey, J. (1938) *Experience and Education*, Kappa Delta Pi.

Dolence, M.G., and Norris, D. M. (1995) *Transforming Higher Education: A Vision for Learning in the Information Age*, Society for College and University Planning (SCUP).

Dolence, M.G., and Norris, D. M. (1996) "IT Leadership Is Key to Transformation," *Cause/Effect* (Spring): 12–20. Available at: http://net.educause.edu/ir/library/pdf/CEM9615.pdf.

Donoghue, F. (2008) *The Last Professors: The Corporate University and the Fate of the Humanities*, Fordham University Press.

Dori, Y., and Belcher, J. (2004) "How Does Technology-Enabled Active Learning Affect Undergraduate Students' Understanding of Electromagnetism Concepts," *Journal of the Learning Sciences* 14 (2): 243–279. Available at: http://web.mit.edu/edtech/casestudies/pdf/teal1.pdf

Downes, S. (2012) *Connectivism and Connective Knowledge: Essays on Meanings and Learning Networks*. Available at: http://online.upaep.mx/campusTest/ebooks/CONECTIVE KNOWLEDGE.pdf.

Duderstadt, J.J. (2000) *A University for the 21st Century*, University of Michigan Press.

Duderstadt, J., J. (2007) *The View from the Helm: Leading the American University during an Era of Change*, University of Michigan Press.

Duffy, F. (1997) *The New Office*, Conran Octopus.

Dugdale, S. (2009) "Space Strategies for the New Learning Landscape," *EDUCAUSE Review* 44 (2): 51–63. Available at: www.educause.edu/ir/library/pdf/ERM0925.pdf.

Dyckhoff, A.L., Zielke, D., Bültmann, M., Chatti, M.A., & Schroeder, U. (2012) "Design and Implementation of a Learning Analytics Toolkit for Teachers," *Educational Technology & Society* 15 (3): 58–76. Available at: www.ifets.info/journals/15_3/5.pdf.

Dyer-Witheford, N. (2002) "Cognitive Capitalism and the Contested Campus," in G. Coxand J. Krysa (Eds.) *Engineering Culture: On 'The Author as (Digital) Producer,'* Autonomedia (DATA browser 02), 71–93

Educause (n.d.) *What Campus Leaders Need to Know about MOOCs*. Available at: http://net.educause.edu/ir/library/pdf/PUB4005.pdf.

ELI (2011) *Seven Things You Should Know About First Generation Learning Analytics*, Educause Learning Initiative. Available at: www.educause.edu/library/resources/7-things-you-should-know-about-first-generation-learning-analytics.

Ellis, R.A. (2011) *Educational Planning Provision, Management and Evaluation of University Learning and Teaching Space—Learning Space Review Final Report*, University of Sydney, Camperdown.

Ellis, R.A., and Goodyear, P. (2010) *Students' Experiences of e-Learning in Higher Education: The Ecology of Sustainable Innovation*, Routledge.

Ernst and Young (2012) *University of the Future. A Thousand Year Old Industry on the Cusp of Profound Change*, Ernst and Young Australia.

Ernst, D.J., Katz, R.N., and Sack, J.R. (1994) *Organisational and technological strategies for Higher Education in the Information Age*, CAUSE Professional Papers Series No. 13, Educause.

Facer, K. (2011) *Learning Futures. Education, Technology and Social Change*, Routledge.

Ferguson, R. (2012) *The State of Learning Analytics in 2012: A Review and Future Challenges*, Technical Report, Knowledge Media Institute, The Open University. Available at: http://kmi.open.ac.uk/publications/pdf/kmi-12–01.pdf.

Ferrari, A. (2012) *Digital Competence in Practice: An Analysis of Frameworks*, Joint Research Centre Technical Report, European Commission. Available at: http://ftp.jrc.es/EURdoc/JRC68116.pdf.

Ferrari, A. (2013) *DIGCOMP: A Framework for Developing and Understanding Digital Competencies in Europe*, JRC European Commission. Available at: http://ftp.jrc.es/EURdoc/JRC83167.pdf.

Fielden, J., Middlehurst, R. Woodfield, S., and Olcott, D. (2010) *The Growth of Private and For-Profit Higher Education Providers in the UK*. London: Universities UK. www.universitiesuk.ac.uk/highereducation/Documents/2010/PrivateProviders.pdf

Florida, R. (2002) *The Rise of the Creative Class: And How It's Transforming Work, Leisure, Community and Everyday Life*, Perseus Book Group.

Florida, R. (2012) *The Rise of the Creative Class—Revisited* (10th anniversary ed.), Basic Books.

Forward, M.L. (2012) "Open CourseWare," in D. G. Oblinger (Ed.) *Game Changers: Education and Information Technologies*, Educause, 291–300.

Fraser, K. (Ed.) (2014) *The Future of Learning and Teaching in Next Generation Learning Spaces*, International Perspectives on Higher Education Research Vol. 12, Emerald.

Freire, P. (1996) *Pedagogy of the Oppressed*, Penguin.

Freire, P. ([1974] 1997). *Education for Critical Consciousness*, Continuum.

Gentleman, A. (2013) "The £54,000 Degree: How Well Is AC Grayling's College Doing?" *The Guardian*, October 26. Available at: www.theguardian.com/education/2013/oct/26/degree-ac-grayling-university-new-college (accessed January 12, 2014).

Goddard, J., and Vallance, P. (2013) *The University and the City*, Routledge.

Gornall, L., Cook, C., Daunton, L, Salisbury, J., and Thomas B. (Eds.) (2013) *Academic Working Lives: Experience, Practice and Change*, Bloomsbury Academic.

Greenberg, M. (2004) "A University Is Not a Business (and Other Fantasies)," *Educause Review Online* 39 (2). Available at: www.educause.edu/ero/article/university-not-business-and-other-fantasies.

Greene, M. (1995) *Releasing the Imagination*, Jossey-Bass.

Greller, W. (2012) "Translating Learning into Numbers: A Generic Framework for Learning Analytics," *Educational Technology and Society* 15 (3): 42–57. Available at: www.ifets.info/journals/15_3/4.pdf.

Greller, W., and Drachsler, H. (2012) "Translating Learning into Numbers: A Generic Framework for Learning Analytics," *Educational Technology and Society* 15(3): 42–57. Available at: www.ifets.info/journals/15_3/4.pdf.

Hager, Y. (2008) "A Town Called Science," *Chemistry World* (February). Available at: www.rsc.org/chemistryworld/Issues/2008/February/ATownCalledScience.asp (accessed February 12, 2014).

Harding, A., Scott, A., Laske, S., and Burtscher, C. (Eds.) (2007) *Bright Satanic Mills: Universities, Regional Development and the Knowledge Economy*, Ashgate.

Harley, D., Krzys Acord, S., Earl-Novell, S., Lawrence, S., and Judson King, M.A.C. (2010) *Assessing the Future Landscape of Scholarly Communication: An Exploration of Faculty Values and Needs in Seven Disciplines*, CSHE University of California, Berkeley.

Harrison, A., and Cairns, A. (2008) *The Changing Academic Workplace*, DEGW UK Ltd. Available at: http://exploreit.sfc.ac.uk/content/the_changing_academic_workplace.pdf.

Harrison, A., and Hutton, L. (2013) *Design for the Changing Educational Landscape: Space, Place and the Future of Learning*, Routledge.

Hartmann, E. (Ed.) (2011) *The Internationalisation of Higher Education. Towards a New Research Agenda in Critical Higher Education Studies*, Routledge.

Hawawini, G. (2011) *The Internationalisation of Higher Education Institutions: A Critical Review and a Radical Proposal*, INSEAD Faculty & Research Working Paper. Available at: www.insead.edu/facultyresearch/research/doc.cfm?did=48726.

Hollister, R.M. and Gearan, M.(2013) "Moving beyond the Ivory Tower." In *Forum* Spring European Association for International Education, 11–13.

Hollister, R.M., Pollock, J.P., Gearan, M., Reid, J., Stroud, S., and Babcock, E. (2012) "The Talloires Network: A Global Coalition of Engaged Universities," *Journal of Higher Education Outreach and Engagement* 16 (4): 81–102.

Holmwood, J. (2011) *A Manifesto for the Public University*, Bloomsbury Academic.

Hooper-Greenhill, E. (2007) *Museums and Education: Purpose, Pedagogy, Performance*, Routledge.

Hoyt, L. (Ed.) (2013) *Transforming Cities and Minds through the Scholarship of Engagement: Economy, Equity and Environment*, Vanderbilt University Press.

Hoyt, L., and Hollister, R. (2014) "Moving Beyond the Ivory Tower: The Expanding Global Movement of Engaged Universities." In: Hall, B., and Tandon, R. (Eds.) *Knowledge, Engagement and Higher Education: Rethinking Social Responsibility*. Palgrave Macmillan.

Hung, D., and Khine, M. S. (2006) *Engaged Learning with Emerging Technologies*, Springer.

Iiyoshi, T., and Vijay Kumar, M. S. (Eds.) (2008) *Opening Up Education: The Collective Advancement of Education through Open Technology, Open Content, and Open Knowledge*, MIT Press.

Jamieson, P. (2008) *Creating New Generation Learning Environments on the University Campus*, Woods Bagot Research Press. Available at: www.woodsbagot.com/en/Documents/Public_Research/WB5307_U21_FA-7_final.pdf.

Jamieson, P., Fisher, K., Gilding, T., Taylor, P. G., and Trevitt, C.F. (2000) "Place and Space in the Design of New Learning Environments," *Higher Education Research & Development* 19 (2): 221–236. Available at: www.oecd.org/education/innovation-education/2675768.pdf.

Jaschick, S., and Lederman, D. (2013) "The 2013 Inside Higher Ed Survey of Faculty Attitudes on Technology," *Inside Higher Ed*, September 12. Available at: www.insidehighered.com/audio/2013/09/12/2013-survey-faculty-attitudes-technology#sthash.drfhdrwh.dpbs.

Johnson, L., Adams, S., and Cummins, M. (2012) *The NMC Horizon Report: 2012 Higher Education Edition*, New Media Consortium. Available at: www.nmc.org/pdf/2012-horizon-report-HE.pdf

Johnson, L., Adams Becker, S., Cummins, M., Estrada, V., Freeman, A., and Ludgate, H. (2013) *NMC Horizon Report: 2013 Higher Education Edition*, New Media Consortium.

Johnstone, B., and Marcucci, P. M. (2010) *Financing Higher Education Worldwide: Who Pays? Who Should Pay?*, John Hopkins University Press.

Johnstone, S. (2002) "The Complexity of Decision-Making," in *Teaching as E-business? Research and Policy Agendas*, Selected Conference Proceedings, Centre for Studies in Higher Education, University of California, Berkeley. Available at http://cshe.berkeley.edu/sites/default/files/shared/publications/docs/elearning.pdf.

Joint Information Systems Committee (JISC) (2006) *Designing Spaces for Effective Learning*. Available at: www.jisc.ac.uk/eli_learningspaces.html.

Joint Information Systems Committee (JISC) (2007) *Game-Based Learning: A Briefing Paper*, JISC Publications. Available at: www.jisc.ac.uk/media/documents/publications/gamingreportbp.pdf.

Joint Information Systems Committee (JISC) (2009) *A Study of Effective Evaluation Models and Practices for Technology Supported Physical Learning Spaces*. Available at: www.jisc.ac.uk/media/documents/projects/jels_final_report_30.06.09.doc.

Jones-Garmil, K. (1997) *The Wired Museum: Emerging Technology and Changing Paradigms*, American Association of Museums.

Kennedy, G., Ioannou, I., Zhou, Y., Bailey, J., and O'Leary, S. (2013) "Mining Interactions in Immersive Learning Environments for Real-Time Student Feedback," *Australasian Journal of Educational Technology* 29 (2): 172–183.

Kennedy, K., Fairbrother, G., and Zhao, Z. Z. (2014) *Citizenship Education in China: Preparing Citizens for the "Chinese Century,"* Routledge.

Kerr, C. ([1963] 2001) *The Uses of the University*, 5th edition. Cambridge, MA: Harvard University Press.

Khanna, A., and Khanna, P. (2012) *Hybrid Reality. Thriving in the Emerging Human-Technology Civilization*, TED Books.

King, R. (2011) "Globalisation and Higher Education," in J. Brennan and T. Shah (Eds.) *Higher Education and Society in Changing Times: Looking Back and Looking Forward*, Centre for Higher Education Research and Information (CHERI) Open University. 24–35. Available at: www.open.ac.uk/cheri/documents/Lookingbackandlookingforward.pdf.

King, R., Marginson, S., and Naidoo, R. (Eds.) (2011) *Handbook on Globalization and Higher Education*, Edward Elgar.

Kipnis, A. B. (2011) *Governing Educational Desire: Culture, Politics, and Schooling in China*, University of Chicago Press.

Kirschner, A. (1999) "Columbia University's Three-in-One Commercial Venture," *Times Higher Education*, December 17. Available at: www.timeshighereducation.co.uk/news/columbia-universitys-three-in-one-commercial-venture/149346.article (accessed May 2, 2014).

Klemencic, M. (2011) "The Public Role of Higher Education and Student Participation in Higher Education Governance," in J. Brennan and T. Shah (Eds.) *Higher Education and Society in Changing Times: Looking Back and Looking Forward*, Centre for Higher Education Research and Information (CHERI) Open University. 74-83. Available at: www.open.ac.uk/cheri/documents/Lookingbackandlookingforward.pdf.

Knight, E., and Casilli, C. (2012) "Mozilla Open Badges," in D. G. Oblinger (Ed.) *Game Changers: Education and Information Technologies*, Educause, 279–284. Available at: www.educause.edu/research-publications/books/game-changers-education-and-information-technologies.

Knight, J. (2008) *Higher Education in Turmoil*, Sense Publishers.

Kolb, D.A. (1984) *Experiential Learning: Experience as the Source of Learning and Development*, Prentice Hall.

Kortuem, G., Bandara, A., Smith, N., Richards, M., and Petre, M. (2013). "Educating the Internet-of-Things Generation," *Computer* 46 (2): 53–61.

Kurtzweil, R. (2006) *The Singularity Is Near: When Humans Transcend Biology*, Penguin.

Landry, C. (2008) *The Creative City: A Toolkit for Urban Innovators*, Routledge.

Laurillard, D. (1993) *Rethinking University Teaching: A Framework for the Effective Use of Educational Technology*, Routledge.

Laurillard, D. (2012) *Teaching as a Design Science: Building Pedagogical Patterns for Learning and Technology*, Routledge.

Lave, J., and Wenger, E. (1991) *Situated Learning: Legitimate Peripheral Participation*, Cambridge University Press.

Leadbetter, C., and Staropoli, R. (2012) *Innovation in Education: Lessons from Pioneers around the World*, Bloomsbury Qatar Foundation Publishing, World Innovation Summit for Education.

Learning Spaces Collaboratory (LSC) (2013) *A Guide. Planning for Assessing 21st Century Learning Spaces for 21st Century Learners*. Available at: http://pkallsc.org/sites/all/modules/ckeditor/ckfinder/userfiles/files/LSC%20Guide-PlanningforAssessing.pdf.

Levidow, L (2002) "Marketizing Higher Education: Neoliberal Strategies and Counter-Strategies," in K. Robins and F. Webster (Eds.) *The Virtual University? Knowledge, Markets and Management*, Oxford University Press, 227–248.

Levy, M. (2009) "Technologies in Use for Second Language Learning," *The Modern Language Journal* 93: 769–782.

Levy, M., Möllering, M., and Dunne, K. (2009) "An Analysis of Technology Use in First Year Language Teaching at Three Australian Universities," *Prospect* 24 (3): 5–14.

Littlejohn, A., Falconer, I., and McGill, L. (2008) "Characterising Effective eLearning Resources," *Computers & Education*, 50 (3): 757–771.

Long, P., and Siemens, G. (2011) "Penetrating the Fog: Analytics in Learning and Education," *Educause Review Online* 46 (5): 31–40. Available at: www.educause.edu/ir/library/pdf/ERM1151.pdf.

Luckin, R., Bligh, B., Manches, A., Ainsworth, S., Crook, C., and Noss, R. (2012) *Decoding Learning: The Proof, Promise and Potential of Digital Education*, NESTA.

Maassen, P., M., Nerland, Pinheiro, R., Stensaker, B., Vabø, A., and Vukasovik, M., (Eds.) (2012) *The Effects of Higher Education Reforms*, Sense Publishers.

Marginson, S. (2013) "The Impossibility of Capitalist Markets in Higher Education," *Journal of Education Policy* 28 (3): 353–370.

Marginson, S. (2014) "There's Still No Such Thing as a Higher Education Market," *Times Higher Education*, April 10. Available at: www.timeshighereducation.co.uk/comment/opinion/theres-still-no-such-thing-as-a-higher-education-market/2012541.article (accessed May 24, 2014).

Maurrasse, D.J. (2001) *Beyond the Campus: How Colleges and Universities Form Partnerships with Their Communities*, Routledge

McGettigan, A. (2013) *The Great University Gamble: Money, Markets and the Future of Higher Education*, Pluto Press.

McGill, L. (2013) "What Are Open Educational Resources?" JISC InfoKit. Available at: https://openeducationalresources.pbworks.com/w/page/24836860/What%20are%20 Open%20Educational%20Resources.

McGill, L., Falconer, I., Dempster, J.A., Littlejohn, A., and Beetham, H. (2013) *Journeys to Open Educational Practice: UKOER/SCORE Review Final Report*, Joint Information Systems Committee. Available at: https://oersynth.pbworks.com/w/page/60338879/ HEFCE-OER-Review-Final-Report.

McLean, M. (2006) *Pedagogy and the University, Critical Theory and Practice*, Continuum.

McLoughlin, C., and Lee, M.J.W. (2008) "The 3 P's of Pedagogy for the Networked Society: Personalization, Participation, and Productivity," *International Journal of Teaching and Learning in Higher Education* 20 (1): 10–27. Available at: files.eric.ed.gov/fulltext/ EJ895221.pdf (accessed August 20, 2014).

Meister, J.C. (1998) *Corporate Universities: Lessons in Building a World-Class Workforce*, McGraw-Hill.

Melhuish, C. (2011a) "Methods for Understanding the Relationships between Learning and Space," in A. Boddington and J. Boys (Eds.) *Re-Shaping Learning: A Critical Reader*, Sense Publisher, 19–32.

Melhuish, C. (2011b) "What Matters about Space for Learning: Exploring Perceptions and Experiences," in A. Boddington and J. Boys (Eds.) *Re-Shaping Learning: A Critical Reader*, Sense Publishers, 81–92.

Mellander, C., Florida, R., Asheim, B.T., and Gertler, M. (Eds.) (2013) *The Creative Class Goes Global*, Routledge.

Metcalfe, A.S. (2010) "Examining the Trilateral Networks of the Triple Helix: Intermediating Organizations and Academy-Industry-Government Relations," *Critical Sociology*, 36 (4): 1–17.

Meyer, R. (2012) "What It's Like to Teach a MOOC (and What the Heck's a MOOC?)," *The Atlantic*, July 22. www.theatlantic.com/technology/archive/2012/07/what-its-like-to-teach-a-mooc-and-what-the-hecks-a-mooc/260000/ (accessed August 16, 2014).

Mitchell, G., White, B., Pospisil, R., Kiley, S., Liu, C., and Matthews, G. (2010) *Retrofitting University Learning Spaces. Final Report*, Australian Learning and Teaching Council. Available at: http://learnline.cdu.edu.au/retrofittingunispaces/index.html (accessed September 14, 2013).

Molesworth, M., Scullion, R., and Nixon, E. (Eds.) (2010) *The Marketisation of Higher Education and the Student as Consumer*, Routledge.

Moore, R. (2010) "The Rolex Learning Centre, Lausanne," *The Observer*, February 21. Available at: www.theguardian.com/artanddesign/2010/feb/21/rowan-moore-rolex-learning-centre (accessed April 8, 2104).

Morgan, J. (2013) "China on the Fast Track," *Times Higher Education*, December 19. Available at: www.timeshighereducation.co.uk/features/china-on-the-fast-track/2009923.article (accessed January 10, 2014).

Morgan, J. (2014) "Headaches for UCLan over Foreign Campuses," *Times Higher Education*, January 2. Available at: www.timeshighereducation.co.uk/news/headaches-for-uclan-over-foreign-campuses/2010068.article (accessed January 10, 2014).

Murphy, T. (2011) "Toward Enhanced Democratic Learning Spaces: A Case Study from the Republic of Ireland," *Critical Literacy: Theories and Practices* 6 (1): 45–49. Available at: http://criticalliteracy.freehostia.com/index.php?journal=criticalliteracy&page=article&o p=viewArticle&path=94.

Neary, M., and Winn, J. (2009) "Student as Producer," in L. Bell, H. Stevenson, and M. Neary (Eds.) *The Future of Higher Education—Policy, Pedagogy and the Student Experience*, Continuum, 126–138.

Neary, M., and Hagyard, A. (2010) "Pedagogy of Excess: An Alternative Political Economy of Student Life," in M. Molesworth, L. Nixon, and R. Scullion (Eds.) *The Marketisation of Higher Education—The Student as Consumer*, Routledge, 209-224.

Neary, M., Harrison, A., Crellin, G., Parekh, N., Saunders, G., Duggan, F., Williams, S., and Austin, S. (2010) *Learning Landscapes in Higher Education*. Available at: http:// learninglandscapes.blogs.lincoln.ac.uk/files/2010/04/FinalReport.pdf.

New College of Humanities (2013) *Undergraduate Prospectus 2014/15 FSC*. www.nchum. org/sites/default/files/NCH_Prospectus2013.pdf.

Newman, J.H. ([1852] 2014) *The Idea of a University*, Assumption Press.

Newman, F., Couturier, L., and Scurry, J. (2004) *The Future of Higher Education: Rhetoric, Reality, and the Risks of the Market*, Jossey-Bass.

NMC Horizon Report, Higher Education Edition (2012), New Media Consortium and Educause Learning Initiative. Available at: www.nmc.org/pdf/2012-horizon-report-HE.pdf.

Norris, D.M., and Poulton, N.L. (2010) *A Guide to Planning Change*, Society for College and University Planners.

Norris, D., Brodnick, R., Lefrere, P., Gilmour, J., and Baer, L. (2013) *Transforming in an Age of Disruptive Change*, Planning for Higher Education vol. 41, no. 2, Society for College and University Planners.

Nussbaum, M. C. (2012) *Not for Profit: Why Democracy Needs the Humanities*, Princeton University Press.

Oakeshott M. (1950) "The Idea of a University," reprinted in T. Fuller (2001) *The Voice of Liberal Learning*, Liberty Fund, 105–117.

Oblinger, D.G. (Ed.) (2006) *Learning Spaces*, Educause. Available at: http:// www.educause. edu/LearningSpaces/10569.

Oblinger, D.G. (2012) "IT as a Game Changer," in D.G. Oblinger (Ed) *Game Changers: Education and Information Technologies*, Educause. Available at: http://net.educause.edu/ ir/library/pdf/pub7203.pdf.

Odin, J.K., and Manicas, P.T. (Eds.) (2004) *Globalization and Higher Education*, University of Hawaii Press.

O'Hara, M. (n.d.) *Finding the Third Horizon of Innovation in Higher Education*. Available at: www.maureen.ohara.net/pubs/Finding_the_Innovative_Edge.pdf.

O'Hara, M., and Leicester, G. (2009) *Ten Things to do in a Conceptual Emergency*, International Futures Forum. Available at: http://maureen.ohara.net/pubs/TenThings.pdf.

Olds, K., and Thrift, N. (2004) "Cultures on the Brink: Re-Engineering the Soul of Capitalism—on a Global Scale," in A. Ong and S. Collins (Eds.) *Global Anthropology. Technology, Politics, and Ethics as Anthropological Problems*, Blackwell, 270–290.

Organisation for Economic Co-operation and Development (2013) *Education at a Glance 2013: OECD Indicators*, June. www.oecd.org/edu/eag2013%20(eng)--FINAL%2020% 20June%202013.pdf

Osberg, D., and Biesta, G (Eds.) (2010) *Complexity Theory and the Politics of Education*, Sense Publishers.

Painter, S., Fournier, J., Grape, C., Grummon, P., Morelli, J., Whitmer, S., and Cevetello, J. (2012) *Research on Learning Space Design: Present State, Future Directions*, SCUP Publications. Available at: www.scup.org/page/resources/books/rolsd.

Parlett, M.R., and Hamilton, D. (1972) *Evaluation as Illumination: A New Approach to the Study of Innovatory Programmes*, workshop at Cambridge and unpublished report Occasional paper 9, Centre for Research in the Educational Sciences, University of Edinburgh.

Parr, C. (2014) "University of the People Gains Accreditation," *Times Higher Education*, March 2. Available at: www.timeshighereducation.co.uk/news/university-of-the-people-gains-accreditation/2011702.article (accessed May 4, 2014).

Patton, G. (2014) "AC Grayling's Elite University Loses Faith in A-Levels," *Daily Telegraph* February 9. Available at: www.telegraph.co.uk/education/educationnews/10624939/AC-Graylings-elite-university-loses-faith-in-A-Levels.html (accessed February 16, 2014).

Pavlechko, G. M., and Jacobi, K. L. (Forthcoming) Faculty Development: Precursor to Effective Student Engagement in the Higher Education Learning Space," in C. Nygaard, J. Brand., P. Barthlomew, and L. Scott-Webber (Eds.), *Learning Space Design in Higher Education*, Libri Publishing.

Payton, S. (n.d.) *Developing Digital Literacies*, JISC briefing paper, Joint Information Systems Committee Available at: www.jisc.ac.uk/media/documents/publications/briefingpaper/2012/Developing_Digital_Literacies.pdf.

Pearson (n.d.) *Let Learning Flourish: Solutions for Higher Education*, Available at: http://catalogue.pearsoned.co.uk/hip/us/ng/assets/documents/HE_Brochure.pdf

Peck, J. (2005) Struggling with the Creative Class. *International Journal of Urban and Regional Research* 29(4): 740–770.

Persson, B. T. (2000) "Danish University Extension" (Translated by David Hohnen), Available at: www.folkeuniversitetet.dk/default.aspx?pagetype=6&custID=8 (accessed March 30, 2014).

Pinheiro, R., Benneworth, P., and Jones. P. (Eds.) (2012) *Universities and Regional Development, A Critical Assessment of Tensions and Contradictions*, Routledge.

Pinheiro, R., Geschwind, L., and Aarrevaara, T. (2014) "Nested Tensions and Interwoven Dilemmas in Higher Education: The View from the Nordic Countries," *Cambridge Journal of Regions, Economy and Society* 7 (2): 233–250

Pinheiro, R., and Stensaker, B. (2013) "Designing the Entrepreneurial University: The Interpretation of a Global Idea," *Public Organization Review* (5) 1–20.

Pinheiro, R., and Stensaker, B. (2014) "Strategic Actor-Hood and Internal Transformation: The Rise of the Quadruple-Helix University?," in J. Brankovik, M. Klemencik, P. Lazetic, and P. Zgaga, (Eds.), *Global Challenges, Local Responses in Higher Education. The Contemporary Issues in National and Comparative Perspective*, Sense Publishers, 171–189.

Powell, S., and MacNeil, S. (2012) *Institutional Readiness for Analytics A Briefing Paper*, JISC CETIS, December. Available at: http://publications.cetis.ac.uk/wp-content/uploads/2012/12/Institutional-Readiness-for-Analytics-Vol1-No8.pdf.

Prince, C., and Beaver, G. (2001) "The Rise and Rise of the Corporate University: The Emerging Corporate Learning Agenda," *International Journal of Multicultural Education (IJME)* 1 (2): 17–26. Available at: www.heacademy.ac.uk/resources/detail/subjects/bmaf/IJME_vol1_no2_prince.

QAA Good Practice Knowledgebase Case Study (2013), "Improving Higher Education," University of Lincoln, Student as Producer. Available at: www.qaa.ac.uk/ImprovingHigherEducation/GoodPractice/Documents/GPKB-case-study-Lincoln-2.pdf.

Radcliffe, D., Wilson, H., Powell, D., and Tibbetts, B. (Eds.) (2008) *Learning Spaces in Higher Education: Positive Outcomes by Design. Proceedings of the Next Generation Learning Spaces Colloquium*, University of Queensland Press.

Readings, B. (1997) *The University in Ruins*, Harvard University Press.

Rhoades, G., and Slaughter, S (2004) "Academic Capitalism in the New Economy: Challenges and Choices" *American Academic* 1 (1): 37–59. Available at: www.aft.org/pdfs/highered/academic/june04/Rhoades.qxp.pdf.

Rhoads, R. A., and Szelényi, K. (2011) *Global Citizenship and the University: Advancing Social Life and Relations in an Interdependent World*, Stanford University Press.

Robinson, F, and Zass-Ogilvie, I. (2012) *How Can Universities Support Disadvantaged Communities?*, Joseph Rowntree Foundation.

Robinson, K. (2011) *Out of our Minds: Learning to be Creative*, Capstone.

Rodin, J. (2007) *The University and Urban Revival: Out of the Ivory Tower and into the Streets*, University of Pennsylvania Press.

Rolfe, G. (2013) *The University in Dissent: Scholarship in the Corporate University*, Society for Higher Education Research and Routledge.

Roodhouse, S. (2013) (Ed.) *Cultural Quarters: Principles and Practice*, Intellect Books.

Rowan, D. (2013) "On the Exponential Curve; Inside Singularity University," *Wired Magazine*, May 6. Available at: www.wired.co.uk/magazine/archive/2013/05/singularity-university/on-the-exponential-curve/viewgallery/303485 (accessed March 14, 2014).

Rubin, B. (2013) "University Business Models and Online Practices: A Third Way" *Online Journal of Distance Learning Administration* 15 (1). Available at: www.westga.edu/~distance/ojdla/spring161/rubin.html.

Ruch, R. (2004) "Lessons from the Non-Profit Side," in J. Odin and P. T. Manicas (Eds.) *Globalization and Higher Education*, University of Hawaii Press, 82–83.

Salmon, G. (2004) *E-Moderating: The Key to Online Teaching and Learning*, Routledge.

Sandel, M. (2012) *What Money Can't Buy: The Moral Limits of Markets*, Allen Lane.

Savin-Baden, M. (2008) *Learning Spaces: Creating Opportunities for Knowledge Creation in Academic Life*, Open University Press/McGraw-Hill.

Schuller, T., and Watson, D. (2009) *Learning through Life: Inquiry into the Future of Lifelong Learning*, National Institute of Adult Continuing Education.

Sclater, N. L. (2008) "Latest Version of Open University VLE Released," January 10. http://sclater.com/blog/?p=55 (accessed August 16, 2014).

Scott-Webber, L. (2004) *In Sync: Environmental Behavior Research and the Design of Learning Spaces*, Society for College and University Planning.

Scott-Webber, L., Strickland, A., and Ring Kapitula, L. (2013) "Built Environment Impact Behaviours: Results of an Active Learning Post-occupancy Evaluation," *Planning for Higher Education* 42(1). Available at: www.steelcase.com/en/products/category/educational/case-studies/documents/phev42n1_article_built-environments.pdf (accessed August 15, 2014).

SCUP Academic Council (2013) *Report on Trends in Higher Education Planning*. Available at: www.scup.org/page/resources/books/rotihep2013 (accessed August 15, 2014).

Selingo, J. (2013a) "Big Idea 2014: Base Degrees on What We Know, Not How Long We Spent in a Classroom," *Linkedin*, December 10. Available at: www.linkedin.com/today/post/article/20131210000347–17000124-big-idea-2014-base-degrees-on-what-we-know-not-how-long-we-spent-in-a-classroom (accessed March 22, 2014).

Selingo, J.J. (2013b) *College Unbound: The Future of Higher Education and What it Means to Students*, New Harvest.

Selwyn, N. (2011) *Education and Technology: Key Issues and Debates*, Continuum.

Shapiro, S., and Schroeder, C.H. (2008) "Beyond Cost-Benefit Analysis: A Pragmatic Reorientation," *Harvard Environmental Law Review* 32: 432–502. Available at: www.law.harvard.edu/students/orgs/elr/vol32_2/Shapiro%20Final%20Final.pdf.

Sharpe, R., Beetham, H., and de Freitas, S. (2010) *Re-thinking Learning for a Digital Age: How Learners Are Shaping their Own Experiences*, Routledge.

Sharples, M., McAndrew, P., Weller, M., Ferguson, R., FitzGerald, E., Hirst, T., and Gaved, M. (2013) *Innovating Pedagogy 2013: Open University Innovation Report 2*, The Open University. Available at: www.open.ac.uk/blogs/innovating/.

Shattock, M. (2003) *Managing Successful Universities*. Buckingham: The Society for Research into Higher Education and Open University.

Shattock, M. (2010) *Managing Successful Universities*, Open University Press.

Sheets, R., Crawford, S., and Soares, L. (2012) *Rethinking Higher Education Business Models: Steps toward a Disruptive Innovation Approach to Understanding and Improving Higher Education Outcomes*, Center for American Progress and Educause. Available at: www.americanprogress.org/issues/higher-education/report/2012/03/28/11250/rethinking-higher-education-business-models/.

Shiel, C., and Mckenzie, A. (Eds.) (2008) *The Global University: The Role of Senior Managers*, BU/DEA. Available at: http://eprints.bournemouth.ac.uk/10983/1/HE_report_seniormgrs_DEA_1.pdf.

Shirky, C. (2012) "Napster, Udacity and the Academy," November. Available at: www.shirky.com/weblog/2012/11/napster-udacity-and-the-academy/ (accessed March 12, 2014).

Sidhu, R. (2005) "Building a Global Schoolhouse: International Education in Singapore," *Australian Journal of Education* 49 (1): 46–65.

Siemens, G. (2003, October 17) *Learning Ecology, Communities, and Networks: Extending the classroom*. Available at: www.elearnspace.org/Articles/learning_communities.htm (accessed August 15, 2014).

Siemens, G. (2004) "Connectivism: A Learning Theory for the Digital Age," December 12. Available at: www.elearnspace.org/Articles/connectivism.htm (accessed February 12, 2014).

Siemens, G. (2011) "Artifacts of Sensemaking," January 14. Available at: www.learninganalytics. net/?p=94 (accessed March 9, 2014).

Siemens, G. (2013a) "The Complexification of Education," March 4. Available at: www. xedbook.com/ (accessed February 1 2014).

Siemens, G. (2013b) "WISE: The World's Most Important Education Conference," November 3. Available at: www.elearnspace.org/blog/2013/11/03/wise-the-worlds-most-important-education-conference/ (accessed February 12, 2014).

Siemens, G., and Gasevic, D. (2012) "Guest Editorial—Learning and Knowledge Analytics." *Educational Technology & Society* 15 (3), 1–2. Available at: www.ifets.info/journals/ 15_3/1.pdf.

Singh, M., and Little, B. (2011) "Learning and Engagement Dimensions of Higher Education in Knowledge Society," in J. Brennan and T. Shah, eds., *Higher Education and Society in Changing Times: Looking Back and Looking Forward,* Centre for Higher Education Research and Information (CHERI) Open University, 36–45. Available at: www.open. ac.uk/cheri/documents/Lookingbackandlookingforward.pdf.

Simons, M. (2010) "Dangerous Precedent: The Melbourne Model," *The Monthly* no. 54 (March). Available at: www.themonthly.com.au/issue/2010/february/1284956481/margaret-simons/ dangerous-precedent (accessed March 14, 2014).

Singer, A. (2014) "Is Pearson Education in Serious Financial Trouble?," *Huffington Post,* April 25. Available at: www.huffingtonpost.com/alan-singer/is-pearson-education-in-s_b_5212784.html (Accessed May 2, 2014).

Sinha, S. (2012) "Motivating Students and the Gamification of Learning," *Huffington Post,* February 14. Available at: www.huffingtonpost.com/shantanu-sinha/motivating-students-and-t_b_1275441.html (accessed March 10, 2014).

Slaughter, S., and Leslie, L.L. (1997) *Academic Capitalism: Politics, Policies, and the Entrepreneurial University,* John Hopkins University Press.

Slaughter, S., and Rhoades, G. (2009) *Academic Capitalism and the New Economy: Markets, State, and Higher Education,* John Hopkins University Press.

Smith, C. (2004) "Globalization, Higher Education and Markets," in J. K. Odin and P. T. Manicas (Eds.) *Globalization and Higher Education,* University of Hawaii Press, 56–67.

Soares, L. (2013) *Post-Traditional Learners and the Transformation of Postsecondary Education: A Manifesto for College Leaders,* American Council on Education.

Society for College and University Planning (SCUP) Academy Council (2014) *Report on Trends in Higher Education Planning.* Available at: http://www.scup.org/asset/75087/ ReportOnTrendsInHigherEducationPlanning2014.pdf?utm_campaign=report-on-trends-in-higher-education-planning-2014&utm_medium=Webpage&utm_source=webpage-link-TrendsReport2014 Accessed 12/10/14

Space Management Group (2008) *UK Higher Education Space Management Project— Evaluation. A Report to the UK Higher Education Funding Councils.* Available at: www. smg.ac.uk/rep_evaluatoin.html (accessed August 15, 2014).

Sprake, J. (2012) *Learning through Touring: Mobilising Learners and Touring Technologies to Creatively Explore the Built Environment,* Sense Publishers.

Sprake. J., and Rogers, P. (2011) "Located Lexicon: A Project that Explores How User Generated Content Describes Space," in S. Sonvilla-Weiss and O. Kelly (Eds.) *Future Learning Spaces: Designs on E-Learning Conference Proceedings,* Alto University, 219–354. Available at: http://process.arts.ac.uk/sites/default/files/future_learning_spaces.pdf.

Sprake, J., and Rogers, P. (2014) "Crowds, Citizens and Sensors: Process and Practice for Mobilising Learning," *Personal and Ubiquitous Computing* 18 (3): 753–764.

Stachowiak, K., Pinheiro, R., Sedini, C., and Vaatovaara, M. (2013) "Policies Aimed at Strengthening Ties between Universities and Cities," in S. Musterd and Z. Kovács (Eds.) *Place Making and Policies for Competitive Cities,* Wiley-Blackwell, 263–286

Taylor, J.B., Cantwell, B., and Slaughter, S. (2013) "Quasi-Markets in U.S. Higher Education: The Humanities and Institutional Revenues," *Journal of Higher Education* 84 (5): 675–707.

Teaching and Learning Spaces Working Group (TLSWG) (n.d.) *Annual Report FY14: Funding Allocations and Decision Process*, McGill University Teaching and Learning Services. Available at: www.mcgill.ca/tls/sites/mcgill.ca.tls/files/2012–13_tlswg_annual_report_fy14.pdf.

Temple, P. (2008) "Learning Spaces in Higher Education: An Under-Researched Topic," *London Review of Education* 6 (3): 229–241.

Temple, P. (Ed.) (2011) *Universities in the Knowledge Economy: Higher Education Organisation and Global Change*, Routledge.

Temple, P. (Ed.) (2014) *The Physical University: Contours of Space and Place in Higher Education*, Routledge.

Tertiary Education Facilities Management Association (TEFMA) (2006) *Learning Environments in Tertiary Education*. Available at: www.tefma.com/infoservices/publications/learning.jsp.

Thille, C. (2012) *Changing the Production Function in Higher Education*, American Council on Education. Available at: www.acenet.edu/news-room/Pages/Changing-the-Production-Function.aspx.

Thille, C., and Smith, J. (2011) "Cold Rolled Steel and Knowledge: What Can Higher Education Learn About Productivity?" *Change: The Magazine of Higher Learning* (March–April) Available at: www.changemag.org/Archives/Back%20Issues/2011/March-April%202011/cold-rolled-steel-full.html.

Thomas, L. (2012) *Building Student Engagement and Belonging in Higher Education in a Time of Change: Final Report from the What Works? Student Retention and Success Programme*, Higher Education Academy. Available at: www.heacademy.ac.uk/assets/documents/retention/what_works_final_report.pdf.

Thorp, H., and Goldstein, B. (2010) *Engines of Innovation: The Entrepreneurial University in the Twenty-First Century*, University of North Carolina Press.

Thrift, N. (2007) *Non-Representational Theory: Space, Politics, Affect*, Routledge.

Thrift, N. (2008a) *Non-Representational Theory: Space, Politics, Affect*, Routledge.

Thrift, N. (2008b) "University Reforms: The Tension between Form and Substance," in C. Mazza, P. Quattrone, and A. Riccaboni (Eds.) *European Universities in Transition: Issues, Models and Cases*, Edward Elgar, 17–30.

Thrift, N. (2009) "Universities Are Radical," in J. Pugh (Ed.) *What Is Radical Politics Today?*, Macmillan, 204–212.

Uckelmann, D., Harrison, M., and Michahelles, F. (Eds.) (2011) *Architecting the Internet of Things*, Springer.

United Nations Conference on Trade and Development (UNCTAD) (2010) *Creative Economy: A Feasible Development Option*. Available at: http://unctad.org/en/Docs/ditctab20103_en.pdf.

Universities UK (2013) *Patterns and Trends in UK Higher Education*. Available at: www.universitiesuk.ac.uk/highereducation/Documents/2013/PatternsAndTrendsinUKHigherEducation2013.pdf.

US Department of Education (2010) *Evaluation of Evidence-Based Practices in Online Learning*, Center for Technology in Learning.

Usher, R., Bryant, I., and Johnston, R. (1997) *Adult Education and the Post-Modern Challenge: Learning beyond the Limits*, Routledge.

Verger, A (2010) "GATS/WTO and Trade in Higher Education: Tension and Dissension in the Education Community," Global University Network for Innovation. Available at: www.guninetwork.org/resources/he-articles/gats-wto-and-trade-in-higher-education-tension-and-dissension-in-the-education-community (accessed May 24, 2014).

Verger, T., and Robertson, S. (2008) "GATS Basics: Key Rules and Concepts," *GlobalHigherEd*, April 19. Available at: http://globalhighered.wordpress.com/2008/04/19/gats-basics-key-rules-and-concepts/ (accessed May 24, 2014).

Walker, J.D., Brooks, C., and Baepler, P. (2011) "Pedagogy and Space: Empirical Research on New Learning Environments," *Educause Quarterly*. Available at: www.educause.edu/ero/article/pedagogy-and-space-empirical-research-new-learning-environments

Watson, D., Hollister, R., Stroud, S. E., and Babcock, E. (2011) *The Engaged University: International Perspectives on Civic Engagement*, Routledge.

Weller, M. (2011) *The Digital Scholar: How Technology Is Changing Academic Practice*, Bloomsbury Academic.

Wenger, E. (1998) *Communities of Practice: Learning Meaning and Identity*, Cambridge University Press.

Wheelahan, L. (2010) *Why Knowledge Matters in Curriculum: A Social Realist Argument*, Routledge.

White, D., and Manton, M. (2011) *Open Educational Resources: The Value of Re-Use in Higher Education Technology-Assisted Lifelong Learning* (TALL), University of Oxford Department for Continuing Education. Available at: www.jisc.ac.uk/media/documents/programmes/elearning/oer/OERTheValueOfReuseInHigherEducation.pdf.

Wievel, W., and Knaap, G.-J. (Eds.) (2008) *Partnerships for Smart Growth: University-community Collaboration for Better Public Places*, M.E. Sharpe.

Wievel, W., and Kunst, K. (2007) *University Real Estate Development: Campus Expansion in Urban Settings*, Lincoln Institute of Land Policy. Available at: www.lincolninst.edu/subcenters/university-real-estate-development/.

Wievel, W., and Perry, D.C. (Eds.) (2008) *Global Universities and Urban Development*, M.E. Sharpe.

Wildavsky, B., Kelly, A., and Carey, K. (Eds.) (2011) *Reinventing Higher Education: The Promise of Innovation*, Harvard Education Press.

William and Flora Hewlett Foundation (2012) *Deeper Learning Strategic Plan Summary Educational Program*. Available at: www.hewlett.org/uploads/documents/Education Program_Deeper_Learning_Strategy.pdf

William and Flora Hewlett Foundation (2013) *Open Educational Resources: Breaking the Lockbox on Education*, white paper. Available at: www.hewlett.org/sites/default/files/OER%20White%20Paper%20Nov%2022%202013%20Final_0.pdf.

Williams, J. (2012) *Consuming Higher Education: Why Learning Can't Be Bought*, Bloomsbury Academic.

Wilson, T. (2012) *A Review of Business–University Collaboration*, Department for Innovation, Business and Skills. Available at: www.gov.uk/government/uploads/system/uploads/attachment_data/file/32383/12–610-wilson-review-business-university-collaboration.pdf.

Wittman, A., and Crews, T. (2012) *Engaged Learning Economies: Aligning Civic Engagement and Economic Development in Community-Campus Partnerships*, Campus Compact. Available at: www.compact.org/wp-content/uploads/2012/10/Engaged-Learning-Economies-White-Paper-20121.pdf.

Yeo, G. (2003) Singapore: The Global Schoolhouse." Speech by Minister for Trade and Industry, August 16. Available at: www.sedb.com/edbcorp/sg/en_uk/index/in_the_news/2003/20030/singapore_in_the_global.html (accessed August 21, 2014).

Yuan, L., MacNeill S., and Kraan, W. (2008) *Open Educational Resources—Opportunities and Challenges for Higher Education*, JISC CETIS. Available at: http://wiki.cetis.ac.uk/images/0/0b/OER_Briefing_Paper.pdf.

Yuan, L., and Powell, S. (2013) *MOOCs and Open Education: Implications for Higher Education. A White Paper*, JISC CETIS Available at: http://publications.cetis.ac.uk/2013/667.

Yuan, L., Powell, S., and Olivier, B. (2014) *Beyond MOOCs: Sustainable Online Learning in Institutions: A White Paper*, CETIS. Available at: http://publications.cetis.ac.uk/2014/898.

INDEX